LEGENDARY LOCALS

OF

SOUTHBURY

CONNECTICUT

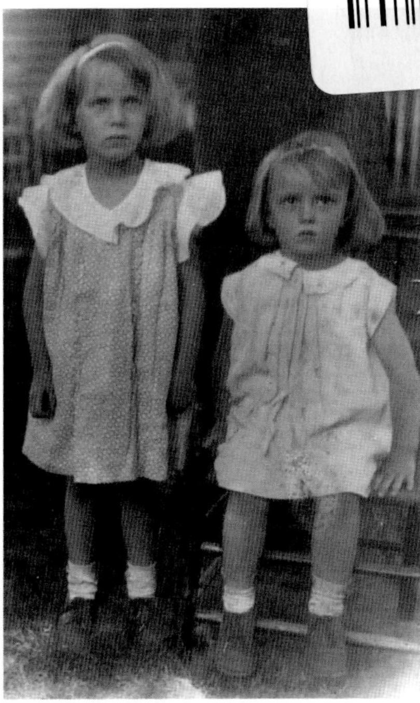

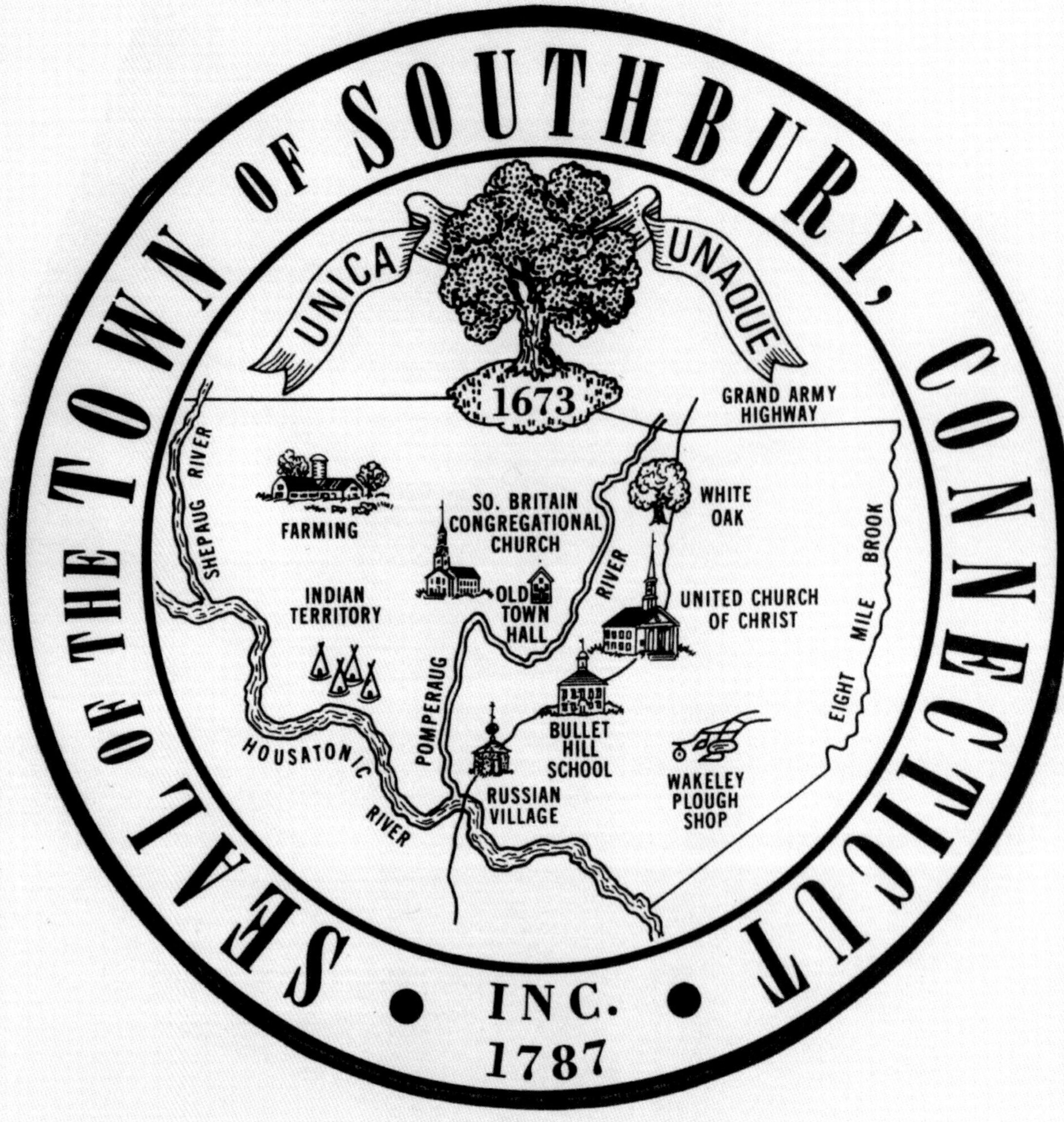

Southbury Town Seal
The town seal reads "Unica Unaque," meaning "the one and only." Southbury is unique in its beauty, people, and magnificent history. It is the only known town of that name in the United States. (Courtesy Town of Southbury.)

Page 1: Jane and Althea Hicock
Jane (left) and Althea's ancestors and descendants were part of the early families of Southbury. Althea was a local nurse at both the Southbury Training School and River Glen. She has served for many years as a docent for Bullet Hill School Days. All of the people who have lived in Southbury, past and present, have helped make it the rich community it is today. (Courtesy Althea McGahie.)

LEGENDARY LOCALS

OF

SOUTHBURY

CONNECTICUT

VIRGINIA PALMER-SKOK

LEGENDARY LOCALS

ISBN 978-1-4671-0068-7

Legendary Locals is an imprint of Arcadia Publishing
Charleston, South Carolina

Printed in the United States of America

Library of Congress Control Number: 2012950193

For all general information, please contact Arcadia Publishing:
Telephone 843-853-2070
Fax 843-853-0044
E-mail sales@arcadiapublishing.com
For customer service and orders:
Toll-Free 1-888-313-2665

Visit us on the Internet at www.arcadiapublishing.com

Dedication

This book is dedicated to Paul and Catherine Palmer, who have taught me the true meaning of community through the many hours they have given to Southbury.

On the Cover: From left to right:
(TOP ROW) George Stone Sr., fire department chief (Courtesy Mark Stone, see page 73); Jane and Althea Hicock, descendants of early families (Courtesy Althea McGahie, see page 1); Peter Homick, owner of Laurel Diner (Courtesy Andrew Skok, see page 75); Nellie Brown, successful businesswoman (Courtesy Samuel Green III, see page 68); John Ludorf, farmer (Courtesy Bullet Hill School Archives, see pages 54–55).
(MIDDLE ROW) Susan Mitchell Meisner, local of South Britain (Courtesy Althea McGahie, see page 16); T.F. Wheeler, town selectman, sheriff, constable, and Connecticut house representative (Courtesy John Dwyer, see page 106); Samuel Green III, first selectman and longtime VFW member (Courtesy VFW Post 1607, see page 111), Samuel Green I, first town doctor (Courtesy Samuel Green III, see page 25), gingham girls, descendants of some of the first families (Courtesy Jane White, see page 63).
(BOTTOM ROW) Elliott Wheeler Hine and George Hine, descendants of an early town family (Courtesy Jane White, see page 14); Gayle O'Neill, successful businesswoman (Courtesy Andrew Skok, see page 77); Harold H. Davis, operated Southford General (Courtesy Harold H. Davis, see page 23); Joyce Hornbecker, town co-historian (Courtesy VFW Post 1607, see page 88); Lt. C. Edward Hine, veteran (Courtesy VFW Post 1607, see page 36).

CONTENTS

ACKNOWLEDGMENTS

The author gratefully acknowledges all of the people who share a love for their hometown of Southbury and have contributed images and stories from their personal and organization collections including, but not limited to, Samuel Green III, Betsey Bette, Ed Wildman Jr., Melinda Elliott, Althea McGahie, Arza Bennett Jr., John Dwyer, the George Newton VFW Post 1607, H. William and Kayanne Davis, and Lisa Gilbert. This book would not have been possible without the many hours of help with proofing from Catherine Palmer and photography from Andrew Skok.

INTRODUCTION

According to area lore, the history of the human habitation of Southbury began in the 1600s with the arrival of the Pootatuck Indians, related to the Mohican tribes and indigenous to the Hudson River area. Undoubtedly, their migration to the Southbury area was necessitated by the quest for additional hunting and fishing grounds. Local accounts indicate the Pootatuck Indians settled in the area now known as the South Britain section of town as well as throughout the area west of the lower reaches of the Pomperaug River. This settlement also encompassed the area just beyond the approach of today's East Flat Hill Road.

Following the Indian migration to this area, Connecticut colonists were in the preliminary stages of settling in this location. In 1668, a minority group attending Connecticut's Stratford Congregational Church engaged Rev. Zachariah Walker to be its minister and represent it in efforts to leave Stratford. The group was dissatisfied with the Stratford church's religious customs and also needed more land to meet the needs of the growing population in Stratford. After several efforts, Reverend Walker and the group were granted permission in May 1672 by the general court, the governing body of the colony, to form a new town. The first transaction by the Stratford group was the purchase of land along the Pomperaug River from the Pootatuck Indians. This first purchase was named Pomperaug Plantation.

Fifteen families signed the original fundamental articles for the site. These articles stated that any number of future settlers who could find accommodations would be allowed in the settlement. The articles further outlined the division of sharing the expenses among the new residents for establishing the site. Each family was allocated between 10 and 25 acres of land. A provision was also included for common land and for saved land to allow space for future settlers. The document was signed by Samuel Stiles Sr., Samuel Stiles, Joshua Curtiss, Israel Curtiss, Lt. Joseph Judson Sr., Titus Hinman, David Jenkins, John Wheeler, Roger Terill, Moses Johnson, John Wyatt, Samuel Munn, John Sherman, John Minor, Eleazur Knowles, and Thomas Fairchild.

In the spring of 1673, the 15 families left Stratford and traveled by foot and boat up the Great River (Housatonic) to the mouth of the Woodbury River, later called the Pomperaug River. They misunderstood their directions and followed the Shippauga River to the falls (now Roxbury). They realized their mistake and climbed east over the hills, arriving on the second night and resting under a large white oak tree in a section of Southbury. Thereafter, that section of town has been called the White Oak section. (A piece of that original white oak tree is on display at the Old Town Hall Museum in the South Britain section of Southbury and has a hand-written paper attached to it stating, "The White Oak fell down and this piece was saved by Shadrack Osborne—8/19/08." The tree was "20 rods from the river by the old house in the corner of the Michell land." (Shadrack Osborne was one of Southbury's selectmen at the first meeting to organize the town on June 20, 1787.)

The May 1674 court of elections session granted the right to call the new town Woodbury, and in many documents, it was noted as "Ancient Woodbury." The original purchasers, called the Proprietors of Ancient Woodbury, bought six parcels of land, five of which involved Southbury and were acquired in 1672, 1685, 1687, 1705, and 1706. Additional purchases included the present town of Bethlehem, Washington, Roxbury, Southbury, and parts of Middlebury, Oxford, and Bridgewater.

The first families settled along the Country Road (Main Street North) in the White Oak section of Southbury and the Middle Quarter section of Woodbury. During the next 90 years, many tracts of land in the various purchases were distributed to the 170 original proprietors.

For a period of 86 years, the Pootatuck Indians and the settlers from Stratford maintained a peaceful coexistence. It should be noted that the Pootatucks did not join in the Indian uprisings during the 1675

King Philip's War against the settlers. However, for fear of their lives, many of the early settlers chose to leave the area and return to Stratford for a period of more than a year. Gradually, they returned to the Pomperaug Plantation to continue their pursuit of settling this new territory. Some historians theorize that the Pootatucks sold the last of the Pomperaug Plantation in the southern part of the purchase area in 1759 and left to join other tribes in Kent, Connecticut, because of dwindling natural resources due to the expansion of the colonist population.

By 1732, White Oak area residents petitioned the court and were granted permission for a separate church parish, which began the separation of Southbury from Ancient Woodbury. In 1761, residents in the South Britain section of Southbury requested and were granted permission for a second parish due to winter traveling conditions.

On October 17, 1786, the Southbury and South Britain parishes petitioned the general assembly to become a separate town. The May 1787 general assembly session granted the request, and Southbury was incorporated as a town separate from Ancient Woodbury.

Soon after, the county lines were changed and Southbury was designated as being part of New Haven County. At the time of incorporation, Southbury's population was 1,738, and the town's grand list was £15,000. The population changed throughout the next centuries, and following World War II and the Korean conflict, it grew to over 9,000. The advent of transportation improvements and, in particular, Interstate 84, brought continuous growth to Southbury. Today the population is close to 20,000. Southbury's ethnicity has also changed and is reflective of changes throughout the nation. Southbury is proud to welcome all the world's citizens to this fair town.

The community's members exhibit a strong commitment to volunteerism. Town boards, commissions, and committees abound with residents participating from all age groups and educational backgrounds with differing political views and life experiences. Regional School District No. 15 announces school volunteers in its annual appreciation publication, including hundreds of Southbury citizens.

Southburians, from those who were born here to those who have migrated here, are proud of their town. The heritage of Southbury's citizens—from the arrival of the Pootatuck Indians to the first settlers to present residents—continues today. It is evidenced as residents and visitors alike reflect and comment on the natural and historical assets that have been enriched throughout the years by those who first set foot here in the 1600s and by all those who have followed.

CHAPTER ONE

They Came Before Us

Settlers from Stratford first camped under a white oak tree in Ancient Woodbury in 1673.

—Virginia Palmer-Skok, Images of America: *Southbury Revisited*

In the spring of 1673, the first colonial settlers arrived in Pomperaug Plantation and rested under a white oak tree. The settlers left Stratford to find religious freedom. Fifteen Stratford families were granted permission from the general court to relocate to the area called Pomperaug Plantation, later known as Ancient Woodbury. The white oak tree was in the southern part of today's Southbury, which became incorporated as a town in 1787. That section extends into Main Street North and is known as the White Oak district. The founding settlers included the Curtis, Judson, Hinman, Jenkins, Wheeler, Terrill, Johnson, Wyatt, Munn, Sherman, Stiles, Minor, Knowles, and Fairchild families.

The early colonists were Congregationalists and were governed by church doctrines. The rules affected the laws of the colony, educational practices, and all social behaviors, in particular the manner of Christian worship. The Congregational Church held sway among Southbury citizens until the late 1700s, when Methodist ministers migrated to the area. In the early 1800s, a Methodist congregation gathered for prayer in the North George's Hill area. Methodist churches were built in both the Southbury and South Britain sections of town across from the Congregational churches.

The addition of new religious entities and individuals' contributions helped to create an environment that fostered advocacy for emerging and developing freedoms in all facets of society. These attitudes extended to the state government, and in 1818, the first state constitution separate from the original English charter was adopted. In Southbury, town meetings were first held in the two Congregational churches, and in the 1840s, at Bullet Hill School. The first Southbury Town Hall was built in South Britain in 1873. As the population and businesses grew, a second town hall was built on the intersection of Peter Road and Main Street South. The third and present town hall was built in 1977. The town's business is actively conducted in this three-story building on Main Street South.

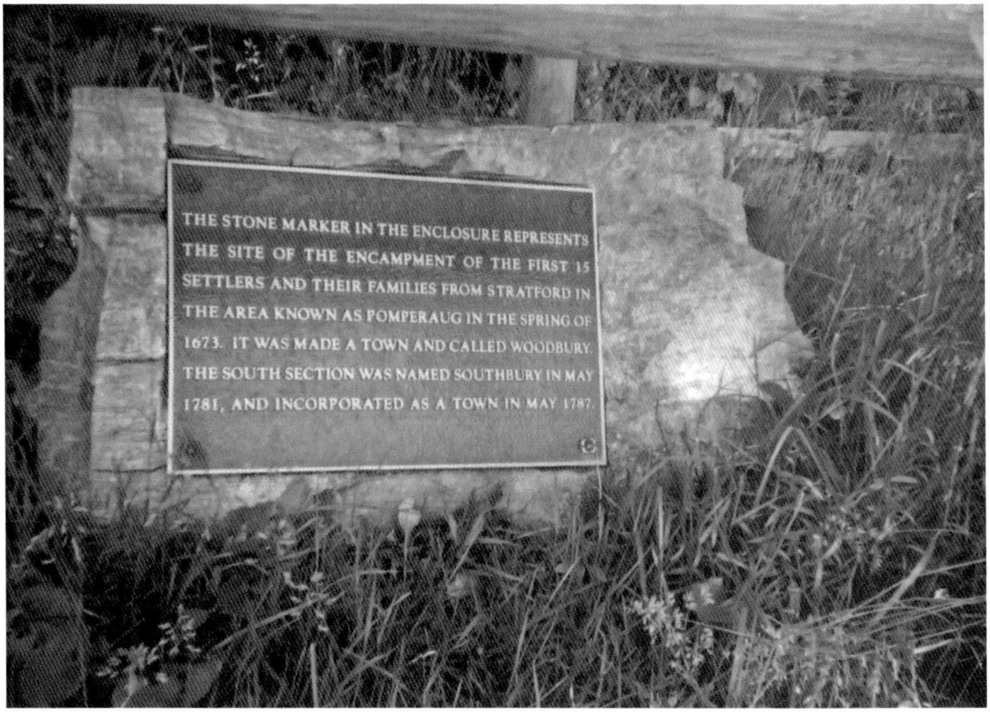

First Colonial Settlers Plaque
Without the first 15 settlers and their families, there would be no community that is known as Southbury today. This plaque is located at the site of the white oak tree where they first rested in the spring of 1673. The plaque was donated by Shirley Garrigus McIlroy and Edmund Schade. The park is located in the White Oak section of Southbury now known as Settlers Park. (Courtesy Catherine Palmer.)

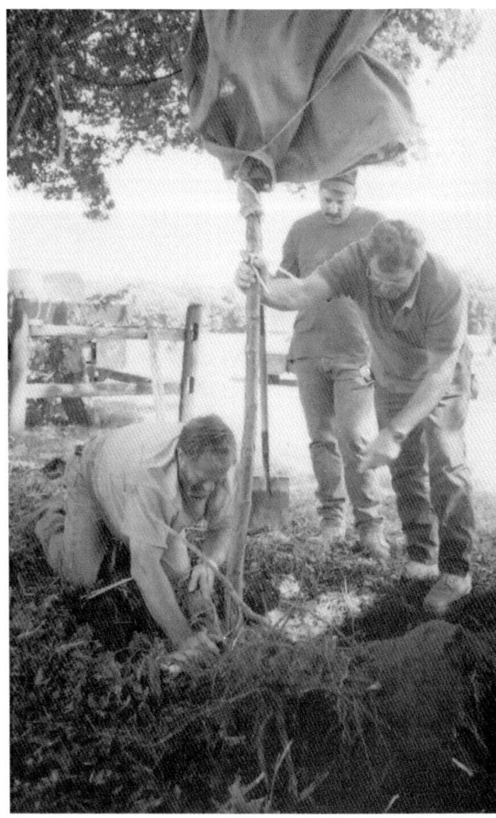

Southbury Public Works Replaces the White Oak
The hardworking Southbury Public Works team replaces the famous white oak. The staff has been responsible for planting at parks and along roadsides, adding aesthetic quality and maintaining public safety. From left to right are George Metcalf, Robert Harmon, and Aaron Lewis, who planted the tree in 1998. They have helped beautify many local areas. The original white oak tree fell down in 1808. Two pieces were saved by the town's First Selectman Shadrack Osborne, and are currently displayed at the Old Town Hall Museum. (Courtesy Catherine Palmer.)

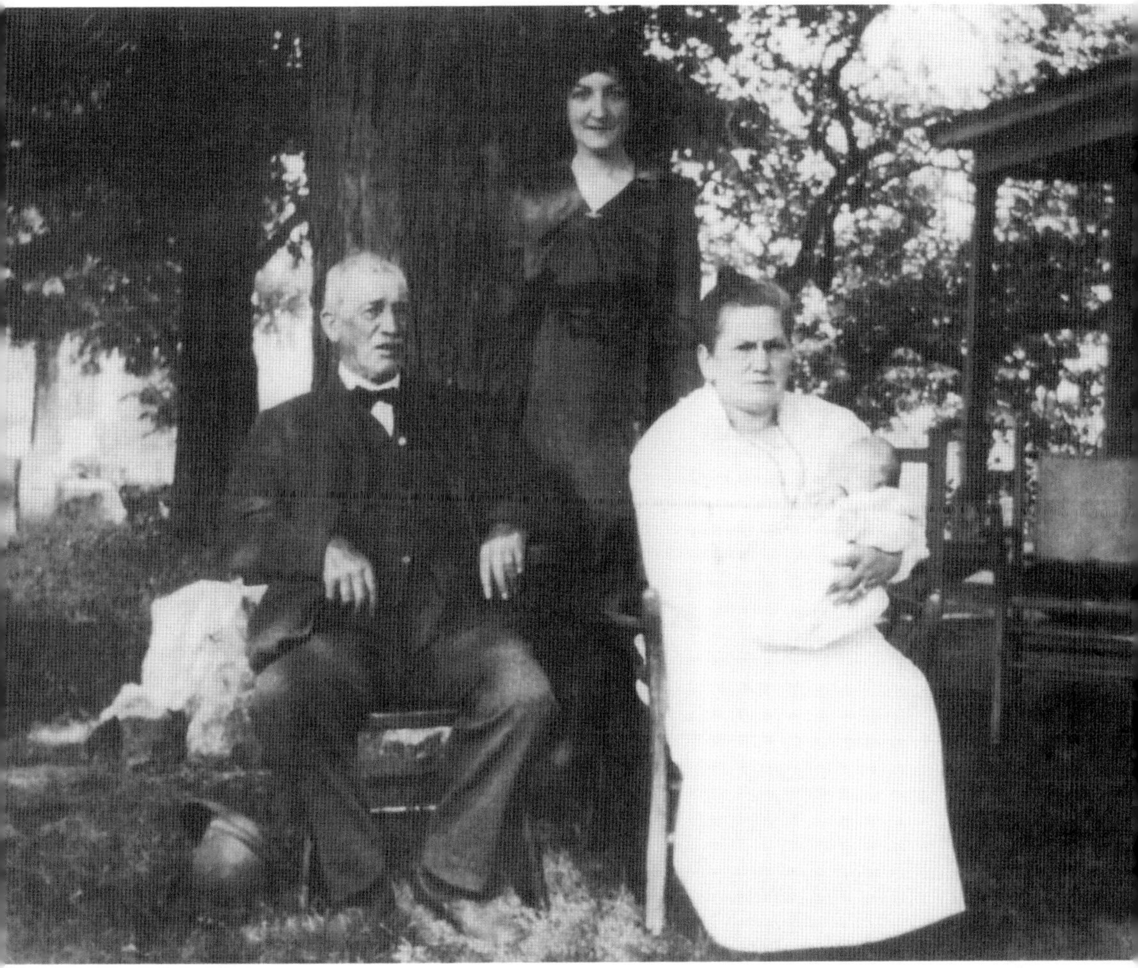

Selectman T.F. Wheeler and Julia Wheeler
Theodore Frielinghison Wheeler, known as "T.F.," was born in 1840. He married Martha Candee, daughter of Samuel Candee Jr. After 1861, T.F. lived at Quaker Farms Road. In 1870, he married Julia Gray. T.F. was a horse-cart grocer and veterinarian and had a feed and grain supply store. He served as first selectman, road inspector, constable, assistant registrar of vital records, Connecticut house representative, and deputy sheriff.

Deputy Sheriff T.F. once found a horse thief from New York when he was visiting friends in Oxford. He cleverly asked the thief if he could buy the horses and promptly arrested him. Family stories state that T.F. had been tempted to use frontier justice and tar-and-feather the thief.

T.F. (pictured here at left), Julia, and family established a farm in the Poverty section of town. Artist Wallace Nutting and celebrity Victory Borge later lived there. It became the site of Heritage Village in the 1960s.

In 1922, two tragedies occurred: T.F. was struck while driving from an inspection. Neighbors noticed him unconscious in the wagon and carried him to his house. A shocked Julia tragically dropped dead in the doorway when he was carried into the house. They are both buried in Southford Cemetery. (Courtesy John Dwyer.)

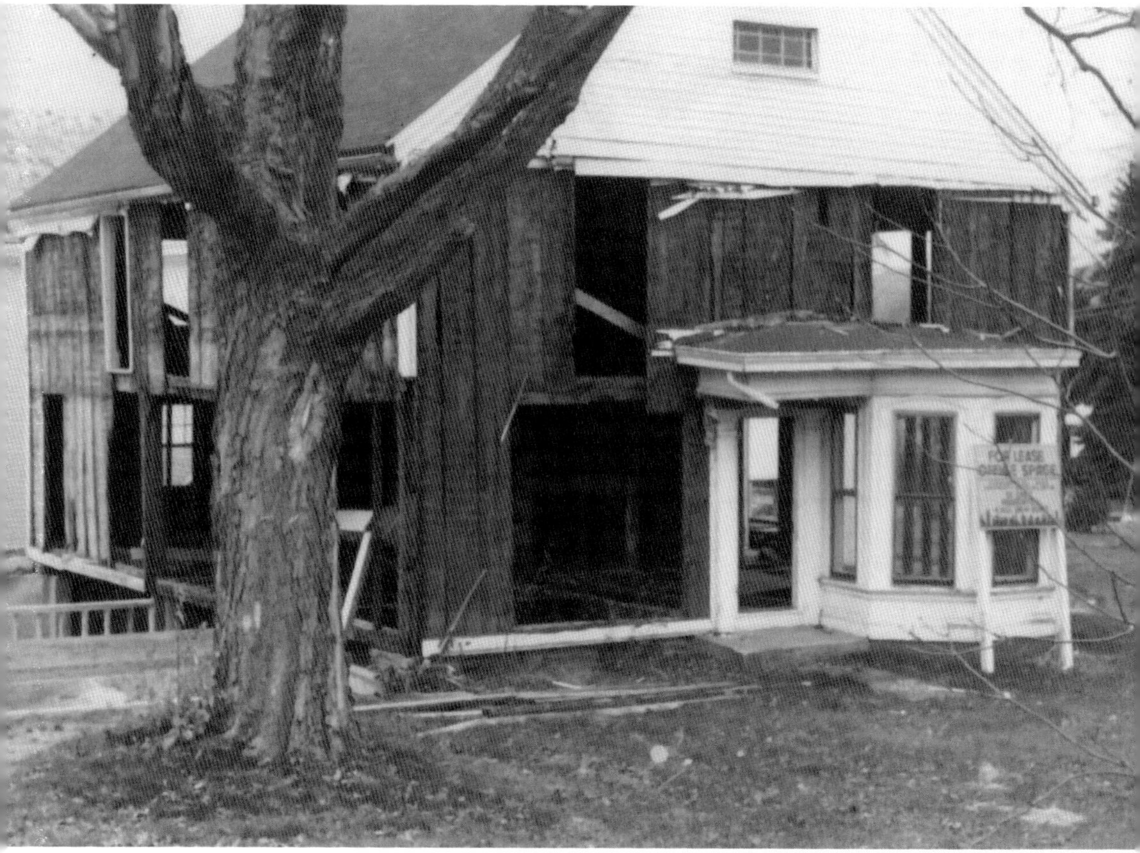

Henry B. Russell

Henry B. Russell owned the home that was located at Poverty Road and Main Street South and which was converted into the popular Leo's Restaurant. Russell was Southbury's Connecticut Constitutional Convention representative. He also served as the town treasurer for 42 years from an office in his home. It was one of the few plank houses in Southbury. (Courtesy Althea McGahie.)

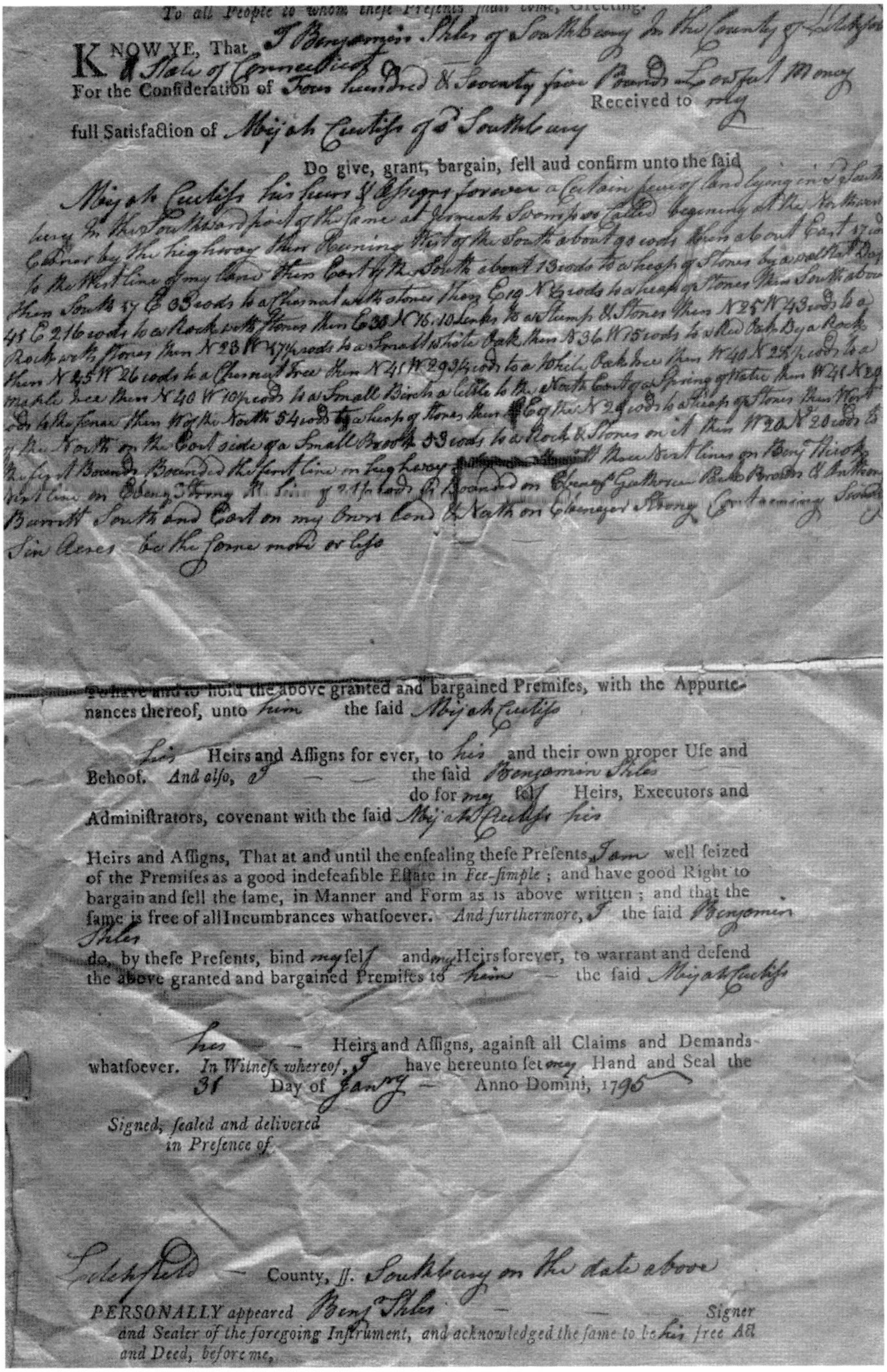

To all People to whom these Presents shall come, Greeting.

KNOW YE, That I Benjamin Stiles of Southbury in the County of Litchfield & State of Connecticut

For the Consideration of Four hundred & Seventy five Pounds Lawful Money Received to my full Satisfaction of Abijah Curtiss of sd Southbury

Do give, grant, bargain, sell and confirm unto the said Abijah Curtiss his heirs & Assigns forever a Certain piece of land lying in sd Southbury ...

To have and to hold the above granted and bargained Premises, with the Appurtenances thereof, unto him the said Abijah Curtiss his Heirs and Assigns for ever, to his and their own proper Use and Behoof. And also, I the said Benjamin Stiles do for my self Heirs, Executors and Administrators, covenant with the said Abijah Curtiss his Heirs and Assigns, That at and until the ensealing these Presents, I am well seized of the Premises as a good indefeasible Estate in Fee-simple; and have good Right to bargain and sell the same, in Manner and Form as is above written; and that the same is free of all Incumbrances whatsoever. And furthermore, I the said Benjamin Stiles do, by these Presents, bind myself and my Heirs forever, to warrant and defend the above granted and bargained Premises to him the said Abijah Curtiss his Heirs and Assigns, against all Claims and Demands whatsoever. In Witness whereof, I have hereunto set my Hand and Seal the 31 Day of Janry Anno Domini, 1795

Signed, sealed and delivered in Presence of

Litchfield County, ss. Southbury on the date above

PERSONALLY appeared Benj Stiles Signer and Sealer of the foregoing Instrument, and acknowledged the same to be his free Act and Deed, before me,

Benjamin Stiles

Benjamin Stiles was reported to be the first lawyer in Old Woodbury and was a large landowner with properties in the South Parish and throughout Southbury. His son was also a prominent citizen with a law degree from Yale and an elegant Georgian Colonial on Main Street. Pictured is the deed to Benjamin Stiles Jr.'s property in the Jeremy Swamp section of Southbury. (Courtesy Melinda Elliott.)

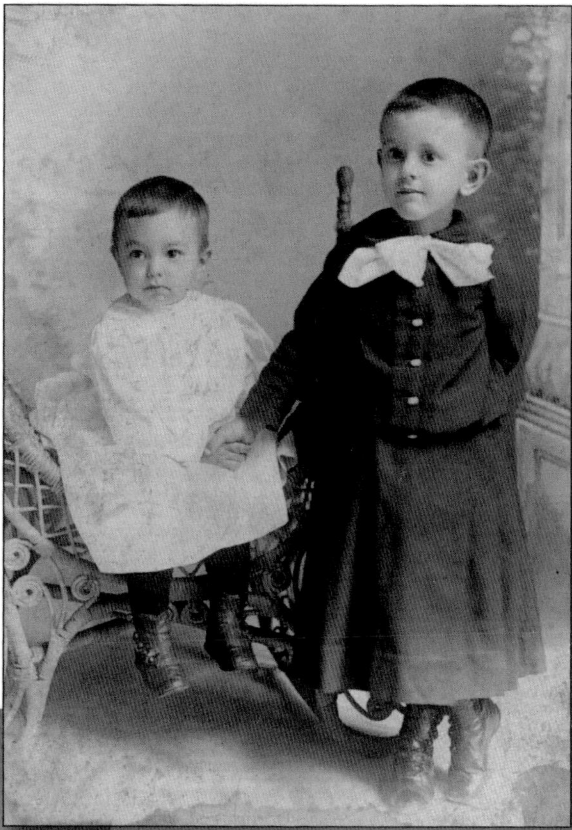

Hicock Brothers
The Hicock brothers, Ely (left) and Henry, are pictured in their Sunday best complete with bowties. Ely was a regular fixture throughout town as the town garbage collector. He took the garbage home to feed to his pigs. Ely also worked at the Southbury Training School. Ely and Henry were raised by their grandfather Henry B. Russell, a Connecticut Constitutional Convention representative, since their stepmother did not want to raise stepchildren. (Courtesy Althea McGahie.)

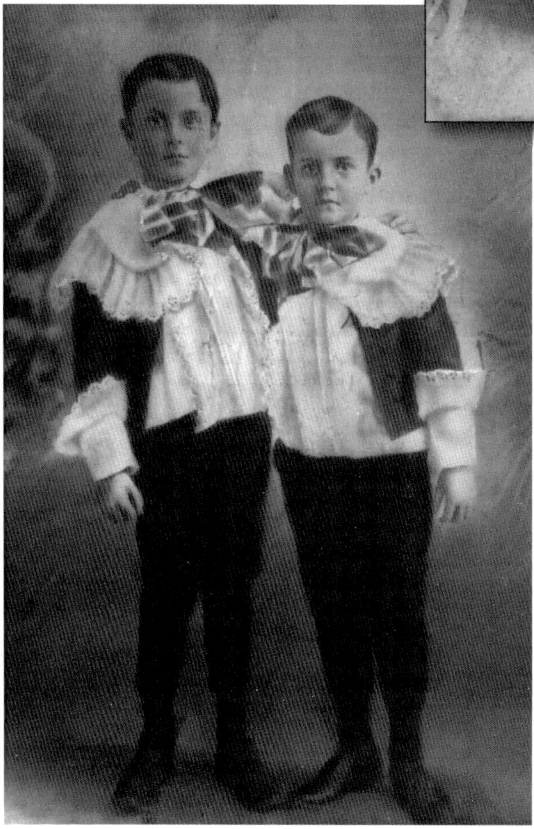

Elliott Wheeler Hine and George Hine, c. 1880s
Elliott Wheeler Hine (left) and George Hine were the sons of Charles and Ann Estella Hine. Elliott was in charge of the Hine family sawmill located in an area called "Out East" in Southford. The mill was operated by a large steam engine. Elliott's family made railroad ties for the new railroad that came to town and ran a dairy farm on Main Street North. Milk cans were placed on a special platform to be picked up every morning in front of their farm. George went on to what was then considered college. He came back and drove the family milk truck. Their father, Charles E. Hine, was Southbury's first selectman in 1916. (Courtesy Jane Ewald White.)

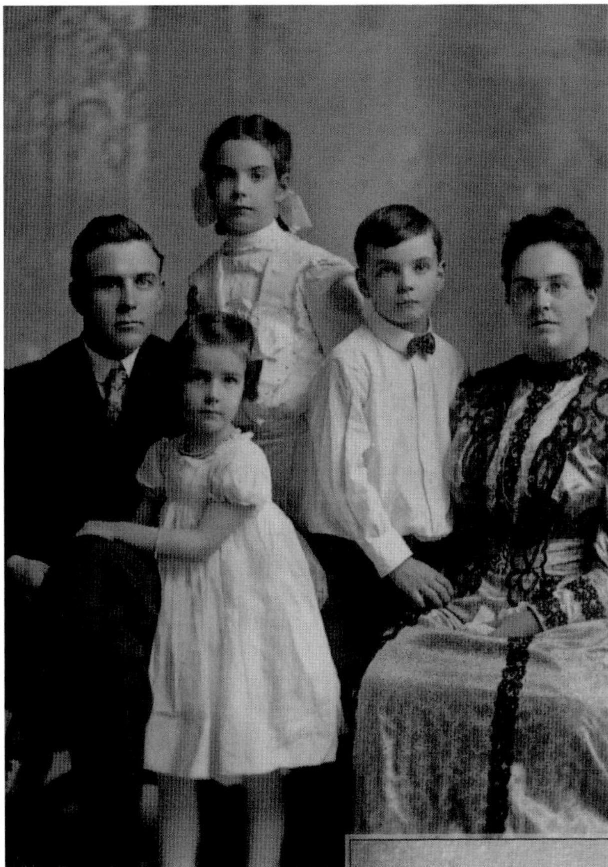

Abbie Williams
Abbie Williams served as a correspondent for both the *Newtown Bee* and *Waterbury American* newspapers for more than 35 years. She wrote her columns from a desk in the dining room. She was also the first librarian at the South Britain Library and was an assessor for the town for 30 years. Abbie married Charles Williams on New Year's Day in 1897. Pictured from left to right are Charles, Evelyn (in front), Winifred, Roger, and Abbie Williams. Evelyn married Ely Pierce Hicock in 1917. Their children were Richard, Priscilla, Thalia, Ely, Amos, Charles, Jane, and Althea. (Courtesy Althea McGahie.)

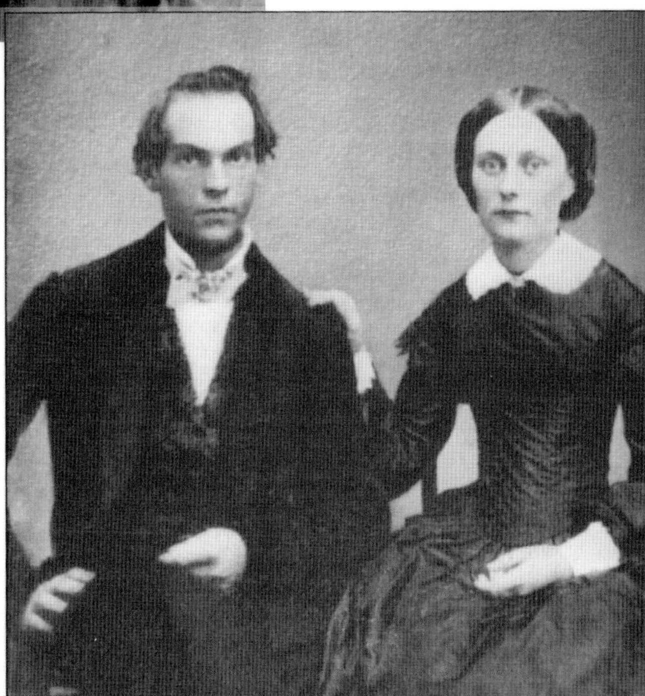

Local Harness Maker and Teamster Sylvester Bennett
Sylvester Bennett married Harriett Canfield, the sister of his first wife, Mary, during the 1860s after Mary died young. Sylvester provided Southbury important hauling services with a horse and wagon. He was from one of the early families in the town. He held a lot of land, with parcels on Mansion House Road, Crook Horn Road, Main Street, Bates Rock Road, Great Hollow in Ragland, and several other Ragland parcels. Pictured are Sylvester and Harriett. (Courtesy Arza Bennett Jr.)

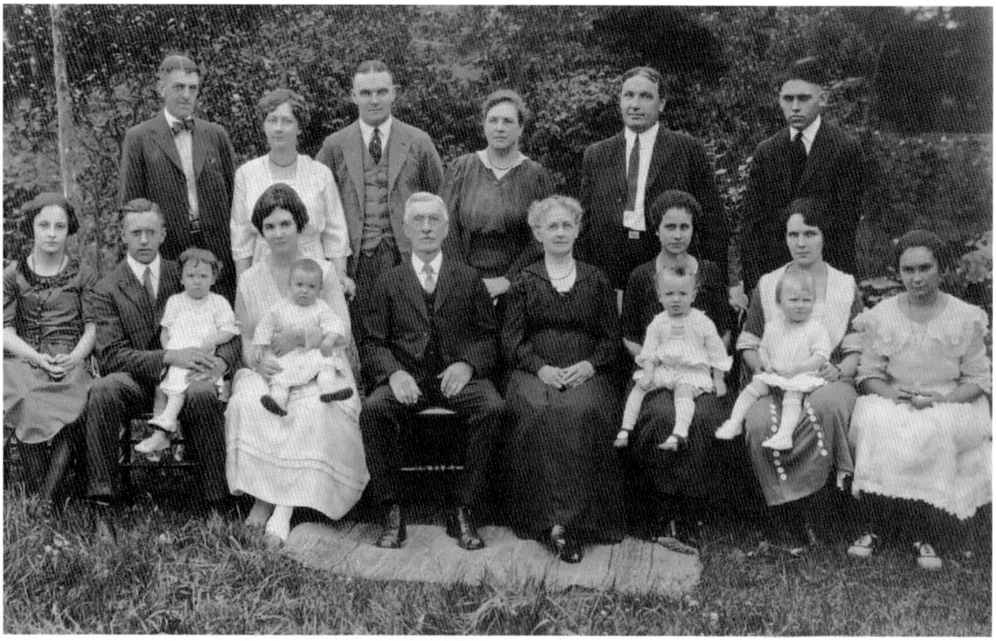

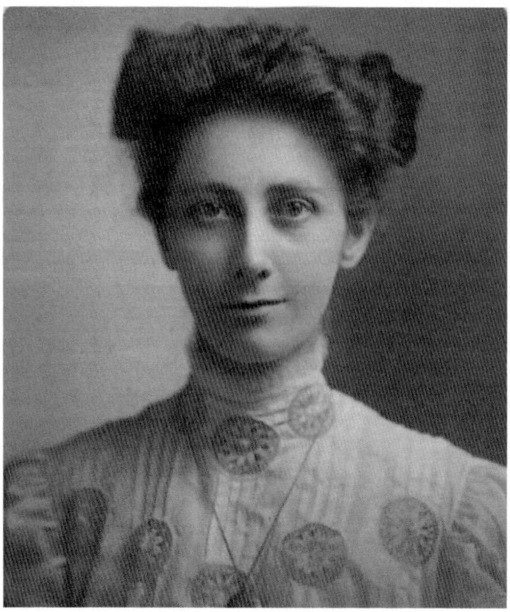

Mitchell Family

The Mitchell family was an important part of South Britain as the general store, the hub of community conversation, was run by a Mitchell for years. Members in attendance at George W. and Julia Platt Mitchell's golden wedding anniversary, from left to right, are (first row) Julia Mitchell Schielke, Ely P. Hicock holding Rachel Hicock Stillings, Evelyn Mitchell Williams Hicock holding Priscila Hicock Schoeffer, George Walter Mitchell, Julia Eliza Platt Mitchell, Florence Hubbard Mitchell holding Barbara Brewer Green, Winifred Williams Brewer holding Roberta Brewer Bertz, and Grace Mitchell Hubbell; (second row) Charles Meisner, Susan Mitchell Meisner, Roger Perry Williams, Abbie Evelyn Mitchell Williams, Hubert George Mitchell, and Robert Brewer. (Courtesy Althea McGahie.)

Susan Mitchell Meisner

Susan typified the industrious, honorable women of her era and contributed her skills to family, community, and church. The South Britain Congregational Church was the center of the community, and Susan supported it, especially with fundraising activities. She made innumerable baked goods for each bake sale and prepared food for the summer Family Days picnics. According to family lore, she was a perfect lady and always came out of her bedroom impeccably dressed. She attended the South Britain Select School. When widowed, she moved back to the Mitchell homestead and lived with her widowed sister Abby Mitchell Williams. They both carried on the family tradition of contributing their many talents to their church and community fundraising events. (Courtesy Althea Hicock McGahie.)

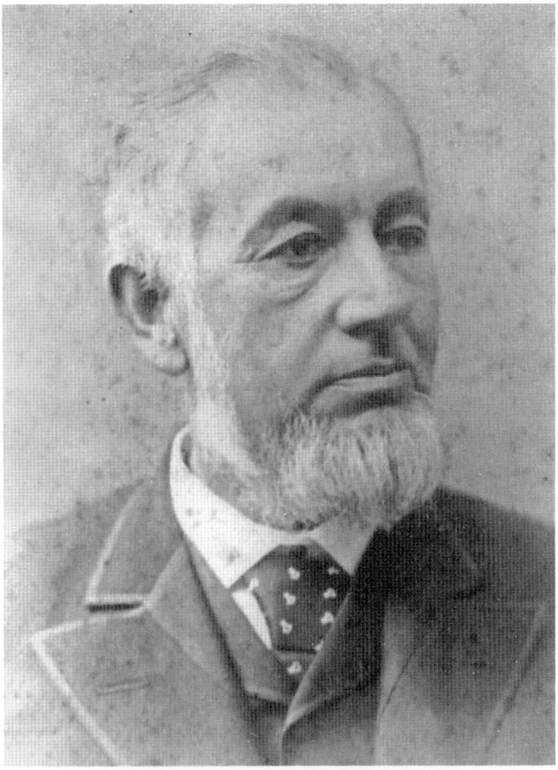

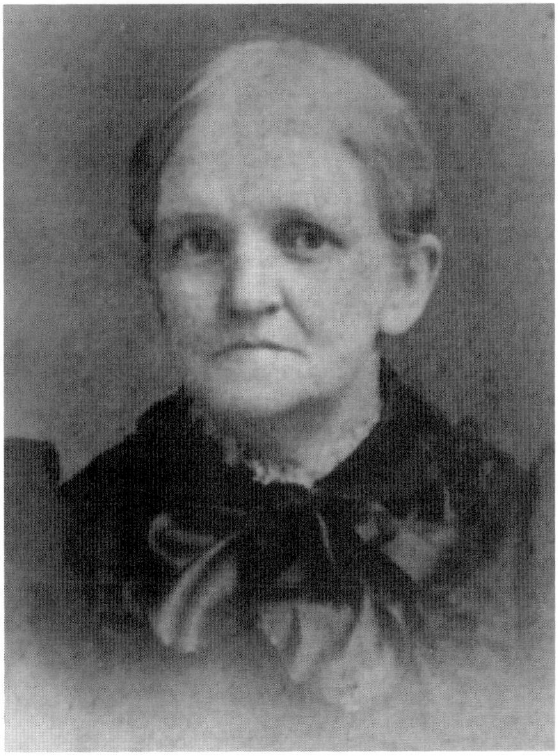

Elliott Perry Hine,
Local Carpenter
Elliott Perry Hine was born in 1827 and was unnamed for a long time. His parents called him "Boy." He visited a Mrs. Perry at the local orchard and she pinned a note to his shirt urging his parents to name him Elliott Perry Hine. Elliott Perry Hine became a carpenter and married Angeline. Pictured are Elliott and Angeline Hine. (Courtesy Jane Ewald White.)

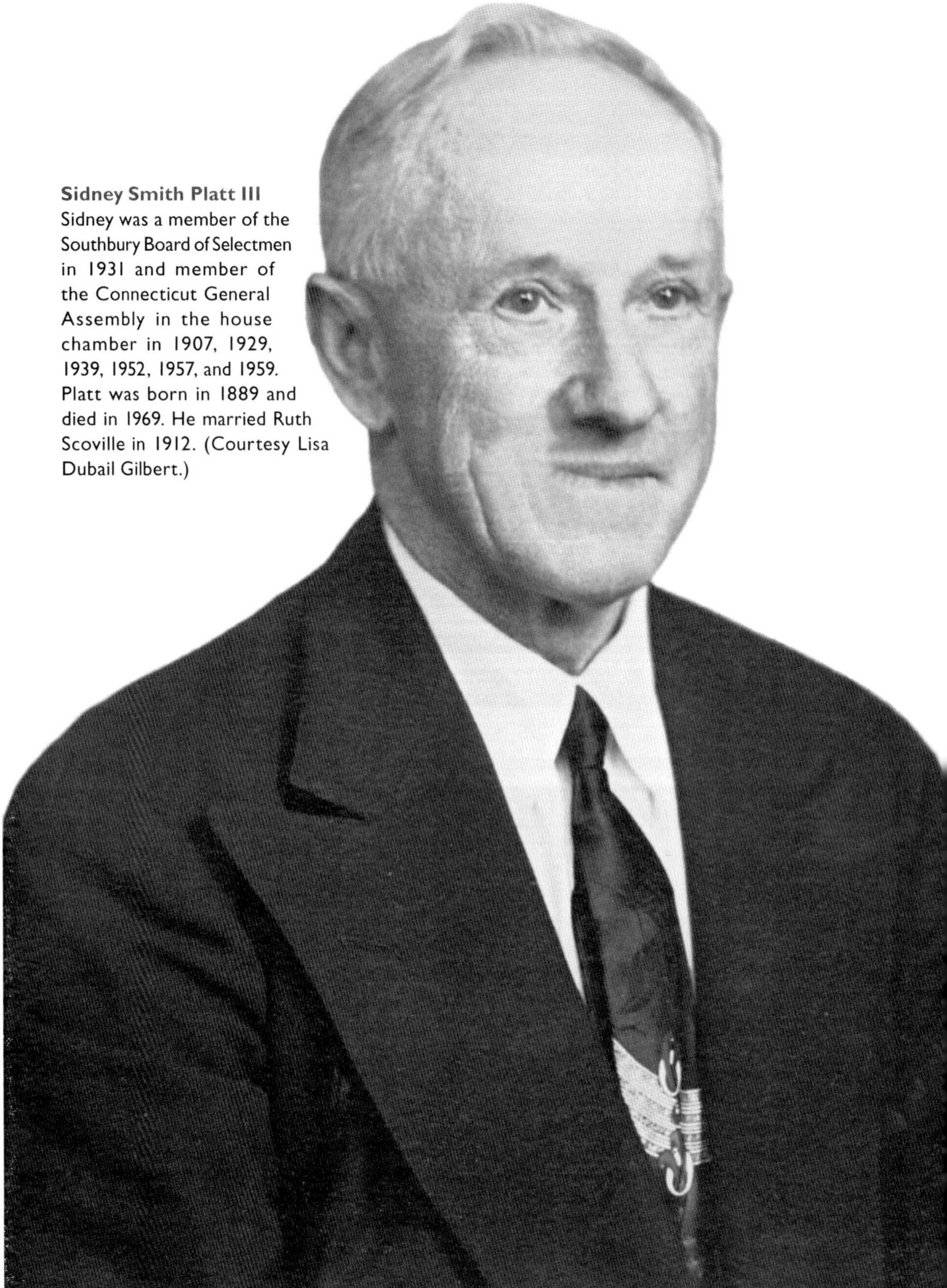

Sidney Smith Platt III
Sidney was a member of the Southbury Board of Selectmen in 1931 and member of the Connecticut General Assembly in the house chamber in 1907, 1929, 1939, 1952, 1957, and 1959. Platt was born in 1889 and died in 1969. He married Ruth Scoville in 1912. (Courtesy Lisa Dubail Gilbert.)

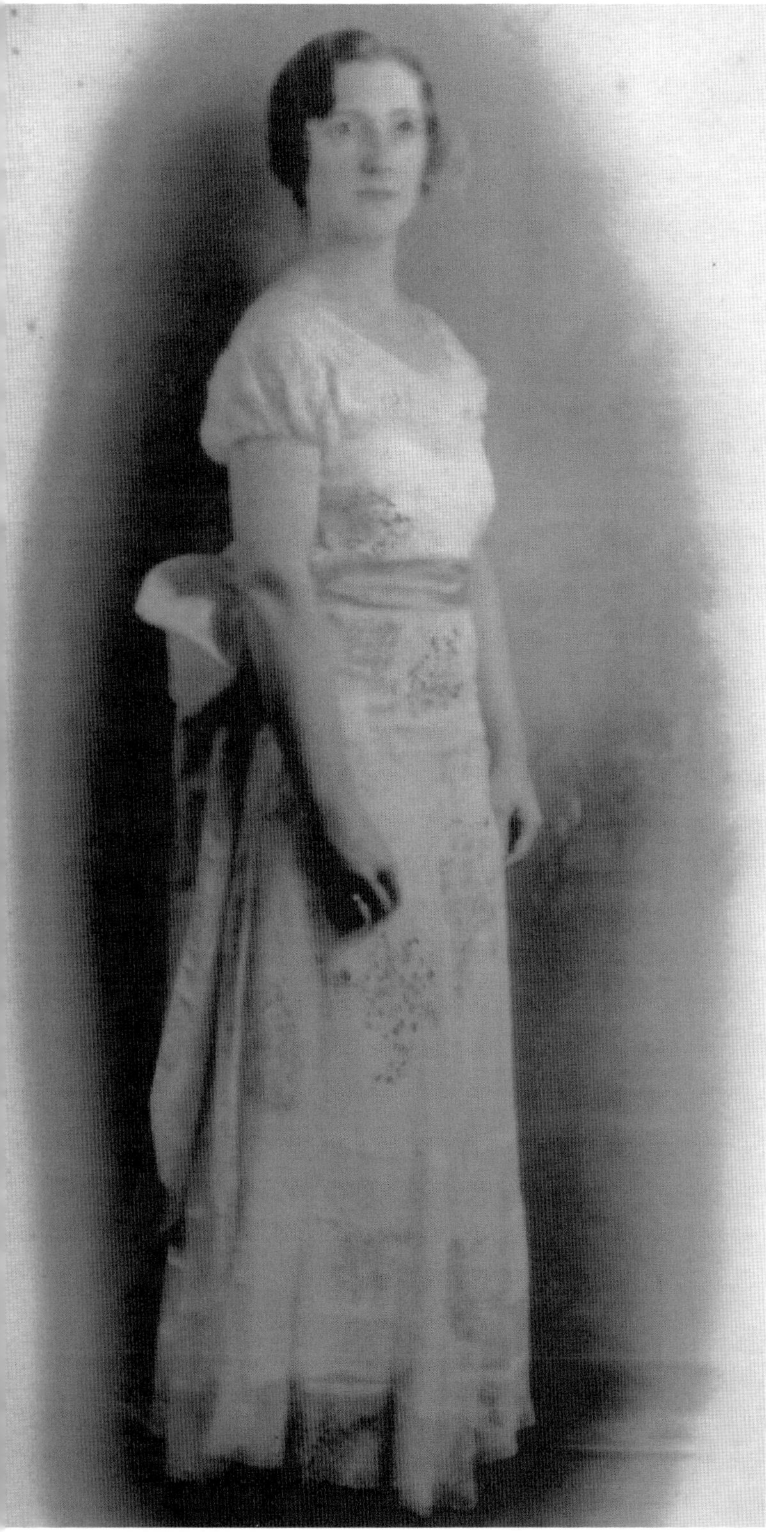

Rosamond Platt, Avid Gardener
Sidney Platt's sister Rosamond typified the lovely "country girl" of the early 1900s. The Platt farm always displayed a variety of beautiful flowers. The farm was sold but still continues the tradition with John Platt managing the Wisteria Gardens on the same property. Rosamond and sisters Laura and Marie were maiden ladies and were interested in gardening. They traveled extensively throughout America to learn about its natural resources. (Courtesy Lisa Dubail Gilbert.)

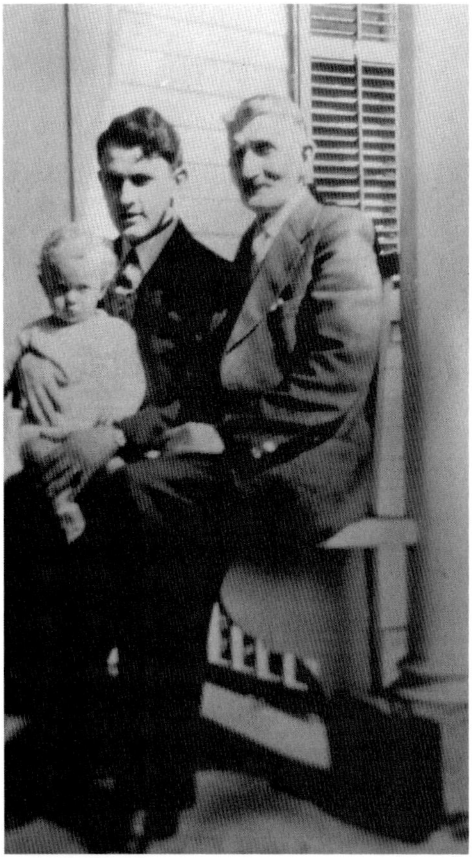

Three Generations of the Green Family
Three generations of the Samuel Green family all contributed to the community. The senior Green was the town's first doctor. The second ran a popular general store. Following in his elders' steps, Samuel Green III served as Southbury first selectman in 1968 and 1969. From left to right are Samuel II holding Samuel III, and Samuel I. (Courtesy of Samuel Green III.)

Public Works Team Restores Trees at Historic Kingsland
The public works team is seen beautifying another historic landmark. From left to right are Aaron Lewis, Dan Troya, foreman George Metcalf, Woody Chapman, John Gradowich, and Dan LaFlamme. The team planted sugar maples in 1996 to initiate tree restoration on Main Street North. Andrew Graham was granted use of this "commons" area to reward his service in colonial times. Graham tired of taxes and turned the land back over to the king, hence the name Kingsland. (Courtesy Catherine Palmer.)

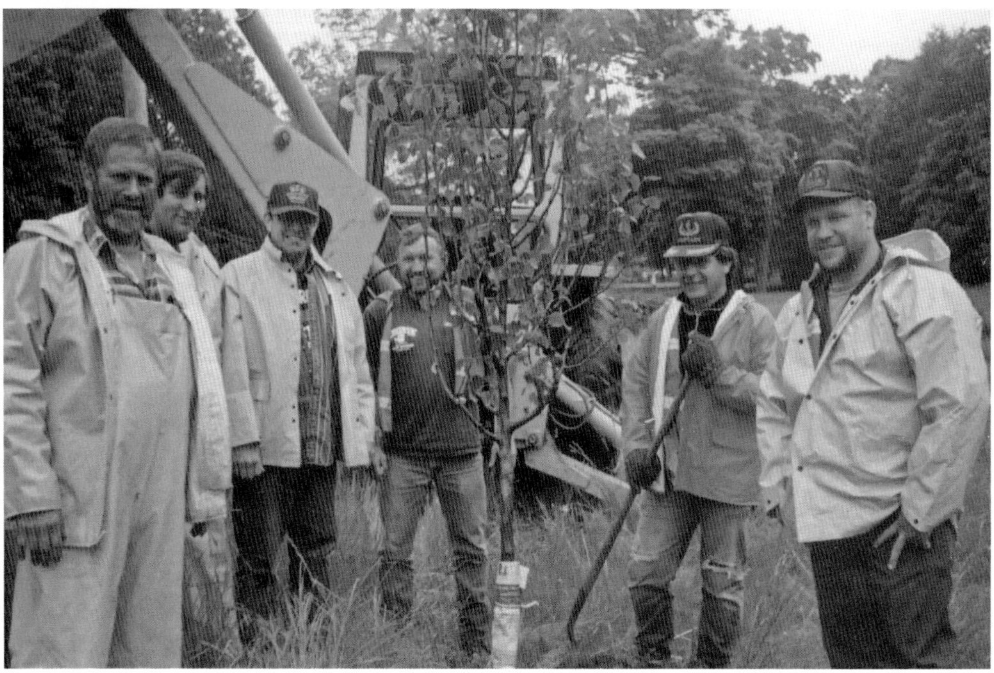

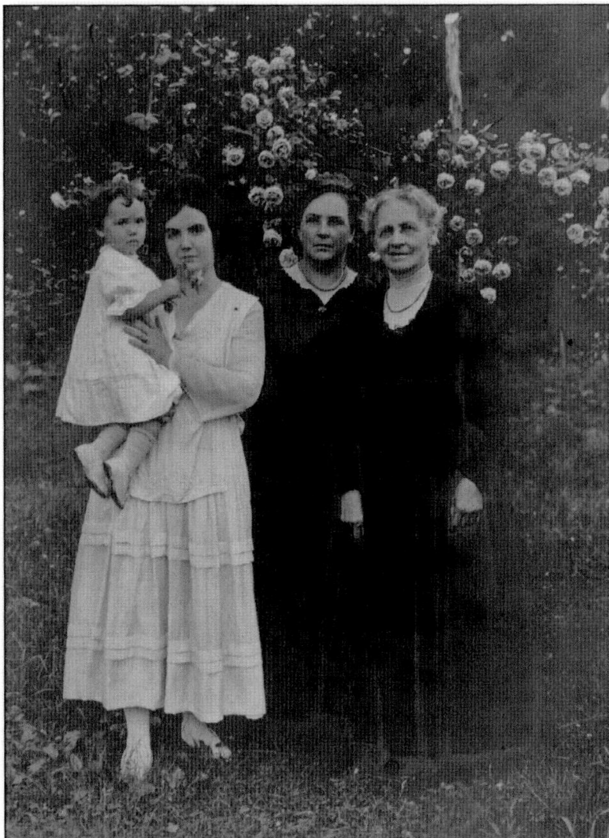

Evelyn Hicock
Evelyn Hicock was a teacher at the Pierce Hollow School. During World War I, she knitted thick sweaters, socks, and blankets for soldiers. She was the Southbury town treasurer for 23 years. She is pictured with her sister and friends. The South Britain ladies typified get-togethers of family and friends in the early 1900s in small towns. From left to right are Rachel Anne Hicock, Evelyn Hicock, Abbie Williams, and Julia Mitchell. (Courtesy Althea McGahie.)

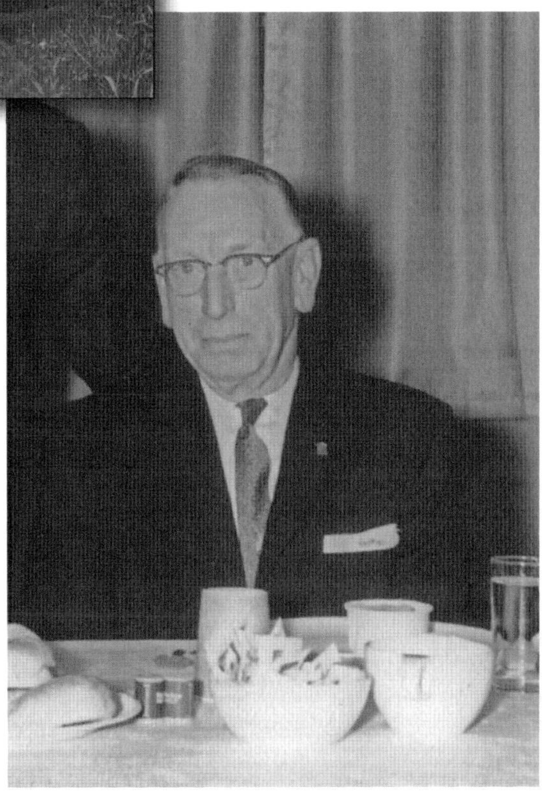

Testimonial Banquet for First Fire Chief of Southbury
Arza Canfield Bennett was the proprietor of St. Pierre's Garage. The building previously housed a blacksmith and a truck body shop. The garage was removed for construction related to Interstate 84 and the widening of Route 6. Arza was a charter member of the Southbury Fire Department and served for 32 years. (Courtesy Arza Bennett Jr.)

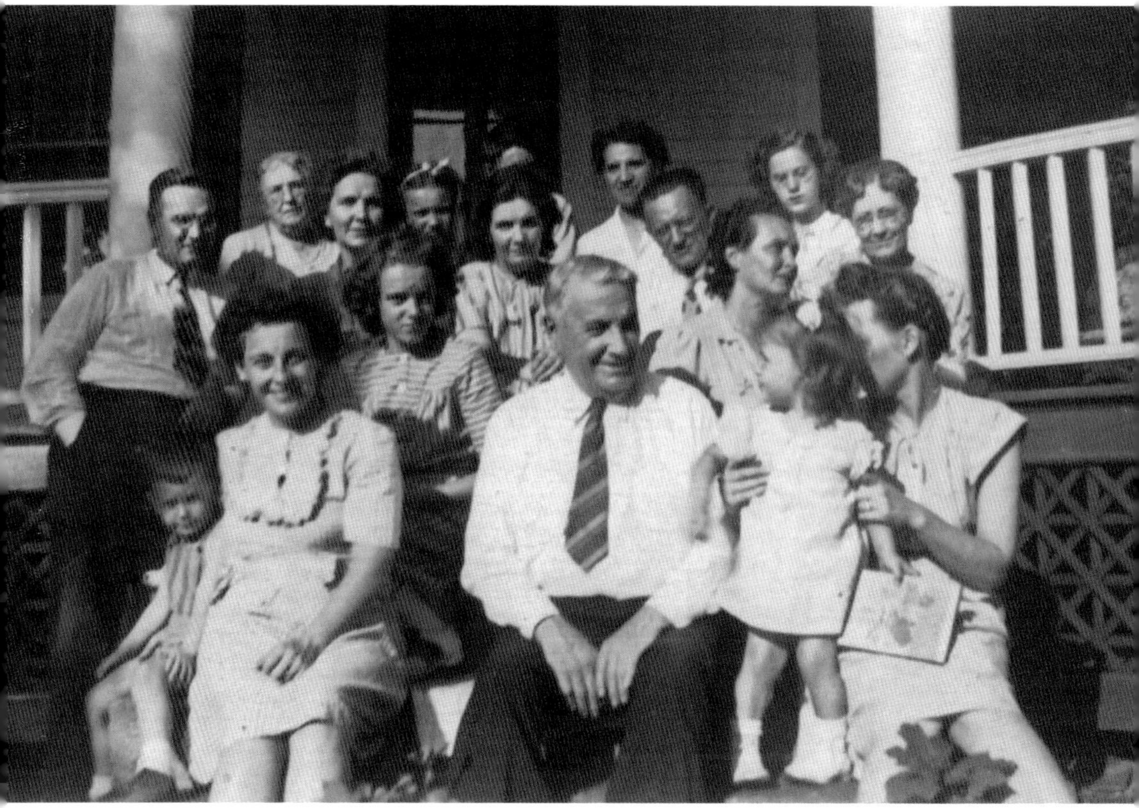

Charles Williams and Family

Charles Perry Williams built the CPW company in South Britain. It is now known as the South Britain General Store. Many of the Williams family descendants live in present-day Southbury and were town officers. Pictured from left to right are (first row) Bob Stilling, Julia Schielke, Hubert Mitchell, Susan Bertz, and Berta Bertz; (second row) Roger Williams, Winifred Brewer, Althea Hicock, Evelyn Hicock, Ely Hicock, Grace Hubbell, and Susan Meisner; (third row) Abbie Williams, Julia Hicock, unidentified, and Jane Hicock. (Courtesy Althea McGahie.)

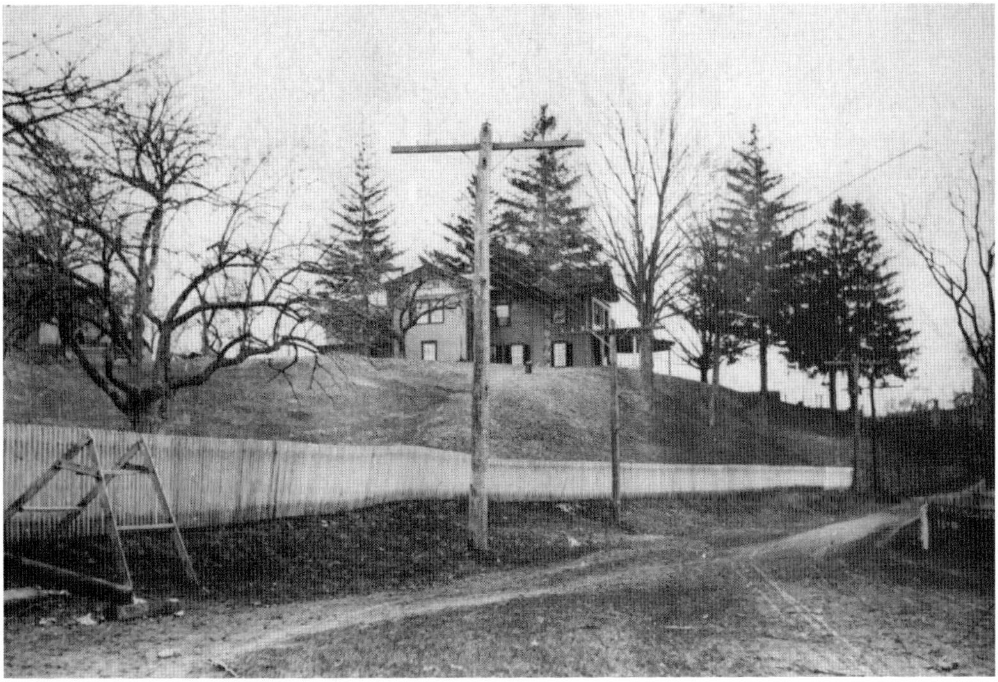

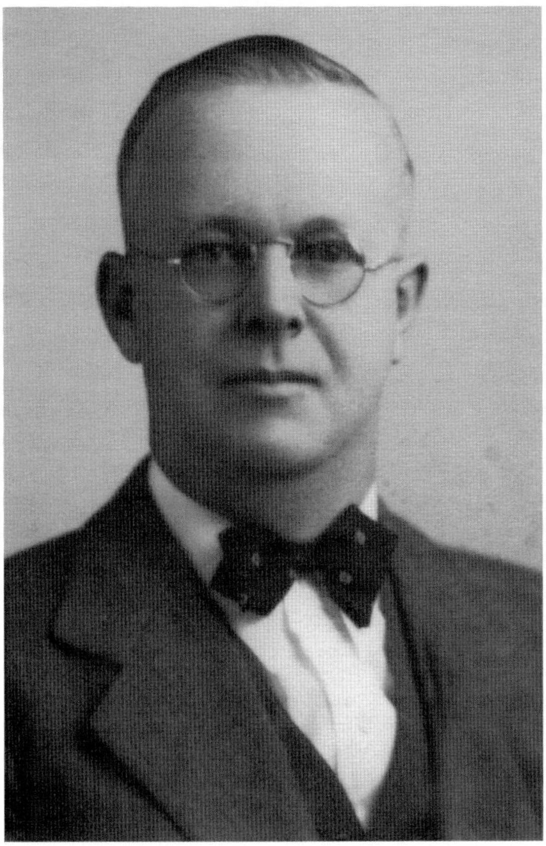

The Williams Family Home in South Britain
The Williams home was located in South Britain and was the site for many holiday parties and family get-togethers. Family members were dedicated churchgoers and citizens whose contributions over the years added to the success of the South Britain and Southbury community. (Courtesy Althea McGahie.)

Harold H. Davis and the Southford General Store
Harold was left the store in 1916, and was the town postmaster. His family remembers him as puritanical and unemotional; he would turn off his hearing aid to avoid arguments. He read the *New York Times* and did well with stock market investments. H. William Davis took over in 1964. (Courtesy H. William Davis.)

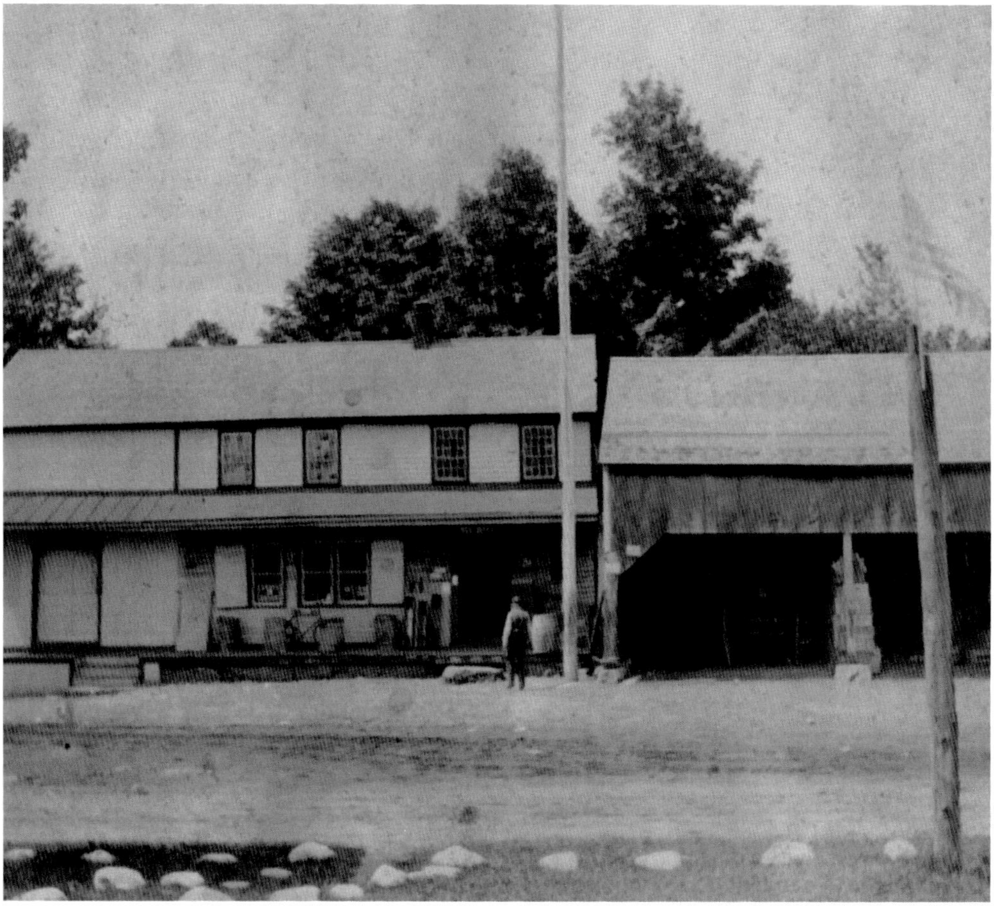

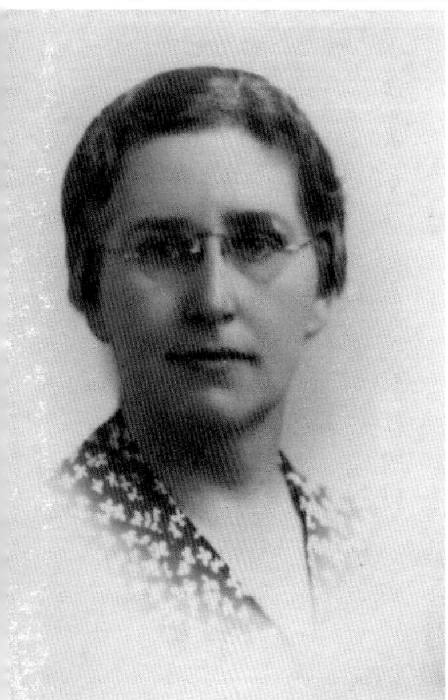

Davis Store with Livery

Founded in 1802 by the Oatman family, the store has been in continuous operation for over 200 years. Since the early 1900s, the store has been run by the Davis family, most recently by former First Selectman H. William Davis. It is located at the Route 188/67 junction and is approximately midway between New Haven and Litchfield. Stagecoach drivers stayed at the Oatman Hotel and rested their horses at the livery purchased in 1895 and attached to the store. (Courtesy Melinda Elliott.)

Delora King Davis

Delora was married to Harold H. Davis and was co-owner of the Southford General Store. Harold would signal Delora when he was ready to leave the store for dinnertime by turning on the well pump that was hooked to the well at home. She would provide milk and cookies to neighborhood children and cook with nasturtiums from her garden. Delora's father, John B. King, was the Diamond Match company foreman and had a company car for traveling in order to regulate the flow of water over the Quassapaug Dam. (Courtesy H. William Davis.)

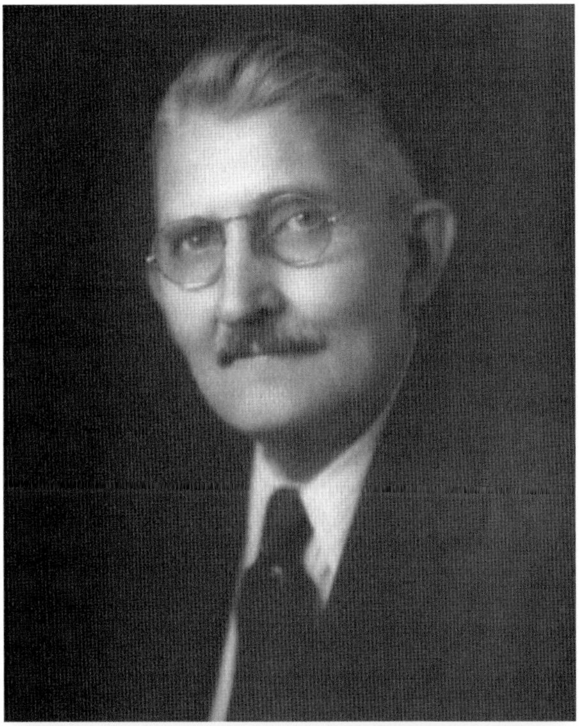

Southbury's First Doctor in 1900
Samuel Green did not go to college to study medicine. He learned and practiced medicine from his college-educated father. When licensing for doctors became mandatory, Samuel had to show proof that he was experienced and had successfully provided appropriate medical treatment to patients for years. (Courtesy Sam Green III.)

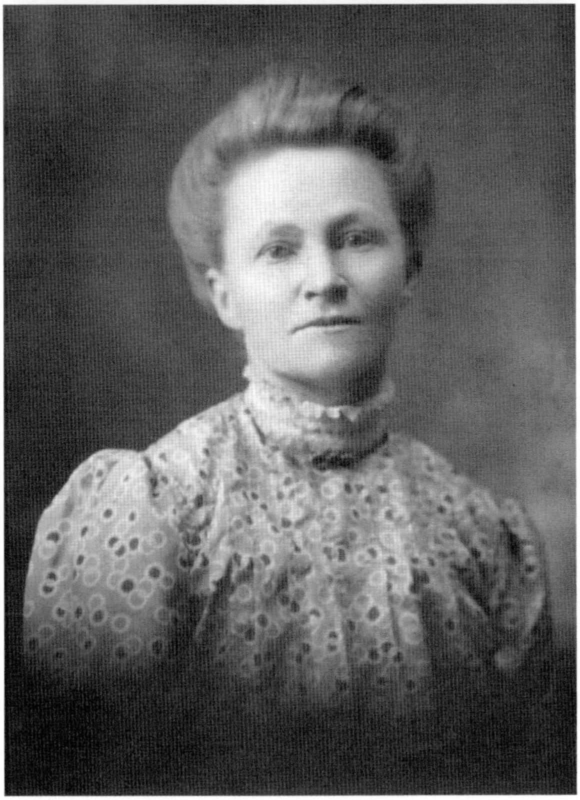

Fannie Green Bennett
Fannie assisted with the birth of many town residents and provided childcare. She married William Alanson Bennett, who owned several feldspar and mica mines in Southbury. They had five children: Arza, George, Homer, Maud, and Thalia. Her father, James, was a Civil War veteran who suffered a bullet wound in his back during the war. (Courtesy Arza Bennett Jr.)

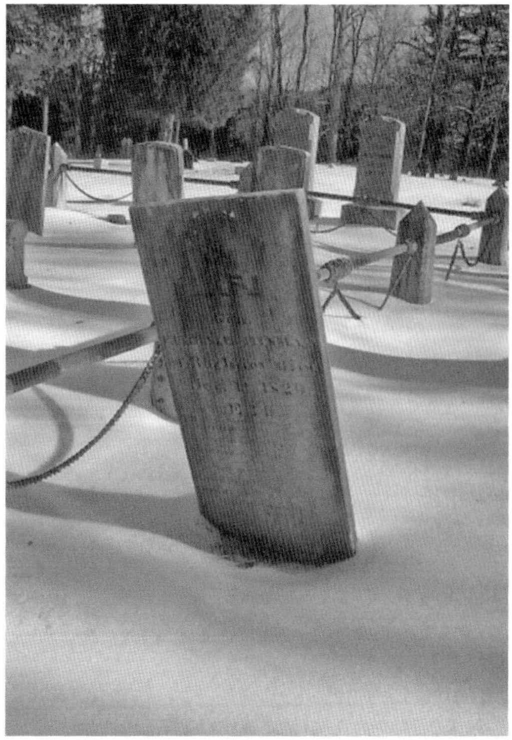

Timothy Hinman and Revolutionary War Soldiers

This 1829 cemetery stone is located in the old Hinman Cemetery. On December 31, 1800, Timothy Hinman transferred a piece of land adjacent to the new Congregational church meetinghouse, completed in 1775, to Benjamin Wildman, the Congregational minister. Seventeen of the 44 Revolutionary War soldiers buried in Southbury are resting at this site. At age 14, Hinman tried three times before he successfully enlisted for service in the war. The Historic Building Survey in 1937 indicated that he gave the land where Bullet Hill School is located today. (Courtesy VFW Post 1607.)

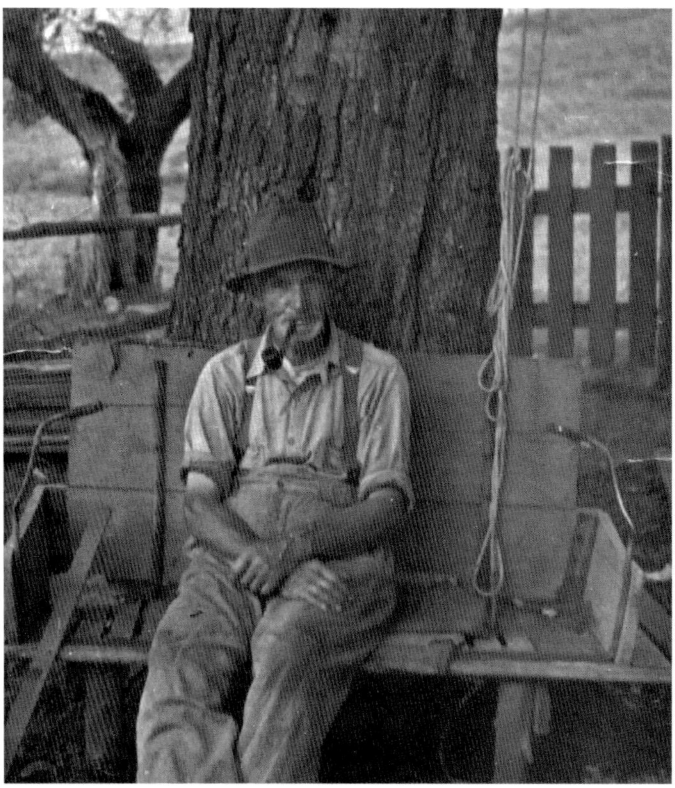

Gus Oberstadt

Gus Oberstadt and other farmers were the bedrock of the community. The Oberstadts owned a dairy farm. Southbury was a rural farming town for most of its history. However, with the development of the interstate system during the Eisenhower period, that changed. In 1963, I-84 opened and Southburians gained access to jobs as far away as New York, Hartford, Danbury, and Waterbury. (Courtesy Ed Wildman Jr.)

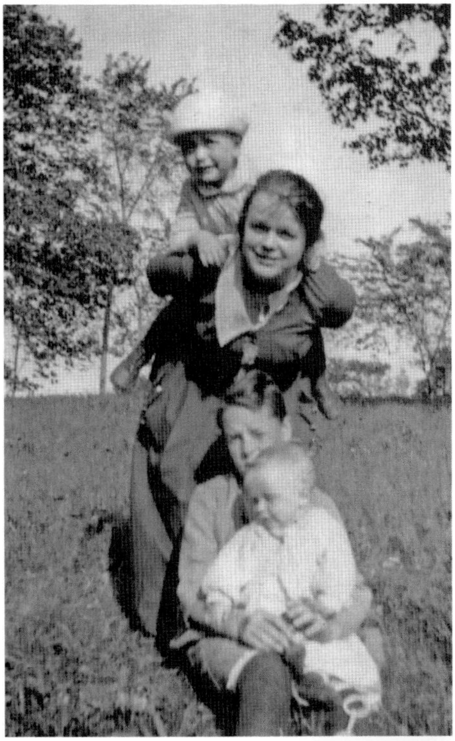

Ethel Droney Bennett
George Bennett was known as "Mr. Conservation" for the town of Southbury, and he believed that all citizens should work to preserve a community's open land. Bennett Park is named after him. Here, Bennett family members and a friend gathered for a picture. From top to bottom are Austin Bennett, Ethel Droney Bennett (a native of England and George Bennett's wife), a family friend, and Reginald Bennett. (Courtesy Arza Bennett Jr.)

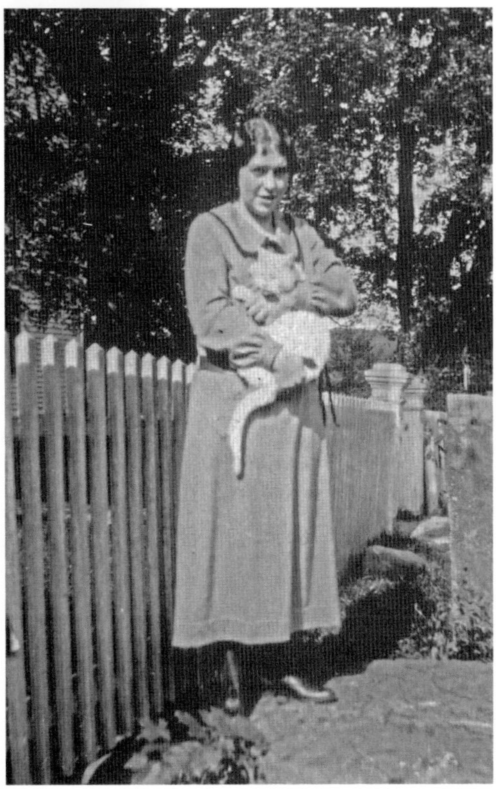

Thalia B. and C. Lewis Anderson
Thalia B. Anderson was a local nurse. She became a nurse at age 17 after attending the Waterbury School of Nursing. This was quite an accomplishment as most started college at age 17. She was born at her parents' home on Crook Horn Road. As a child she got her head caught in a bucket of water and almost drowned. Her husband, C. Lewis Anderson, helped build the present grange hall on Community House Road. She is pictured with her pet cat in the 1920s. (Courtesy Arza Bennett Jr.)

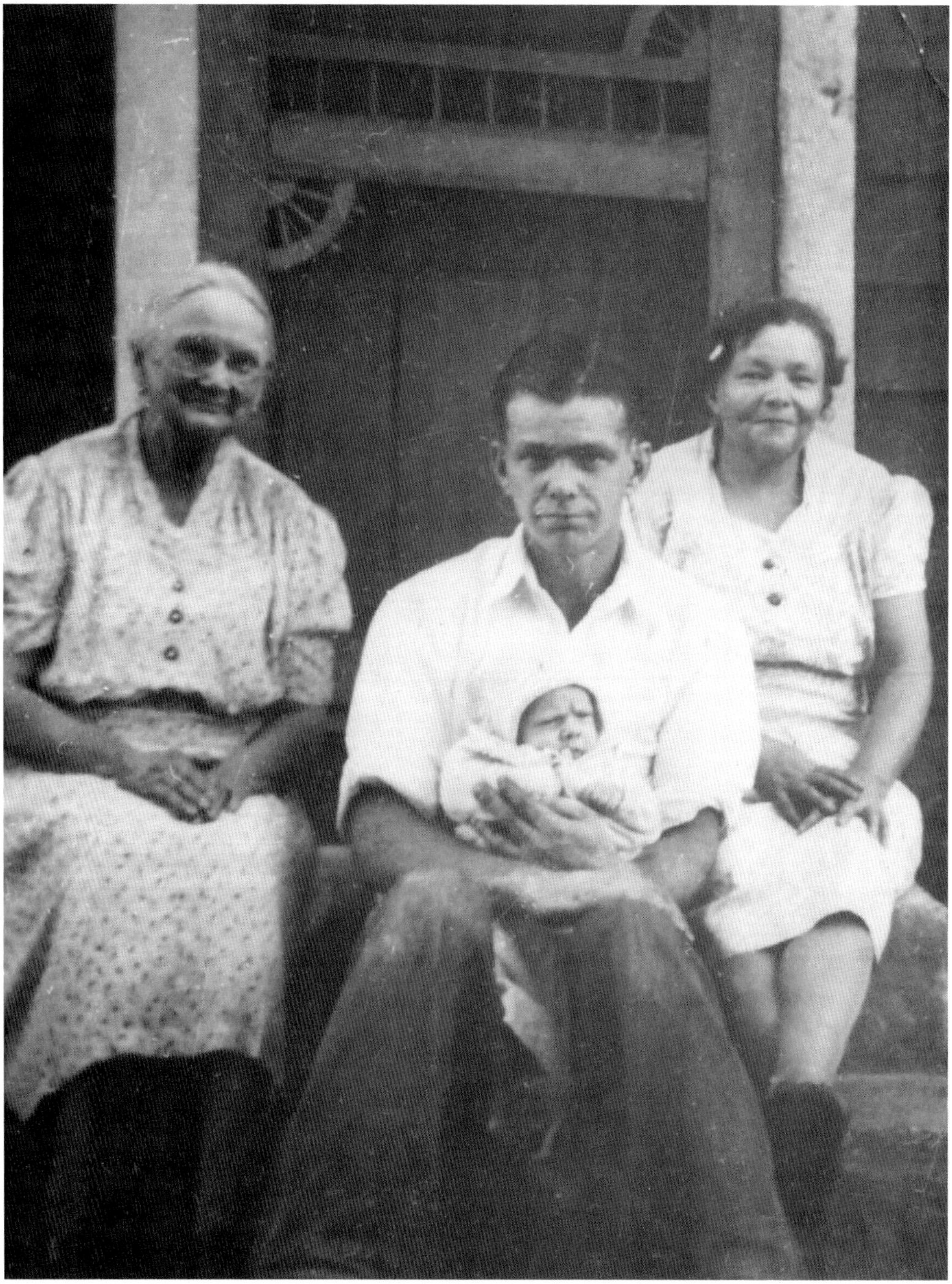

Ed Wildman Sr., Veteran and Master Mason

Ed Wildman Sr. served with the US Navy during World War II in the Pacific theater as a radar seaman. He was a master mason and owned and operated a well-known local masonry and plastering business. Four generations of the Wildman family are pictured here. From left to right are great-grandmother "Grossie" Wildman, Ed Wildman Sr. holding Ed Wildman Jr., and grandmother Augusta Wildman. (Courtesy Ed Wildman Jr.)

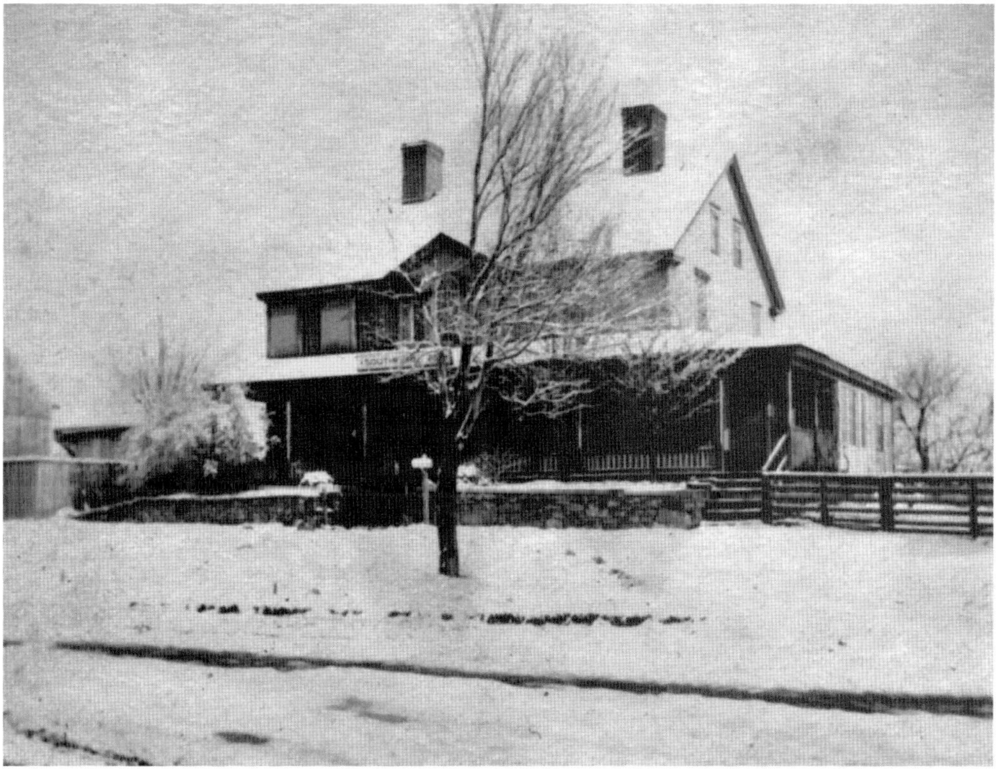

George Thompson and the Oatman Hotel
The Oatman Hotel was built in 1806 by George Thompson in the Southford section of Southbury, and later became Fennbrock Dairy. It was located close to the Davis Store. Visitors traveling between New Haven and Litchfield often enjoyed the comfort of the Oatman Hotel facilities. (Courtesy Melinda Elliott.)

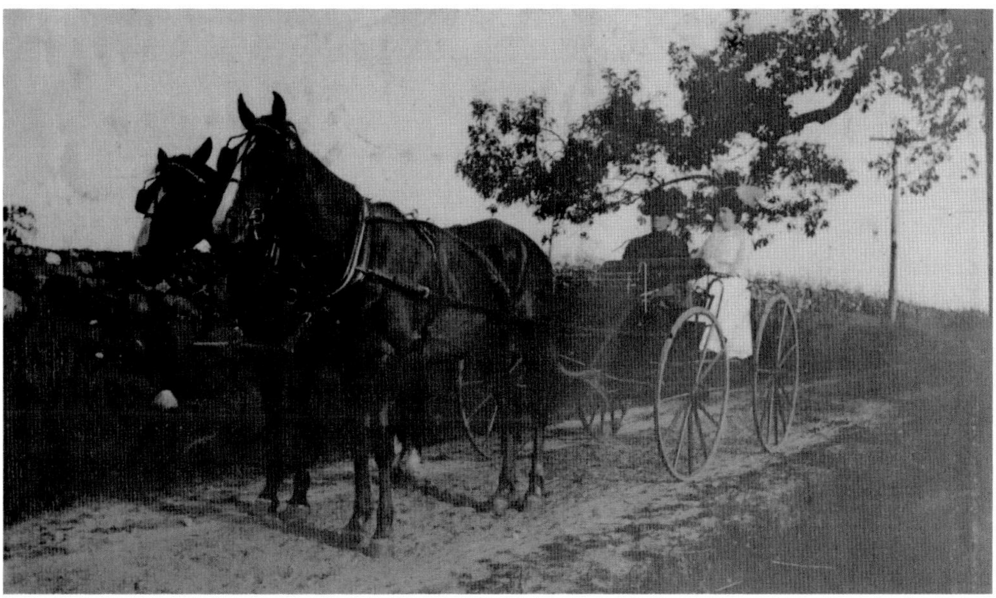

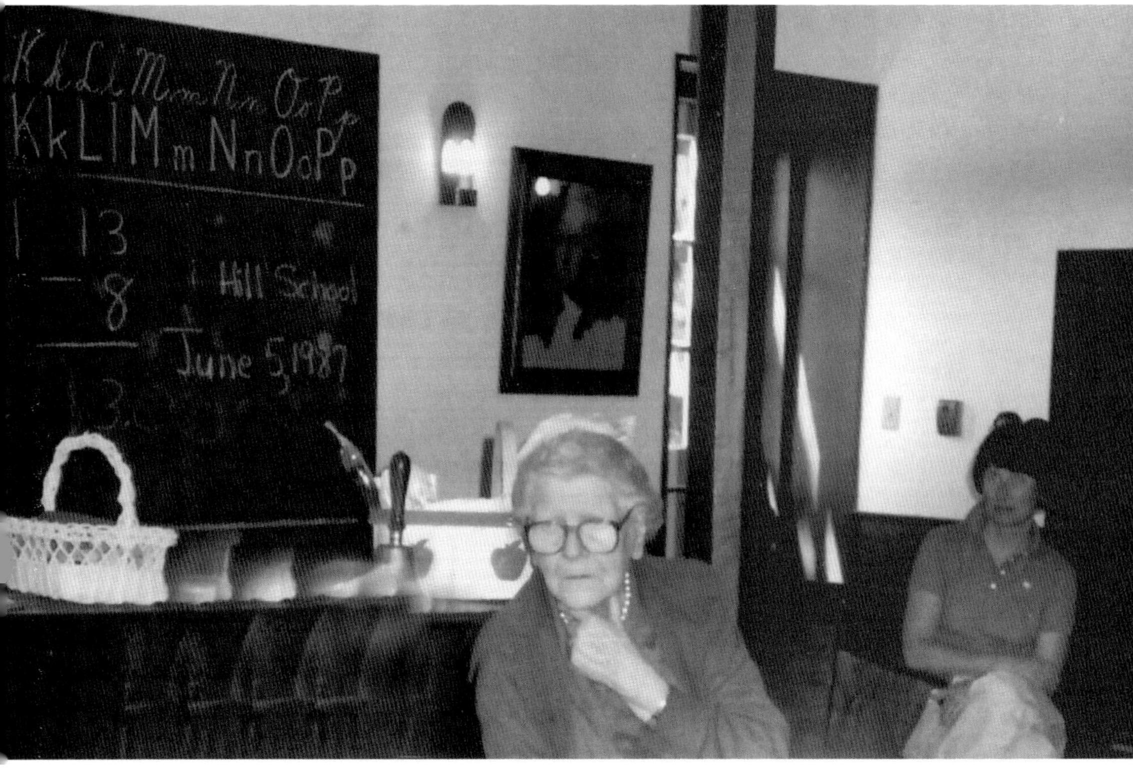

Catherine McCarthy Visiting Bullet Hill School

Catherine lived in an 1800s South Britain home. She was Connecticut's first female principal. In 1942, she became the town welfare director and also bought the nearby Methodist church for $500. The grounds were not cared for, and Catherine did not want snakes near her house from the tall grasses of the untended church grounds. She was Connecticut's oldest town employee before retirement. Upon her death, townsfolk were amazed at her wealth. Her will left more than $1 million to an Icelandic bishop who had visited Southbury. Shortly after he inherited the money, he died, and controversy arose as to whether his church family or real family should get the money. (Courtesy Catherine Palmer.)

CHAPTER TWO

Patriots, Veterans, and Town Heroes

The world is moved along, not only by the mighty shoves of its heroes, but also by the aggregate of tiny pushes of each honest worker.

—Helen Keller

Southbury is reflective of many New England cities that have evolved from small rural villages to fast-growing, bustling towns. The advent of motorized vehicles and the subsequent development of paved roads and state and interstate highways brought an enormous population expansion to Southbury. Despite the population growing from over 6,000 in the 1960s to close to 20,000 today, the spirit of patriotism and appreciation of military heroes, both sung and unsung, has grown and thrived. The number of citizens who are patriots, veterans, volunteers, and local heroes has grown exponentially. When one is standing or sitting in a lawn chair watching the annual Memorial Day parade, the number of marchers and those in admiration is a true study in Southbury Americana and the national pride the community shares.

From the country's first wars, Southbury citizens have pledged their service to America. Members of the George Newton VFW Post 1607 and the American Legion Lt. C. Edward Hine Post 147 exemplify this commitment and pride. The posts honor all veterans and encourage loyalty to the nation. Southbury's volunteer fire department is celebrating more than eight decades of protective services, from the town's first fire chief, Arza Bennett, and his volunteers in 1932 to today, including Fire Marshal Barry Rickert, Fire Chief Rick Lyle, 97 fellow volunteer firefighters, 19 junior firefighters, and 26 members of the ladies' auxiliary. Under the direction of Geralyn Hoyt, chief and president of the Southbury Ambulance Association, and her fellow members, the ambulance corps is celebrating 45 years of assisting citizens in times of great need. A call to 911 brings capable, trained, and compassionate heroes. Connecticut state police Chief Sgt. Michael O'Donnell and police department officers bring protective security to every challenging situation.

Over the years that Southbury has grown from a small village to the present-day town, patriots have served in all forms and have not only been the men and women who serve the country but also the volunteers who make Southbury a better place to live.

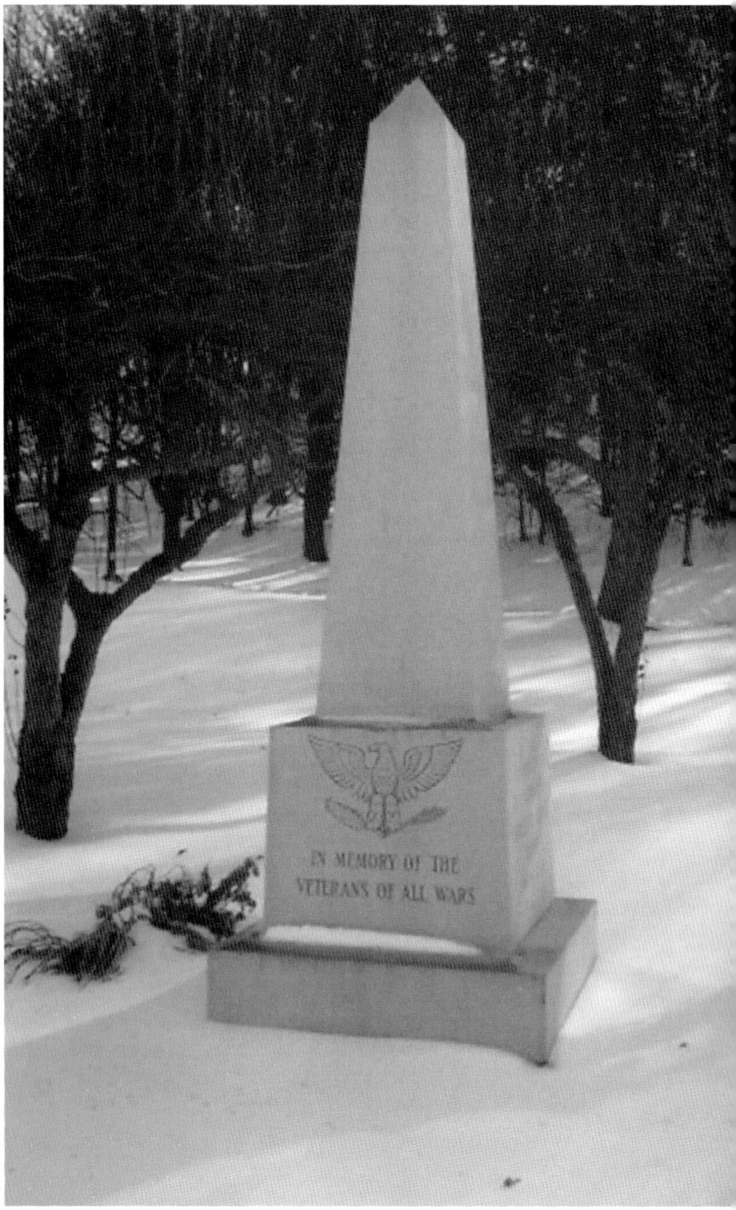

Veterans of All Wars Monument
Many Southbury veterans have fought to protect the rights of citizens. Three monuments are set between town hall and the old public library to honor them. Unlike the other two, the one pictured was not moved from other sites. It is the tallest memorial and was created in 1971 by the American Legion Lt. C. Edward Hine Post 147 and George Newton VFW Post 1607, with a contribution of $3,000 from the town. Two monuments are located at Memorial Park in memory of World War I and World War II veterans, also provided by the local VFW and American Legion posts. The World War I monument honors 65 Southbury veterans who served from 1917 to 1919, including George Newton and Harold Davis, two soldiers who died in World War I. The World War II monument's inscription includes the dates 1941–1945. (Courtesy VFW Post 1607.)

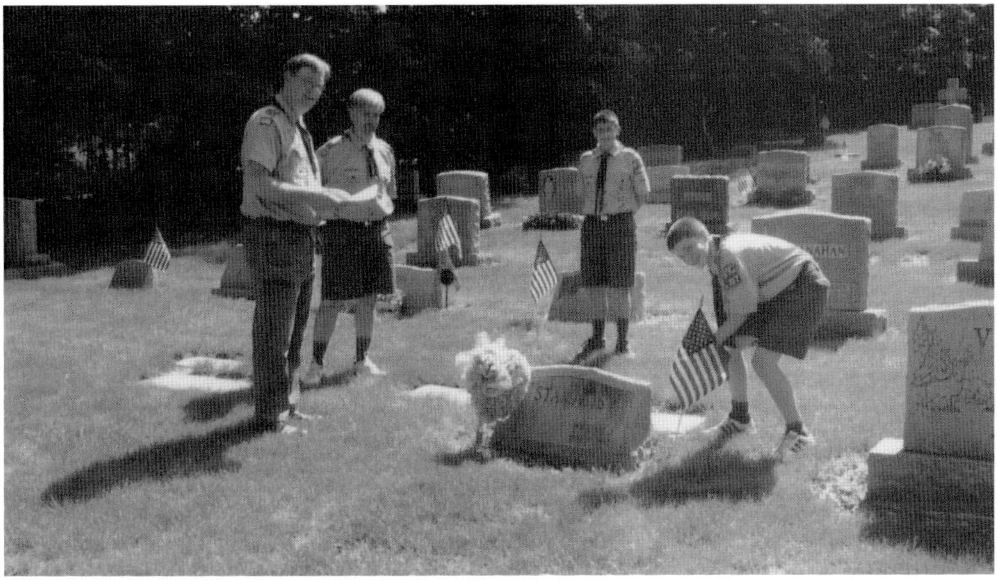

Boy Scouts Placing Flags on Veterans' Graves
Boy Scouts have worked on many community endeavors including building bridges and paths in town parks. During the week before Memorial Day every year, local Boy Scouts place flags on graves in the town's six cemeteries. More than 400 hundred veterans are buried at these sites. (Courtesy VFW Post 1607.)

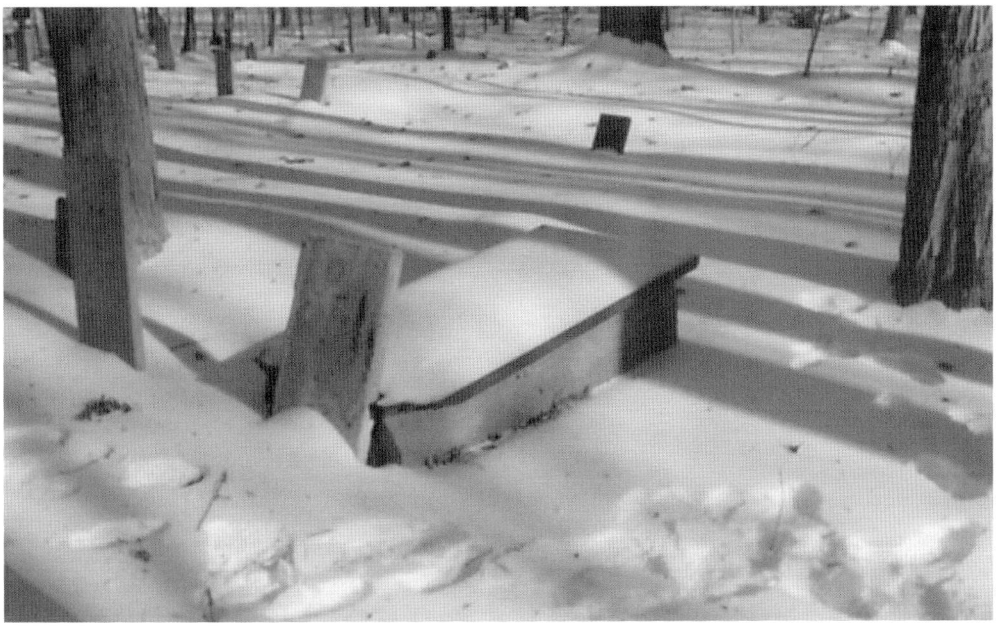

Thomas Solley's Grave
Thomas Solley was a Revolutionary War patriot, and received a pension for the rest of his life. He died in 1840 and is buried in the North George's Hill Cemetery. His family members were the first settlers to immigrate to America with the Solley name. They owned and operated a hat shop near the Kettletown area with local employees making homemade hats. (Courtesy VFW Post 1607.)

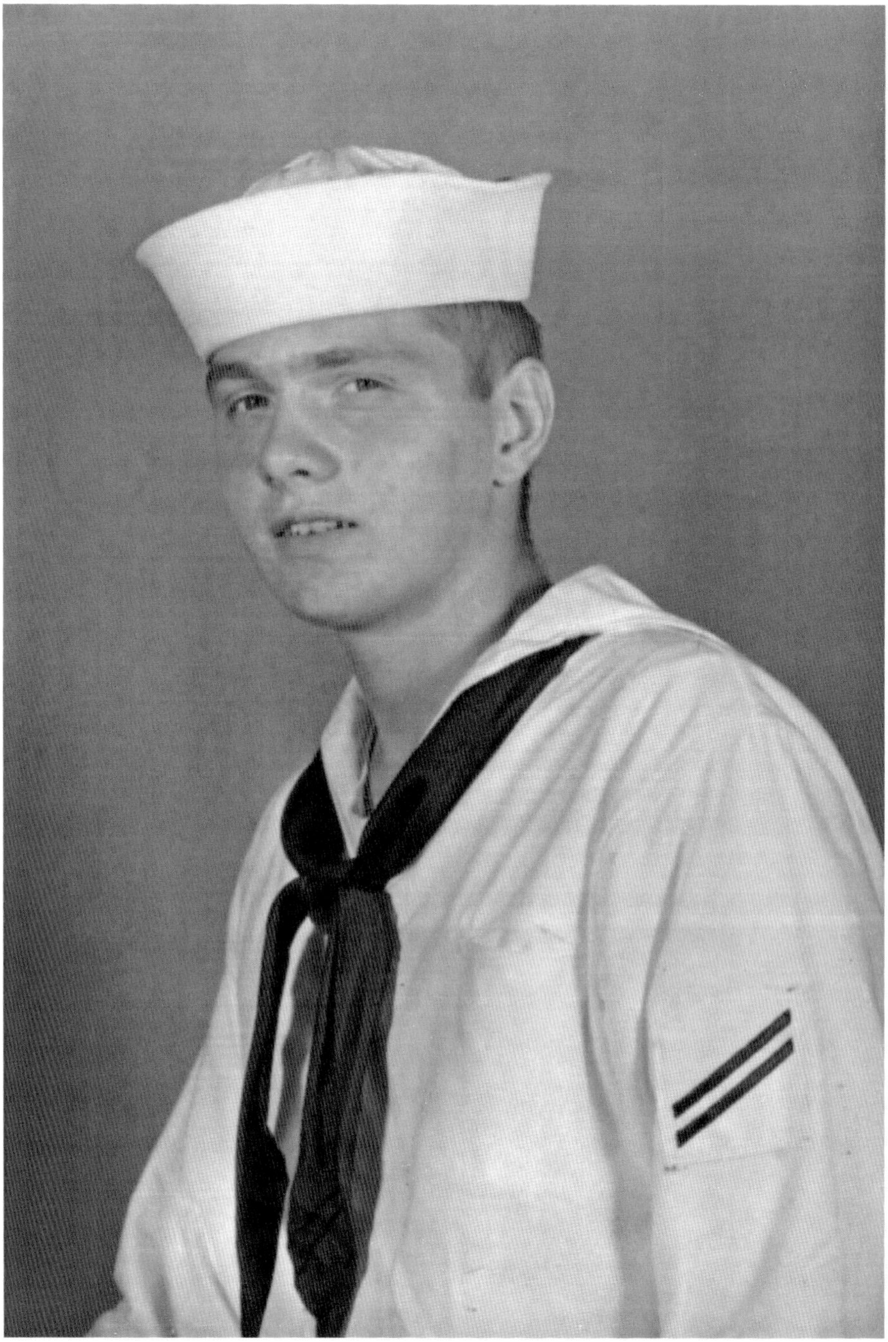

Ed Wildman Jr.

Ed Wildman Jr. has served as chairman of the Zoning Commission and presently serves on the Rural Preservation Commission. Ed was a seaman and trained at Great Lakes Naval Station in Illinois. He served his country in Guam and Adak, Alaska. He also served in Okinawa with the Mobile Construction Battalion. This was the first company of Seabees in Vietnam for the first three months of the war. (Courtesy Ed Wildman Jr.)

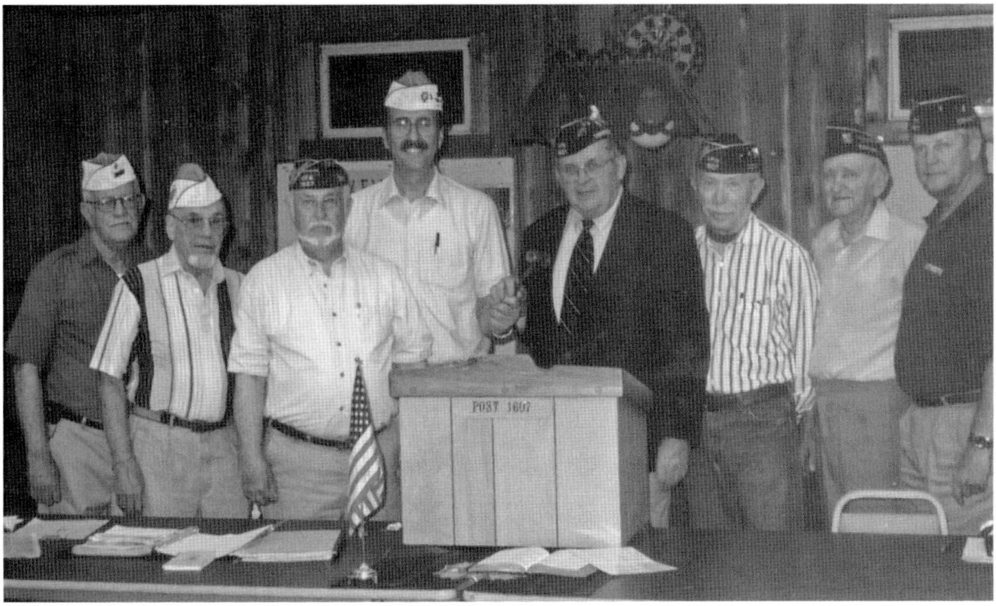

George Newton VFW Post 1607

The 2000 officers of the George Newton VFW Post 1607 are, from left to right, Joseph Jamieson, Richard Heebner, Sam Green, Leslie Hatstat, Comdr. Harmon Andrews, Arthur Murray, Anthony Polmon, and Ken Korsu. The post was named after George Newton, who died in World War I in France. Founded in 1923, the members are proud to be one of approximately 8,500 posts. (Courtesy VFW Post 1607.)

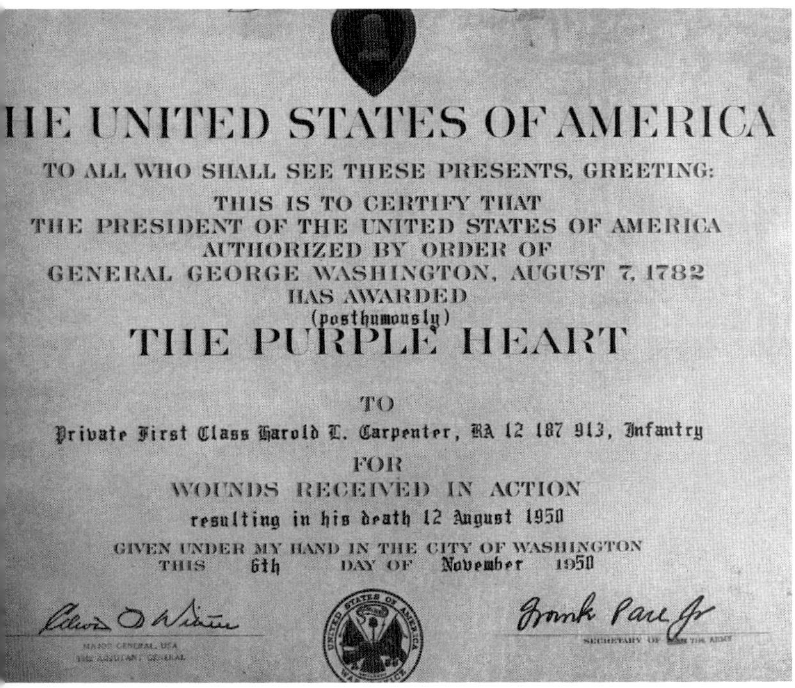

HE UNITED STATES OF AMERICA

TO ALL WHO SHALL SEE THESE PRESENTS, GREETING:

THIS IS TO CERTIFY THAT
THE PRESIDENT OF THE UNITED STATES OF AMERICA
AUTHORIZED BY ORDER OF
GENERAL GEORGE WASHINGTON, AUGUST 7, 1782
HAS AWARDED
(posthumously)

THE PURPLE HEART

TO

Private First Class Harold L. Carpenter, RA 12 187 913, Infantry

FOR

WOUNDS RECEIVED IN ACTION
resulting in his death 12 August 1950

GIVEN UNDER MY HAND IN THE CITY OF WASHINGTON
THIS 6th DAY OF November 1950

MAJOR GENERAL, USA
THE ADJUTANT GENERAL

SECRETARY OF THE ARMY

Harold Carpenter

Harold Carpenter was awarded a Purple Heart medal. He was killed during the Korean conflict. He was the son of Ellis Carpenter, commander of American Legion Post 147. (Courtesy VFW Post 1607.)

Hero Hine
Lt. C. Edward Hine served in World War II. He died during a training mission in Texas when his plane caught fire while he was trying to land. He was the son of Elliott Charles Hine. American Legion Post 147 was named after him. (Courtesy VFW Post 1607.)

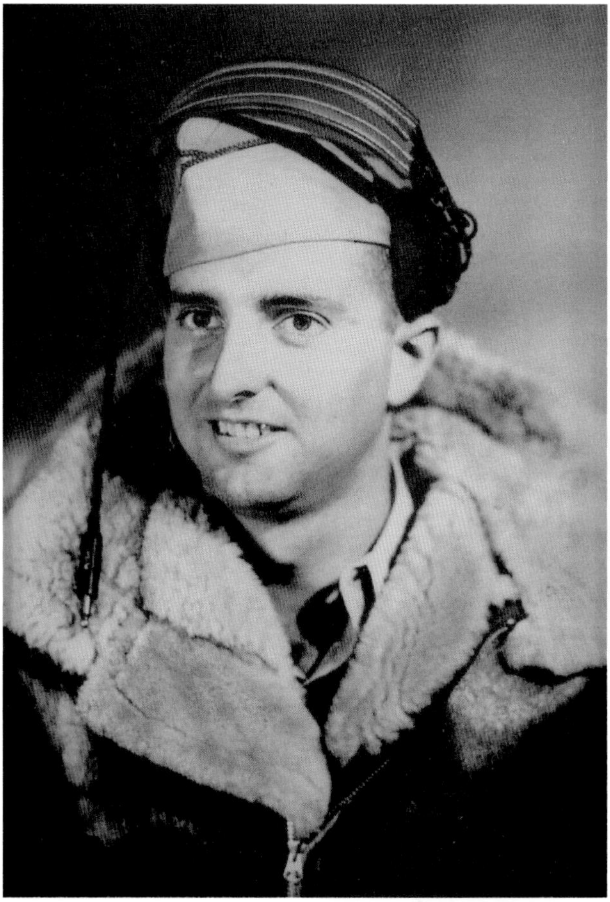

Memorial Day Celebration, 1961
Southbury helmet-wearing veterans proudly represent all who have served and are currently serving their country. (Courtesy VFW Post 1607.)

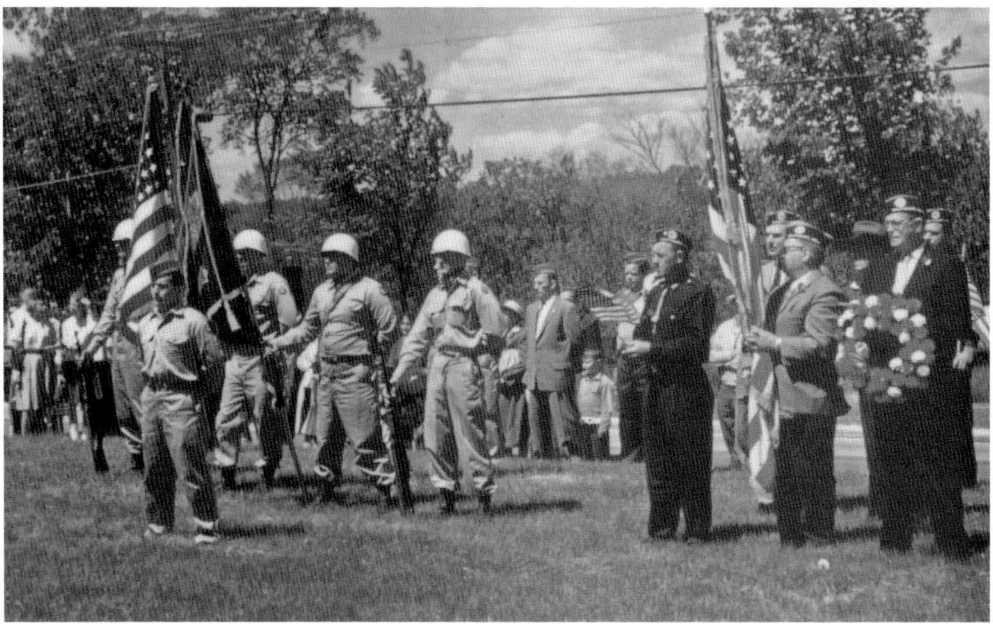

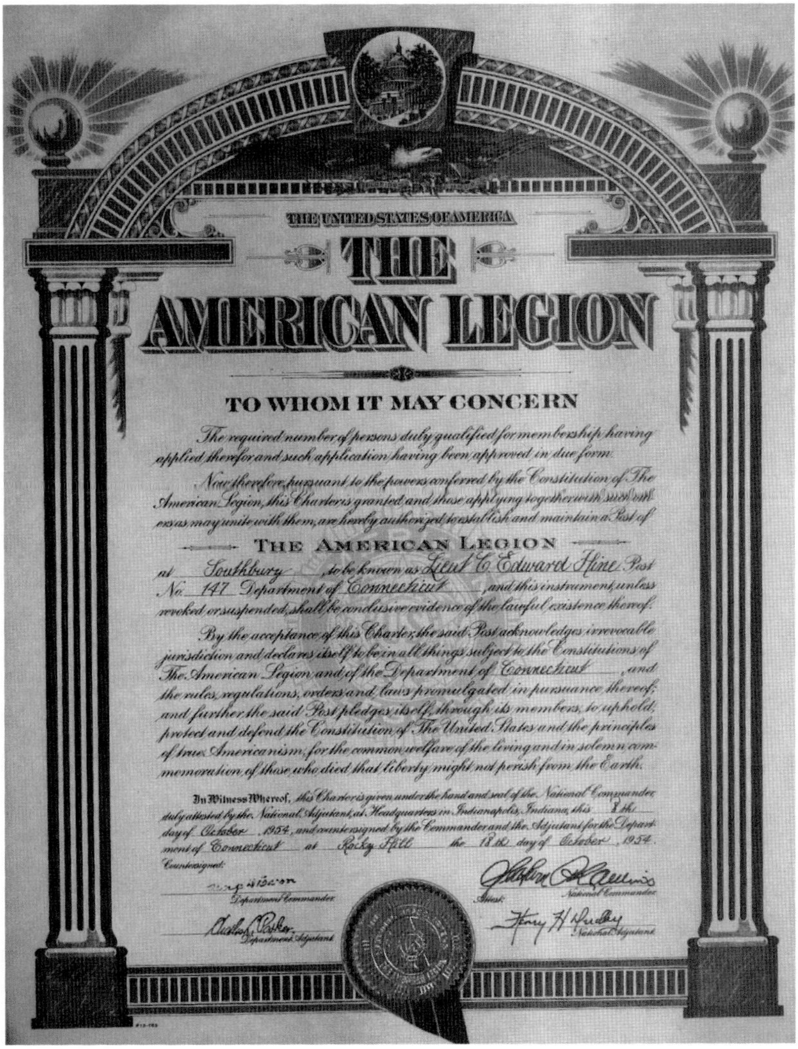

THE UNITED STATES OF AMERICA

THE

AMERICAN LEGION

TO WHOM IT MAY CONCERN

The required number of persons duly qualified for membership having applied therefor and such application having been approved in due form.

Now therefore, pursuant to the powers conferred by the Constitution of The American Legion, this Charter is granted and those applying together with such others as may unite with them, are hereby authorized to establish and maintain a Post of

THE AMERICAN LEGION

at Southbury, to be known as Lieut C. Edward Hine Post No. 147 Department of Connecticut, and this instrument, unless revoked or suspended, shall be conclusive evidence of the lawful existence thereof.

By the acceptance of this Charter, the said Post acknowledges irrevocable jurisdiction and declares itself to be in all things subject to the Constitutions of The American Legion and of the Department of Connecticut, and the rules, regulations, orders and laws promulgated in pursuance thereof, and further the said Post pledges itself, through its members, to uphold, protect and defend the Constitution of The United States and the principles of true Americanism, for the common welfare of the living and in solemn commemoration of those who died that liberty might not perish from the Earth.

In Witness Whereof, this Charter is given under the hand and seal of the National Commander duly attested by the National Adjutant, at Headquarters in Indianapolis, Indiana, this 8th day of October 1954, and countersigned by the Commander and the Adjutant for the Department of Connecticut at Rocky Hill the 18th day of October, 1954.

Countersigned:

Department Commander

Department Adjutant

Attest:

National Commander

National Adjutant

American Legion

Many members of the local American Legion have served in leadership positions within the local government from commissions to boards to first selectman of the town. The American Legion Lt. C. Edward Hine Post 147 has provided an ongoing program of educating Southburians of all ages in developing an awareness and respect for veterans and the essential roles they have played in society. The American Legion members encourage high school students to participate in an annual essay contest on a subject related to patriotism, and present awards for the winners. An additional valuable opportunity is the American Legion Boy's State, a weeklong program for outstanding high school juniors to learn about the mechanics of the federal government as senators and representatives in a dual-party system. Each year, fundraising events are held by selling the symbolic poppy, which benefits veterans by developing the public's appreciation for them. Members represent all branches of service. The American Legion members meet at the VFW Post 1607 building; they used to meet at Kelley's Oak Tree Inn. The American Legion was chartered and incorporated by Congress in 1919 as a patriotic veterans' organization devoted to mutual helpfulness. It is the nation's largest veterans' service organization, and is committed to sponsoring youth programs, instilling patriotism and honor, and encouraging national security and devotion to servicemembers and veterans. (Courtesy American Legion Post 147.)

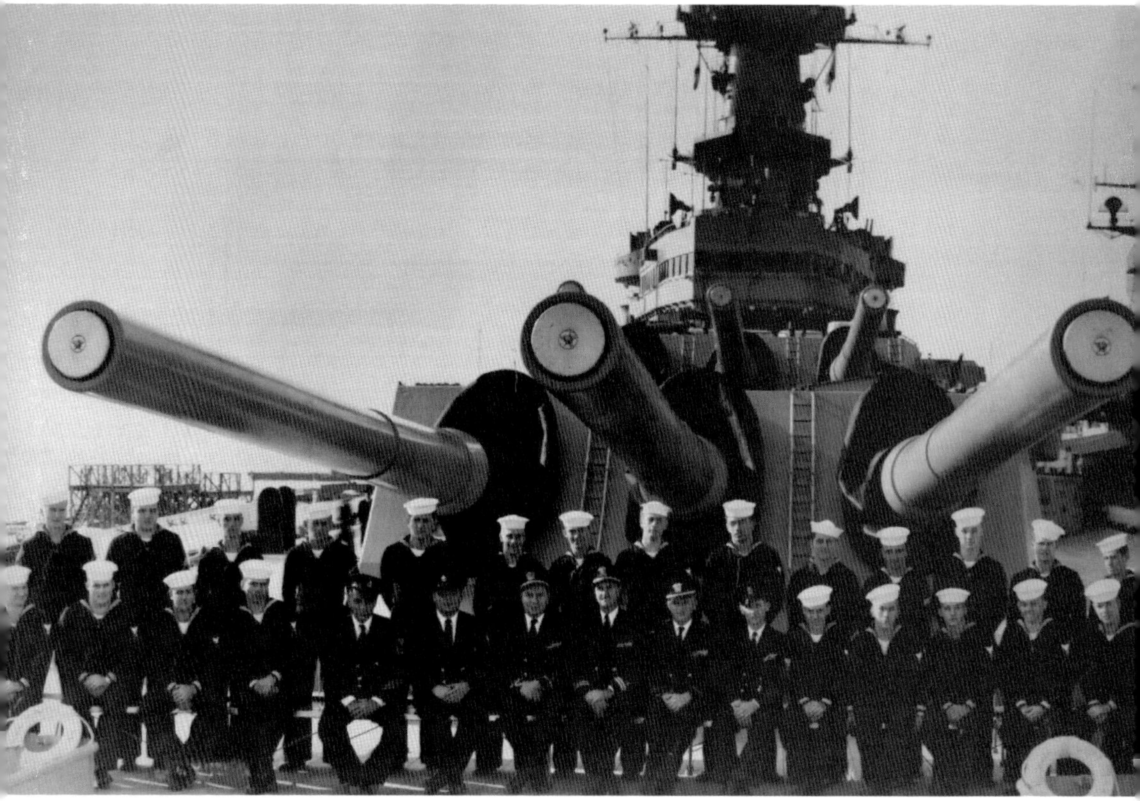

Charles Hicock Scott, Veteran

Shown is a US Navy battleship with one of Southbury's own, Charles "Scotty" Hicock Scott. Scotty's father was a commander of the local VFW post. (Courtesy VFW Post 1607.)

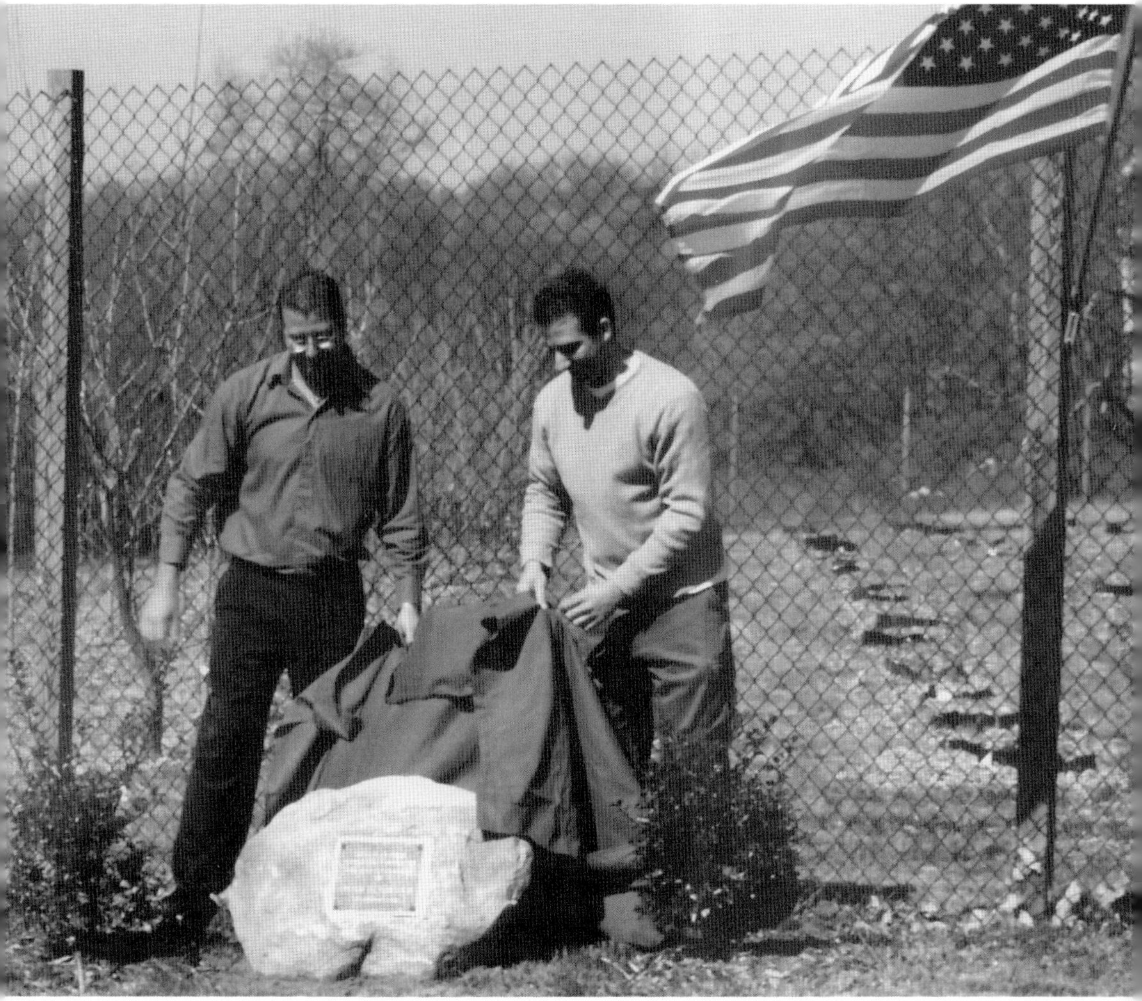

Sean Schielke

Sean Schielke lost his life in the terrorist attacks of 9/11. He was a 27-year-old international bond trader for Cantor Fitzgerald and was trapped on the 105th floor of the north tower. Brandon Schielke (left) and Ken Schielke are pictured at the tree and plaque dedication in honor of their brother at Schielke Park Town Tree Nursery. The brothers grew up working in the family's Schielke Lumber Company with their grandfather Gordon Schielke. (Courtesy Catherine Palmer.)

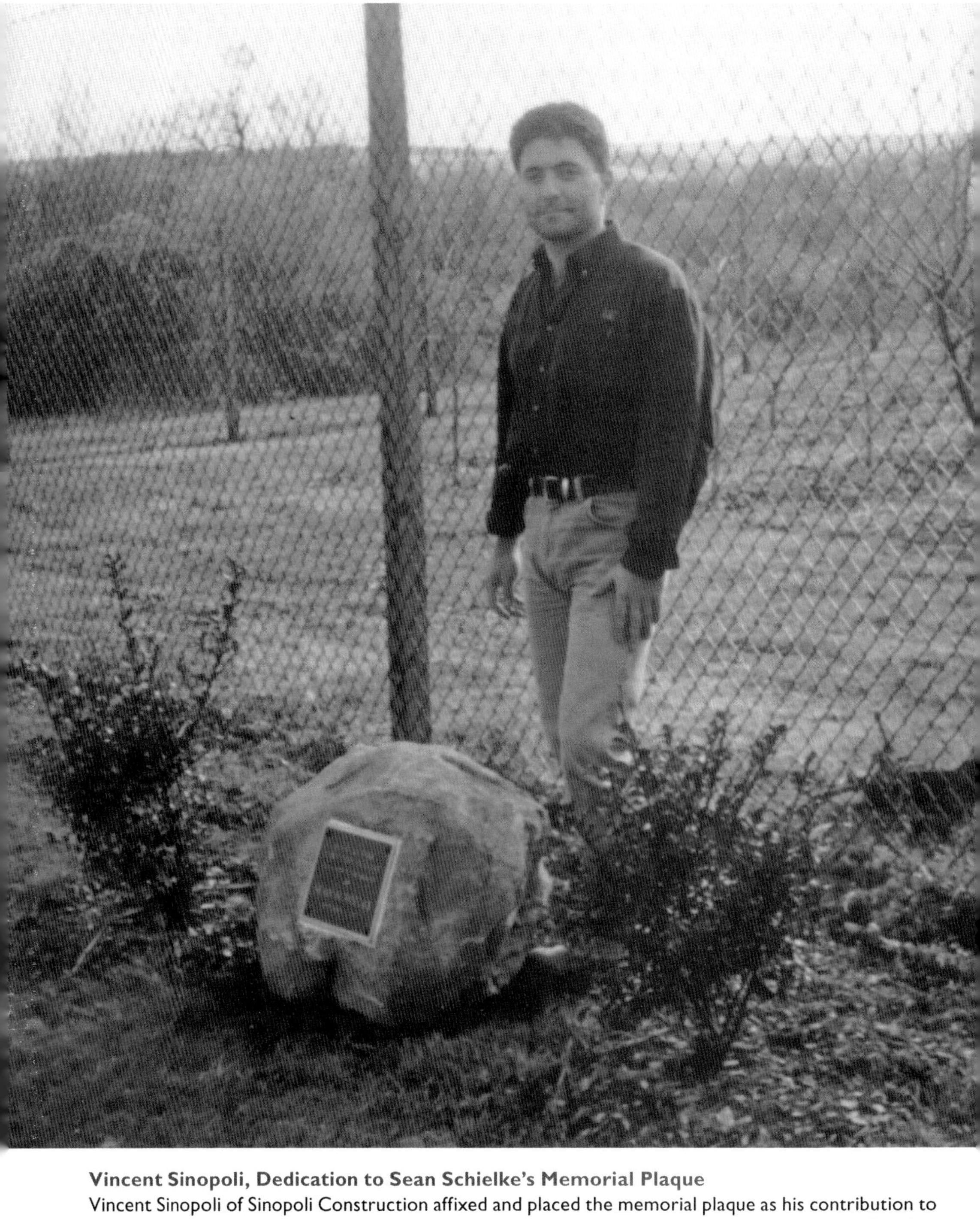

Vincent Sinopoli, Dedication to Sean Schielke's Memorial Plaque
Vincent Sinopoli of Sinopoli Construction affixed and placed the memorial plaque as his contribution to Sean Schielke's memory. Vincent is a major contributor when it comes to assisting the Historic Building Commission. He has assisted with many projects at the town's three historic buildings. Vincent and his wife are very active when it comes to local school business and also Southbury PTO activities. Sinopoli Construction was started by Vincent and his late brother, Anthony. (Courtesy Catherine Palmer.)

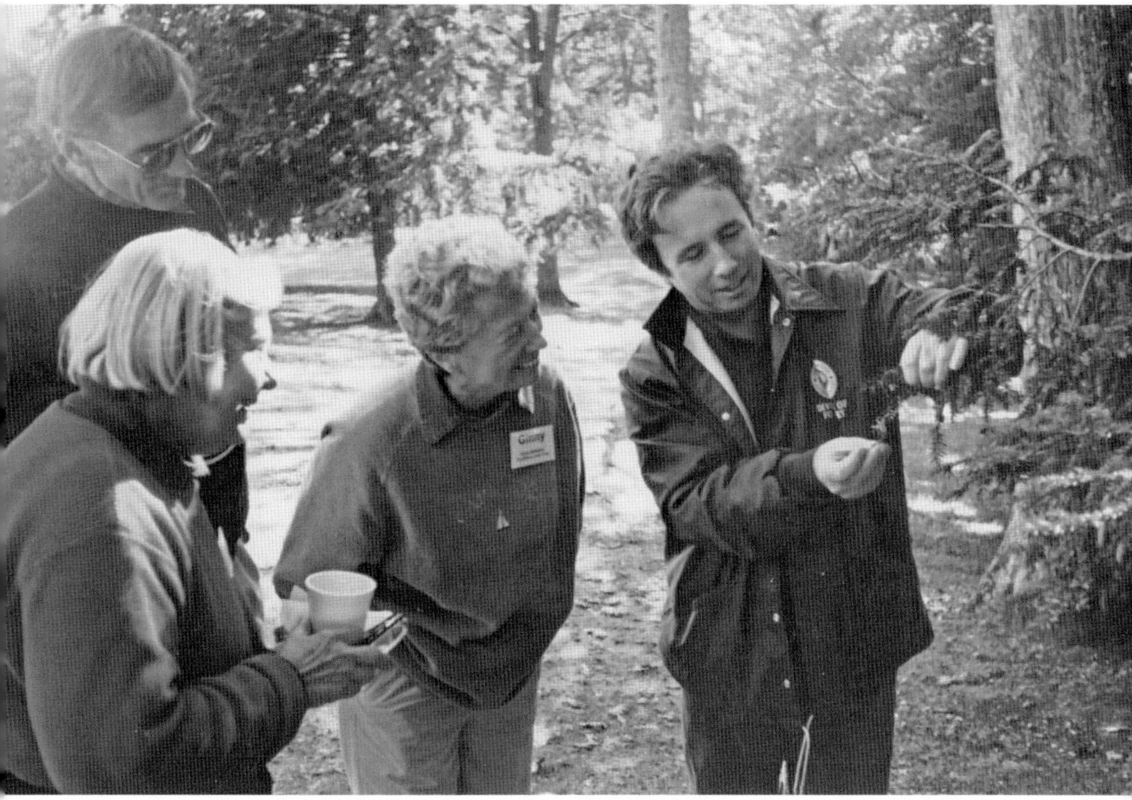

John Ballantine Jr.

In 1924, John H. Ballantine, the famed owner of Ballantine Beer, bought the home that later became the Heritage Village Meeting House. He donated the 25-acre site now known as Ballantine Park in memory of his son John Jr., a Navy flier killed in World War II. This picture was taken at Environmental Awareness Day 2000 at Ballantine Park. The event featured environmental presentations by Connecticut Urban Forestry Program foresters and local arborists. Those in attendance included members of the town's land trust and interested residents. Pictured from left to right are Alberta Pichey, John Middleton, Virginia Middleton, and Christopher Donnelly, a forester with the Urban Forestry Program of the Connecticut Department of Energy & Environmental Protection. (Courtesy Catherine Palmer.)

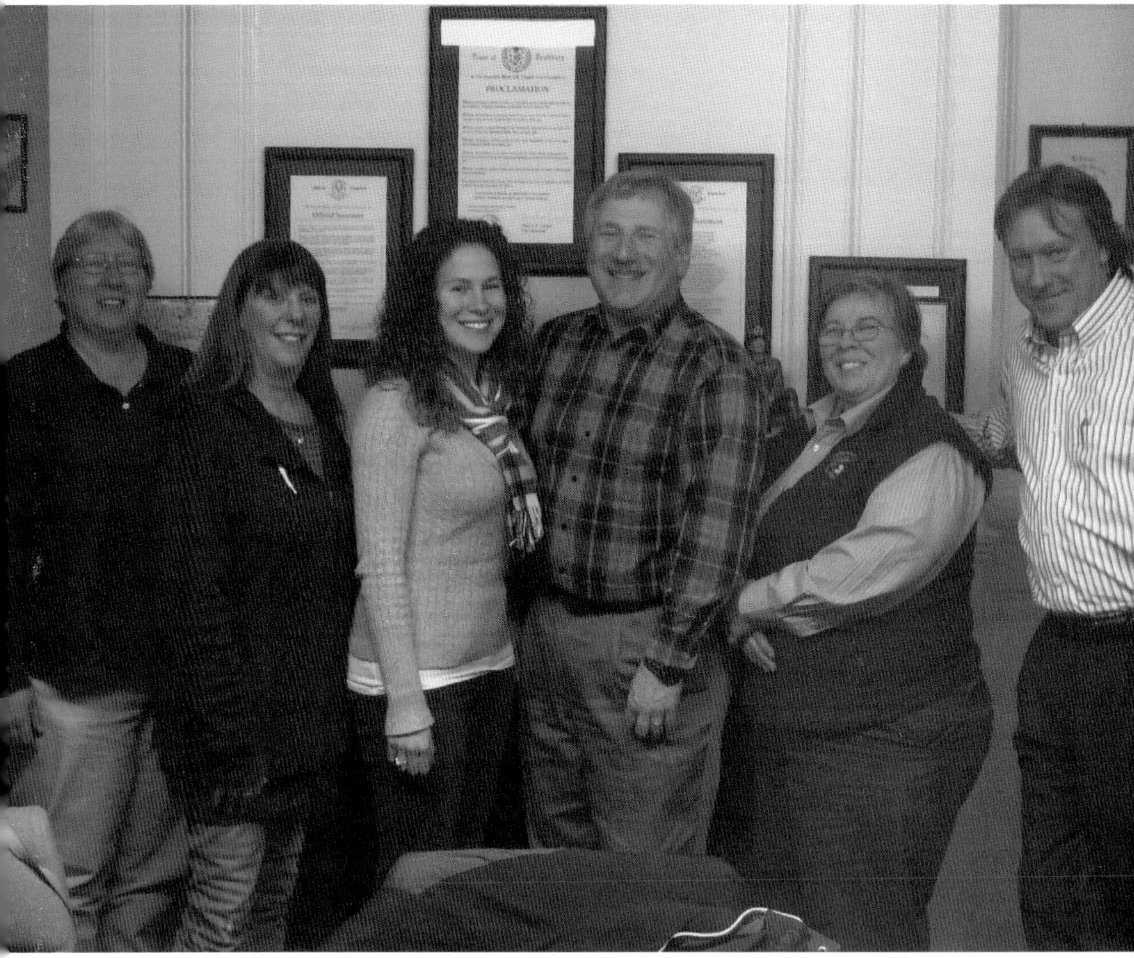

Southbury Ambulance Association Officers
The Southbury Ambulance Association received the Governor's Annual EMS Volunteer Organization Achievement Award in 2012 and also assisted Southbury in earning the prestigious HEARTSAFE Award. Funding is raised through donations from Southbury citizens. Pictured from left to right are Suzanne Vetter, human resources officer; Mandi Trumpp, recruiting and retention officer; Shayna Cieply, training officer; Burt Cieply, vice president; Geralyn Hoyt, chief and president; and Scott Ziegler, secretary and treasurer. (Courtesy Eva Biereder.)

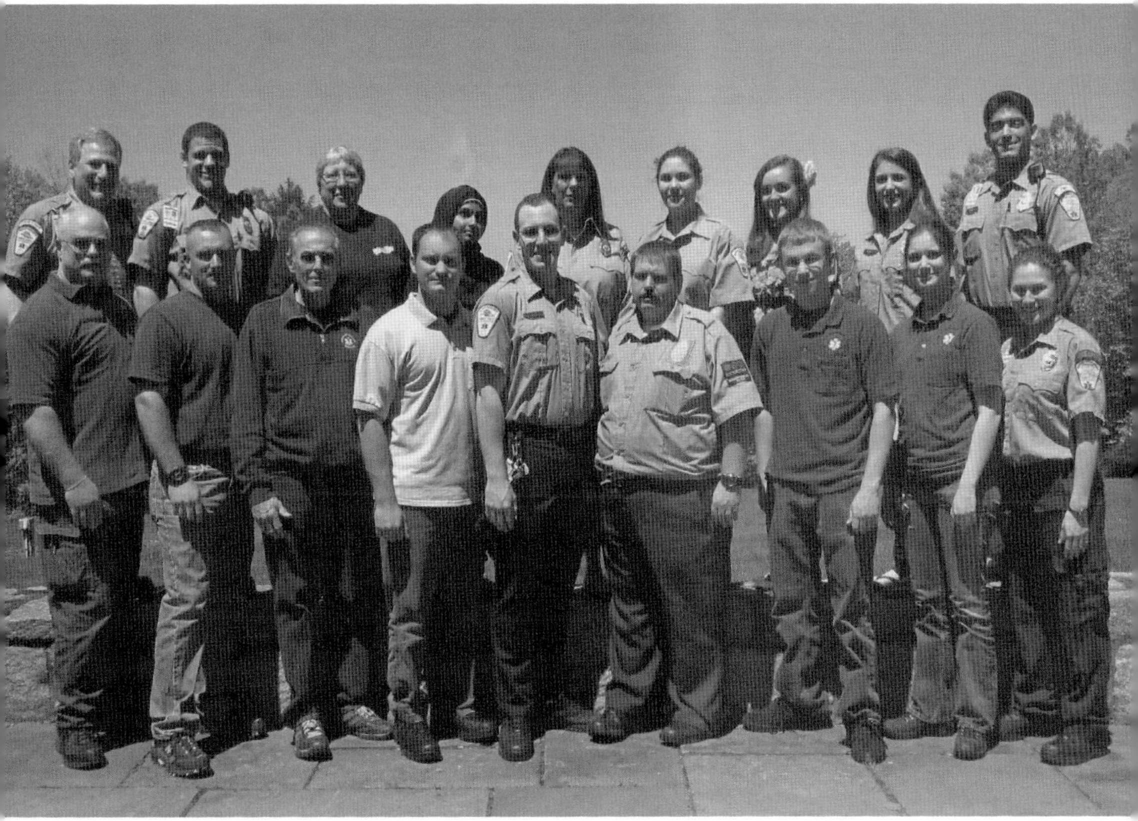

Southbury Ambulance Association OSHA Day

The Southbury Ambulance Association (SAA) was started as a volunteer organization in 1953 by the Southbury Lions Club, handling both Southbury and Woodbury. The SAA had some of the first EMTs in the state in the 1970s. SAA members are trained medical volunteers operating solely to provide emergency medical services to Southbury citizens. Every year, they participate in a special OSHA training day. Pictured from left to right are (first row) Gordon Jones, Tom Gillotti, Wayne King, Martin Rajcok, Alex Tillinghast, Robert Gardner, Kyle Bielanos, Janet Zapor, and Shayna Cieply; (second row) Burt Cieply, Alex Cieply, Suzanne Vetter, Faria Iqbal, Mandi Trumpp, Tori Trumpp, Jennifer Biereder, Maria Mucci, and Roman Massi. (Courtesy Eva Biereder.)

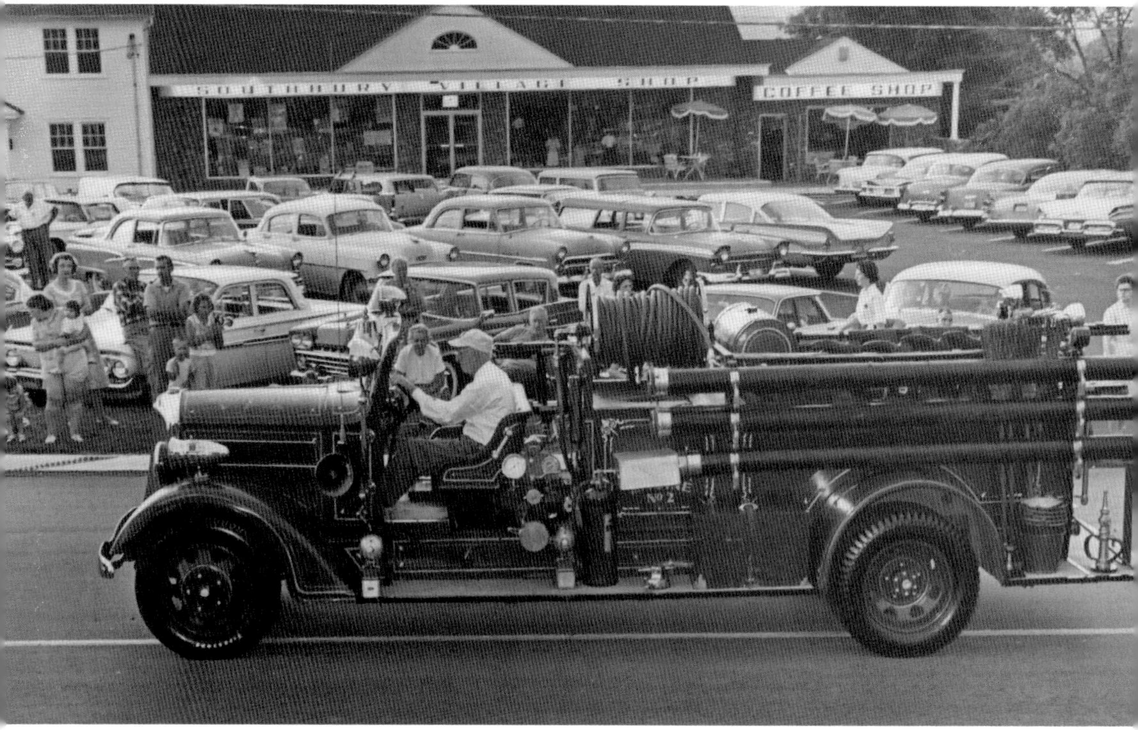

First Chief of the Southbury Volunteer Fire Department
Arza Bennett Sr. is pictured driving a fire truck in front of the Southbury Food Center. Arza was an automobile mechanic for close to 30 years at the location of the present Southbury Shell Station. He was the first Southbury volunteer fire chief in 1932. Arza is representative of all who serve as Southbury Volunteer Fire Department members. (Courtesy Arza Bennett Jr.)

CHAPTER THREE

Creative Spirit

There are painters who transform the sun to a yellow spot, but there are others who with the help of their art and their intelligence, transform a yellow spot into sun.

—Pablo Picasso

Southbury has been the home of many creative icons who have amused, entertained, and inspired the community. The town has been the home to painters, furniture makers, writers, actors and actresses, photographers, and musicians. Some of the more known notables have been Victor Borge, Ed Sullivan, Barbara Hershey, Arleen Francis, and the New York Metropolitan Opera's Gladys Swarthout.

Many times, a visit to the former Southbury Food Center would be an occasion to hear the booming and distinctive voice of Tony Marvin, Arthur Godfrey's "straight man" on an early popular television show, *The Arthur Godfrey Show.* He would regale his fellow grocery shoppers with a warm greeting and a welcoming smile. Tony was often asked to introduce and emcee programs at the Heritage Village condominiums where he lived. These were built in the mid-1960s for those age 55 and older by the Paparazzo brothers. When completed, the condominiums helped add another 2,500 residents to town.

The local drugstore was relocated from Main Street South to the Southbury Plaza and with an expanded parking area provided room for customers from neighboring towns. Local and nationally known celebrities were often noted buying pharmaceuticals and sundries after waiting patiently in line with local residents. On one occasion, a familiar-looking gentleman and his older companion appeared to be selecting toys for younger family members. The older woman commented, "Now, Sonny, I think he would like that color much better." The reply was, "Yes, Mother, I think that is the better choice." The salesperson, a local high school student, stated that the couple always seemed to be in line for another salesman, and he was disappointed that he had not yet waited on them. As they left, the customers noted that the celebrity was Dustin Hoffman and his mother. To be recognized and appreciated for their creative gifts certainly is high praise for well-known celebrities as well as for a community's unsung heroes.

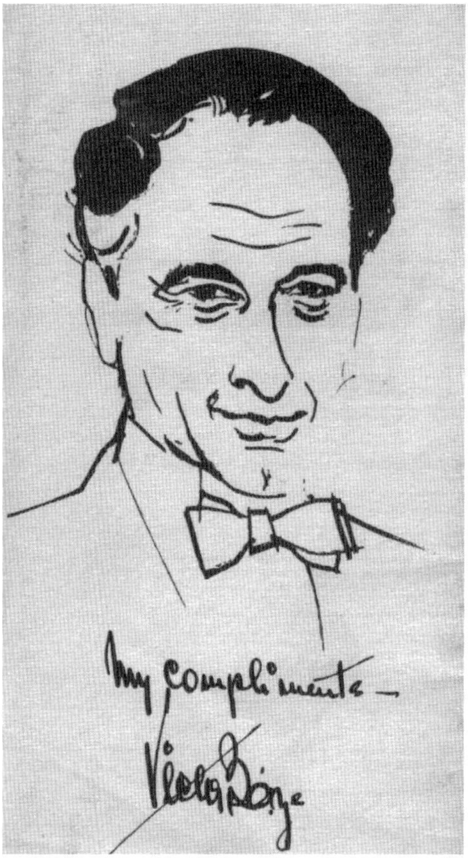

The Danish Clown Prince

Victor Borge, well known for his onstage humorous pianist sketches, purchased the Ballantine Beer family estate in 1953, renamed it the ViBo Farm, and started Pheasants Inc. to raise and sell Rock Cornish game hens. Borge, who was also known as the "Danish Clown Prince," sold the estate in 1965 to the Paparazzo brothers, and it became the center of Heritage Village's first 67 units. (Author's collection.)

Duncan Phyfe, Furniture Maker

Duncan Phyfe, considered one of the finest furniture makers of the Federal period, owned this impressive home, which is now referred to as the Mansion House. His craftsmanship was considered the epitome of American High Style furniture. The Mansion House was built in 1827–1829 by James English, a future Connecticut governor, and was located east of Kingsland. (Courtesy Catherine Palmer.)

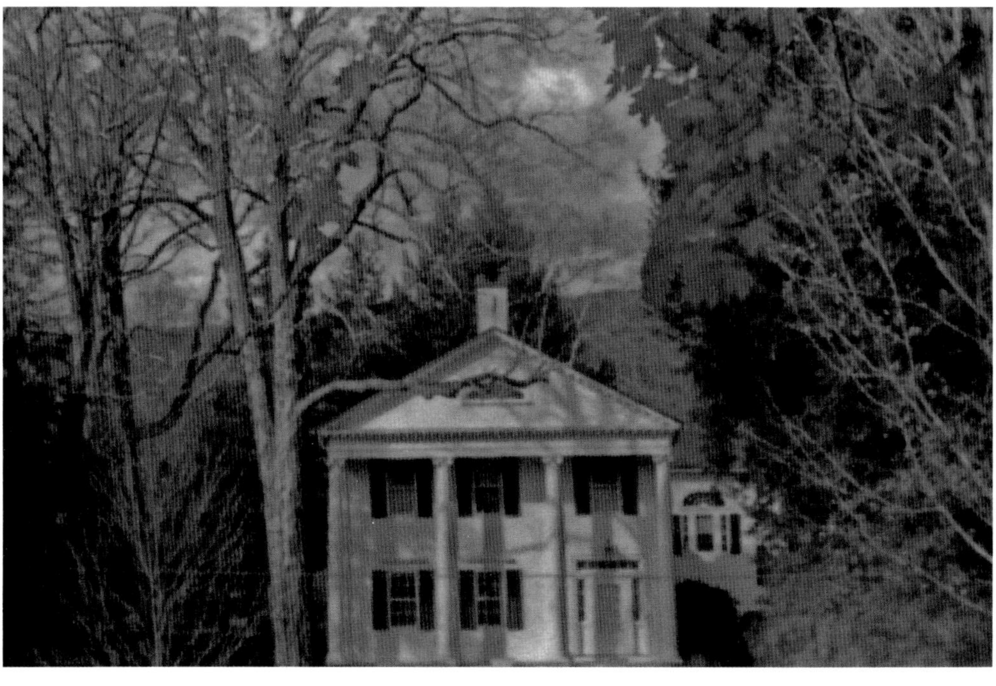

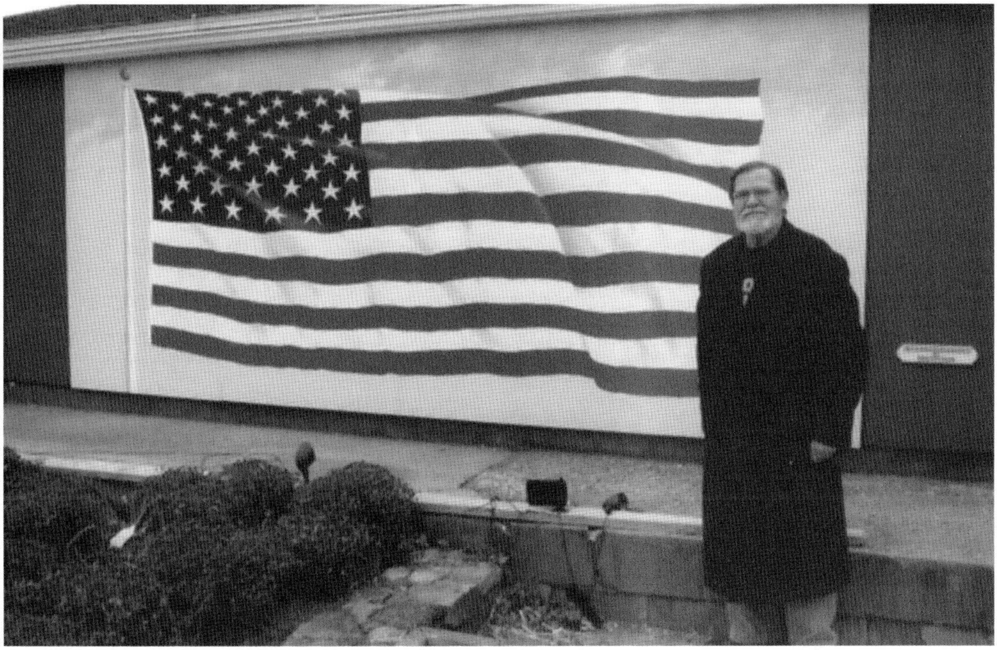

David Merrill, Preservationist of the Past
Merrill painted a series of outstanding murals of 42 local scenes at the Southbury Town Hall. Nearly $9,000 in donations were raised towards Merrill's payment—a small amount for the 10 months it took him to complete this historical tribute. Among his many awards are the Medal of Merit, the Arthur Hooten Memorial Award, seven best in shows, eight first prizes, and five audience choice awards in exhibitions throughout New England. A love for New England inspired Merrill to paint, capturing Southbury in the nostalgic view of an early New England town. (Courtesy VFW Post No. 1607 and Catherine Palmer.)

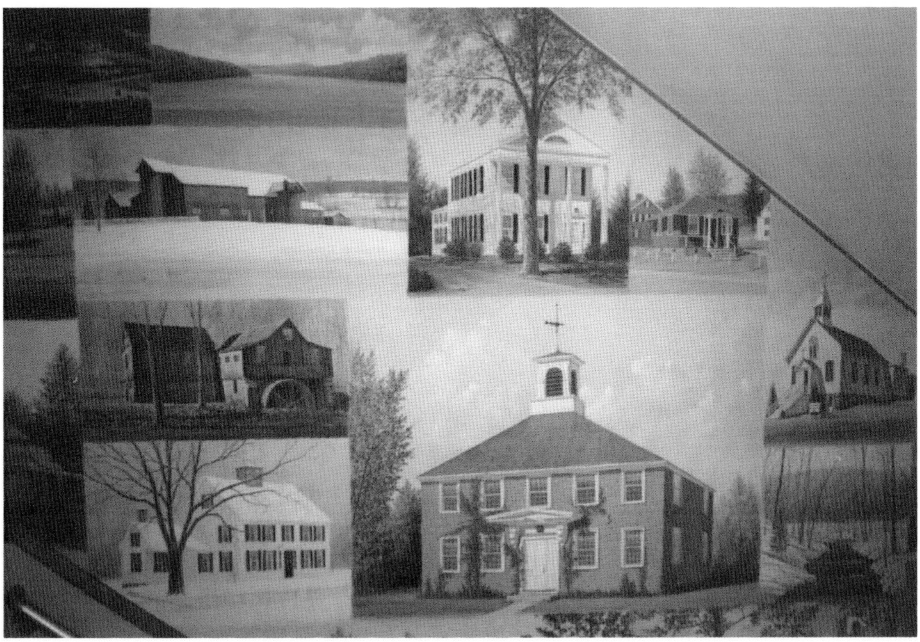

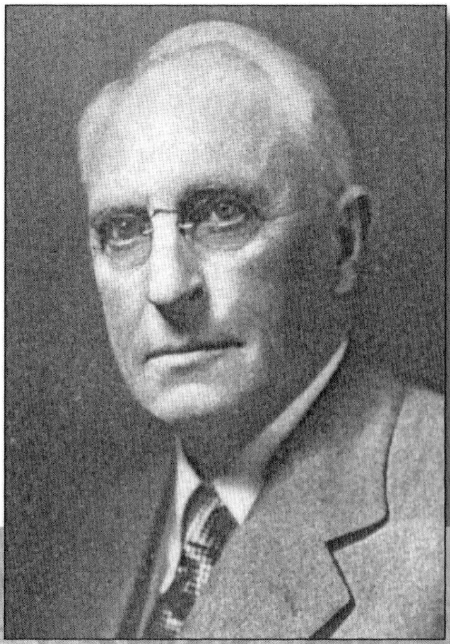

Wallace Nutting and Nuttinghame

Wallace Nutting, a famous photographer, minister, author, and furniture maker, bought Truman Wheeler's property before viewing the house, which he named Nuttinghame. In 1905, he employed local women as colorists for his photographs. Nutting sold the business and farm after seven years and moved to Framingham. Nutting's interior scenes are more rare than his pastoral ones such as those collected in *My Colonial Pictures*. (Author's collection.)

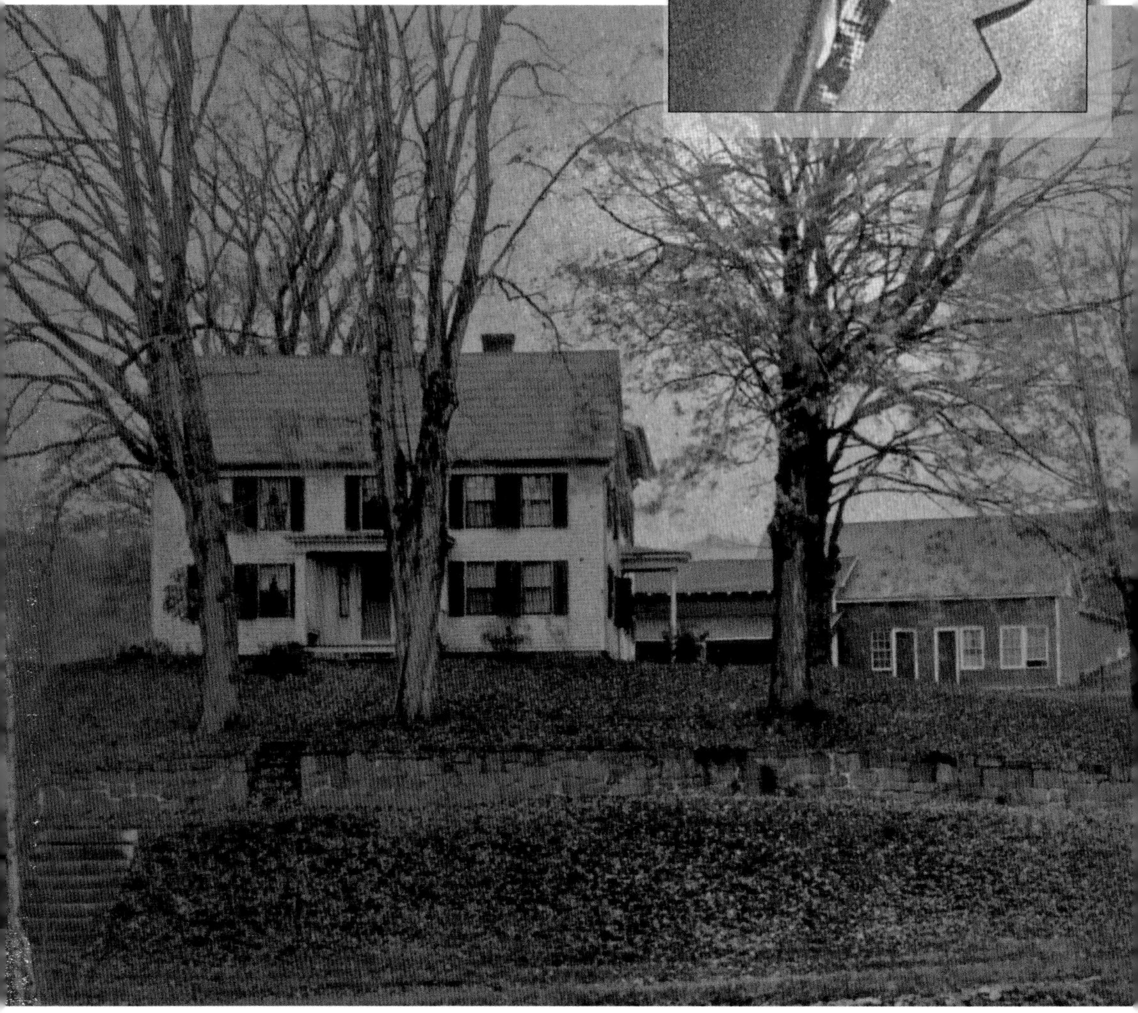

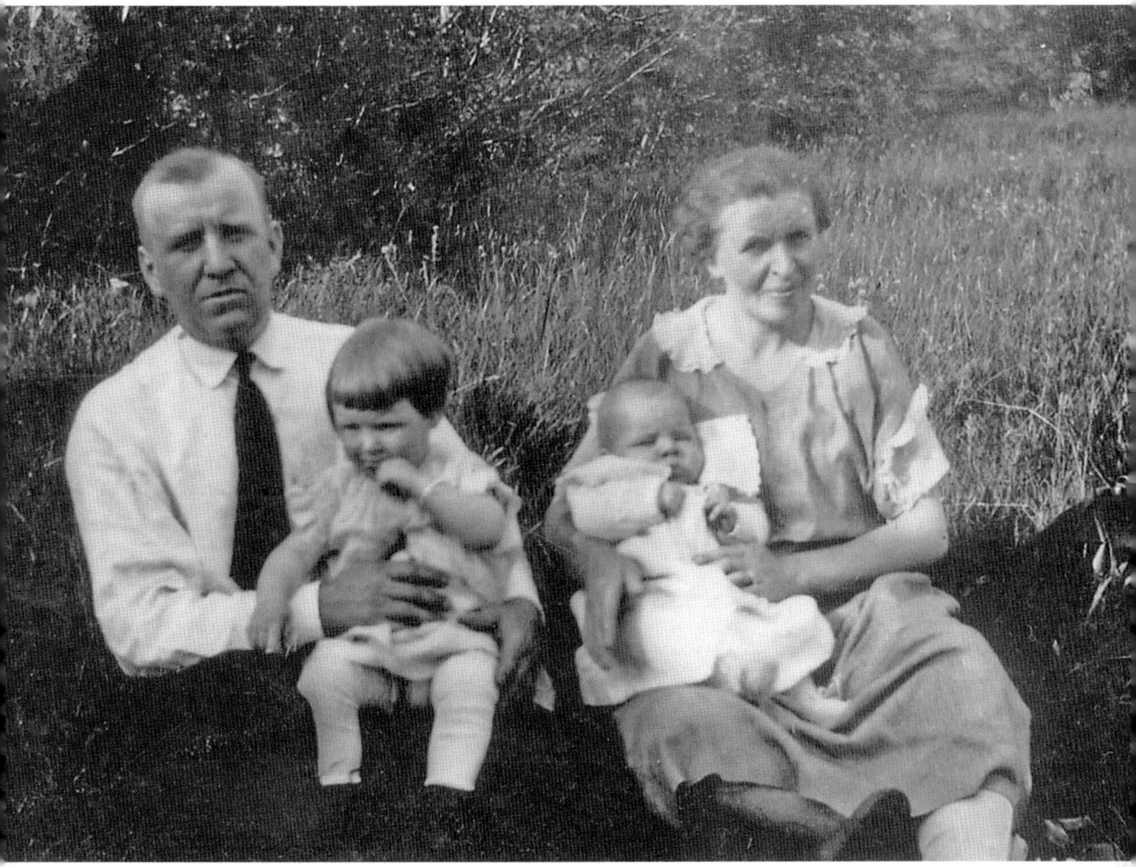

Nutting Colorist
Without the local women who trekked to his studio and colored his photographs, Wallace Nutting might not have been famous. Maud Bennett Kolb, a Nutting colorist, is pictured with her husband, Louis, daughter Doris, and son Harvey, who was named after the local doctor who delivered him. Maud amassed a collection of beautiful Nutting prints that she had most likely colored. (Courtesy Arza Bennett Jr.)

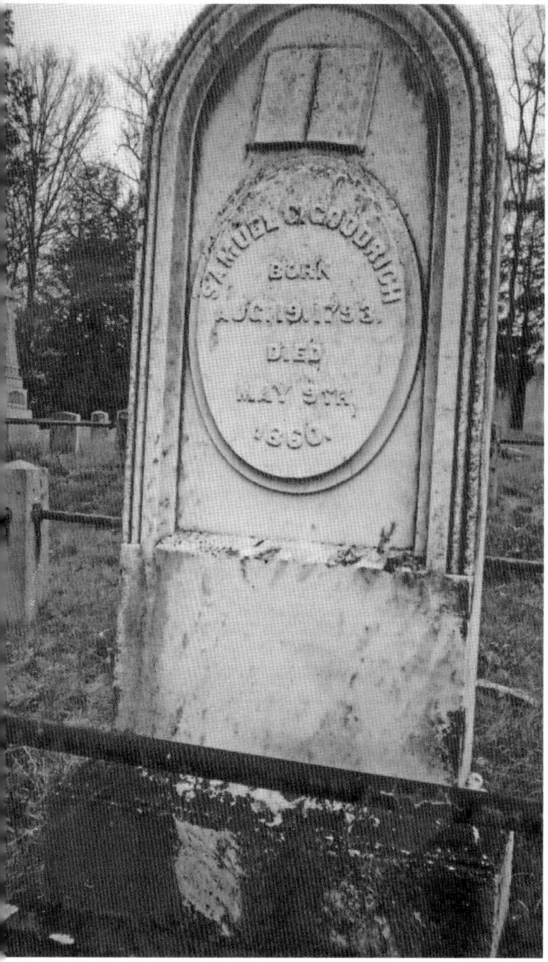

Samuel Goodrich and the Lutheran Home
Goodrich wrote more than 100 children's books with the intent of removing British background and focusing on American subject matter, as in his 1817 book *The Tales of Peter Parley*. A million copies of Peter Parley's method of telling children about geography were published, including *The Adventures of Captain Peter Riley*. Goodrich purchased the Hinman Home in 1857. Many locals have either worked at or spent their last years of life at the Lutheran home. The Lutheran Mission Society for Aged Lutherans purchased the property in 1918. Despite several additions over the years, the Lutheran Home still closely resembles its original appearance when Samuel Goodrich lived there. (Left, author's collection; below, courtesy Catherine Palmer.)

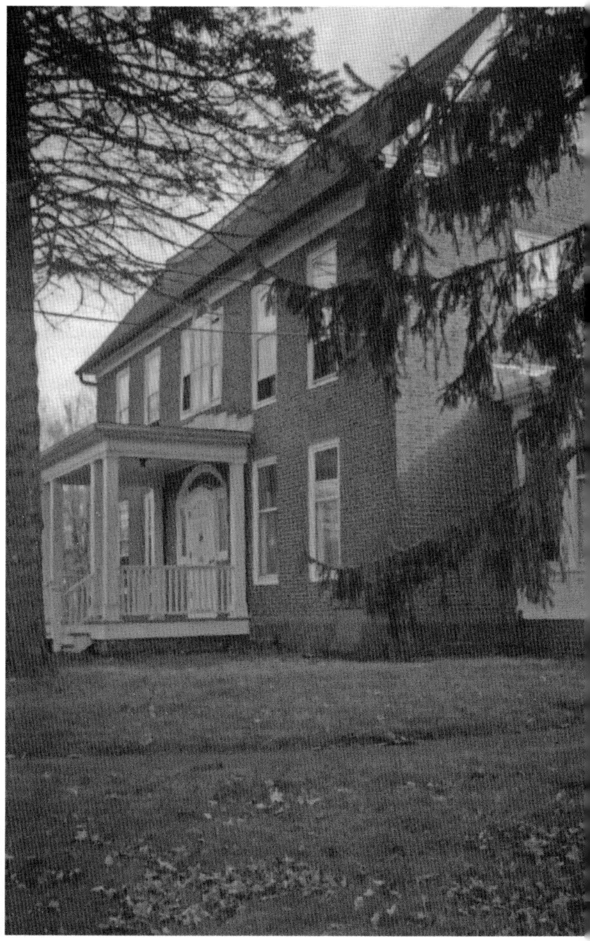

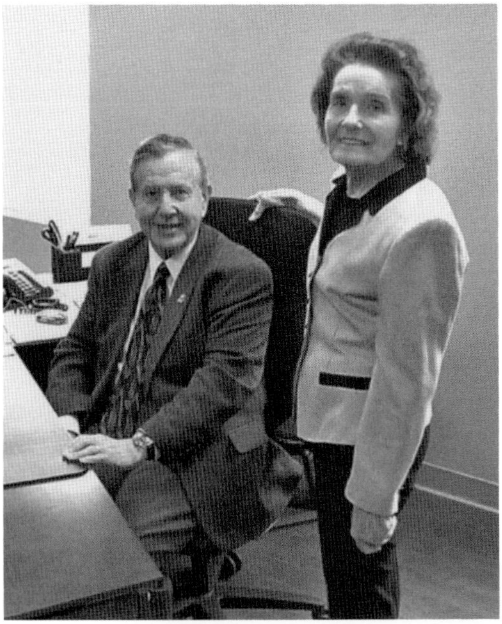

Voices Newspaper

Voices has served the community with local news for many years. The Mazurosky family, owners of Prime Publishers Inc., hosted a ribbon-cutting at the company's new headquarters on Heritage Road in March 2010. Pictured are Rudy and Trudy Mazurosky, the patriarch and matriarch of the family. Rudy, president and publisher, has been in the newspaper business for nearly 60 years. Trudy is the corporate secretary and notary for the Southbury-based newspaper. (Courtesy O'Brien–*Voices*.)

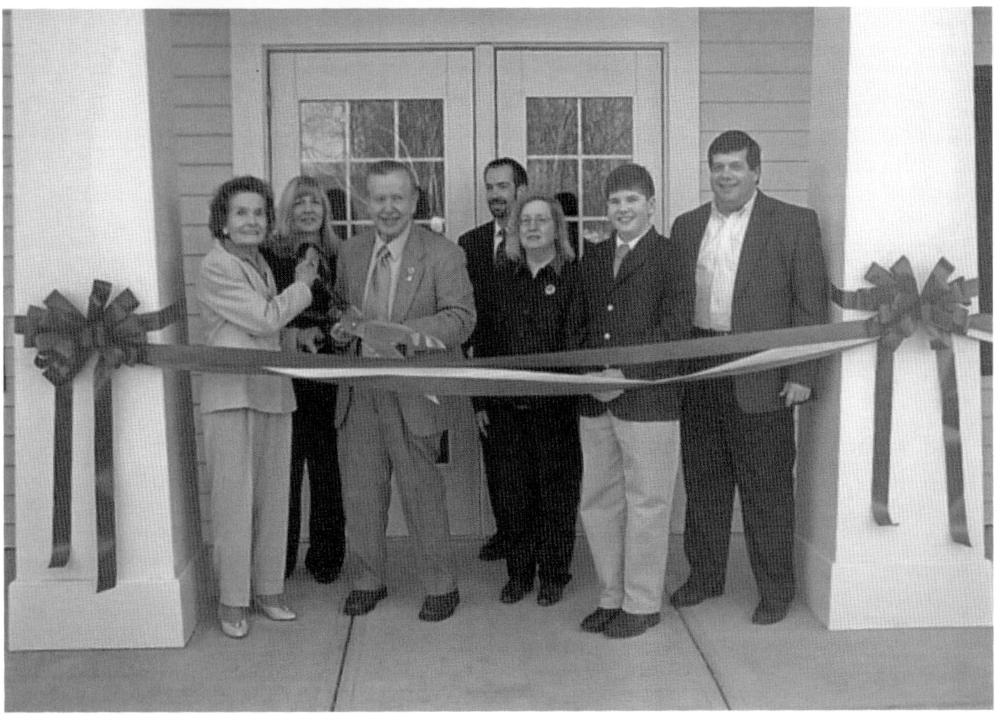

Prime Publishers Staff

The company publishes the *Voices*, *Voices Weekender*, and *Town Times* newspapers. From left to right are Trudy Mazurosky, corporate secretary and notary; Annette (Mazurosky) Linster, chief financial officer; Rudy Mazurosky, publisher; Walter Mazurosky, circulation and classified manager; Laura Mazurosky, business office; William Linster, special projects; and Kurt Mazurosky, operations director. (Courtesy O'Brien–*Voices*.)

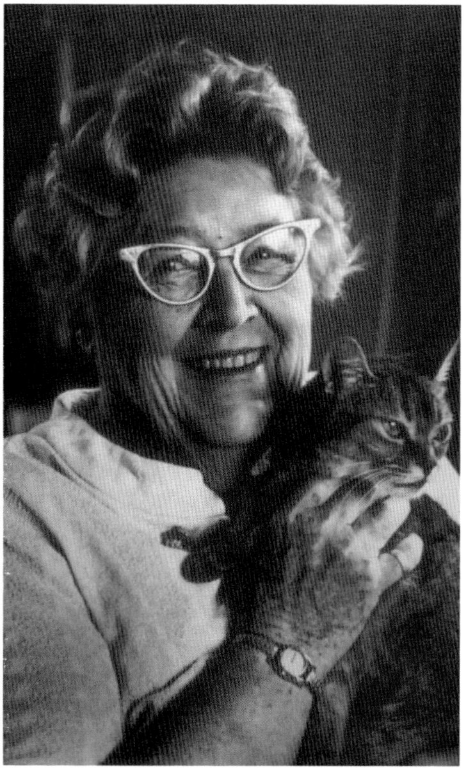

Gladys Taber at Stillmeadow
Gladys Taber became a Southbury resident in 1933. She wrote her many books and a column for the *Ladies Home Journal* from her 1690s farmhouse called Stillmeadow, located off Jeremy Swamp Road. She penned 59 books on various subjects such as cooking, cats and dogs, and flower arranging. Her writings still have a large following, including the faithful Gladys Taber Fan Club. (Author's collection.)

Jack Quinn and the Southbury Playhouse
The Playhouse, which was located on what is now known as Playhouse Corner, was opened in the early 1950s and brought art and famous actors and actresses to Southbury. The original director, Jack Quinn, who was a former professional ballet dancer, ran the establishment for several years. After not running for a period, W. Thomas Littleton took over in 1968 and staged more than 500 shows for almost two decades. Local high school girls in formal dress were ushers (including this author) for each of the summer plays. The entire Playhouse Corner closed in 1985 and was sold to real estate developer G. Thomas Nettleton. The Playhouse was demolished due to disrepair. (Author's collection.)

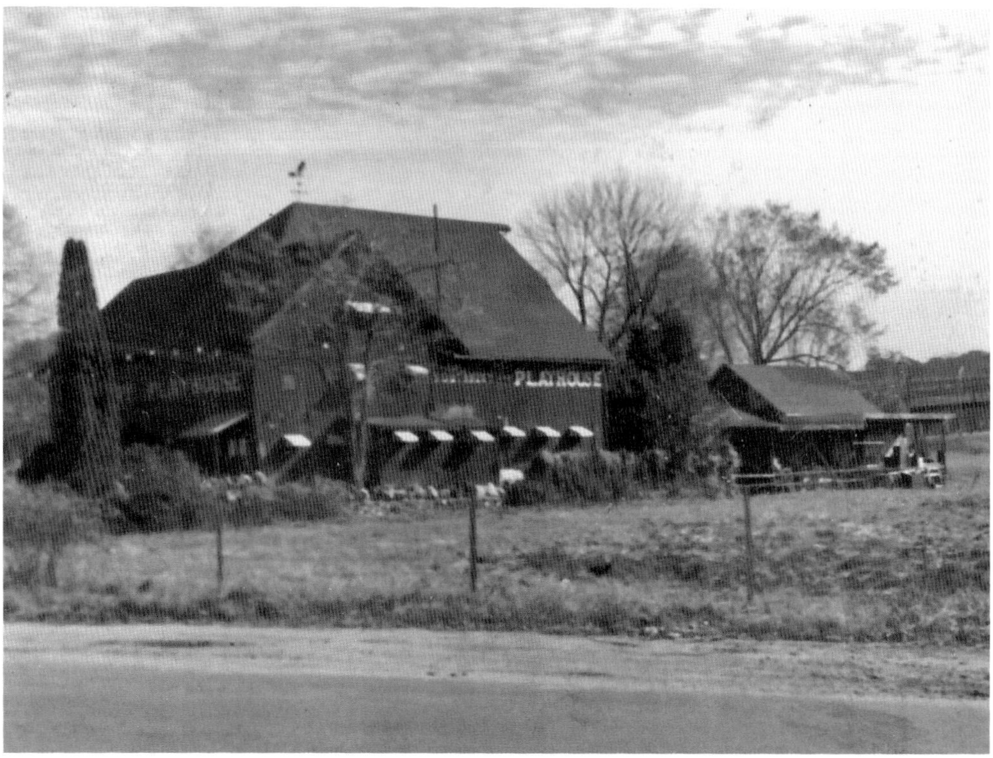

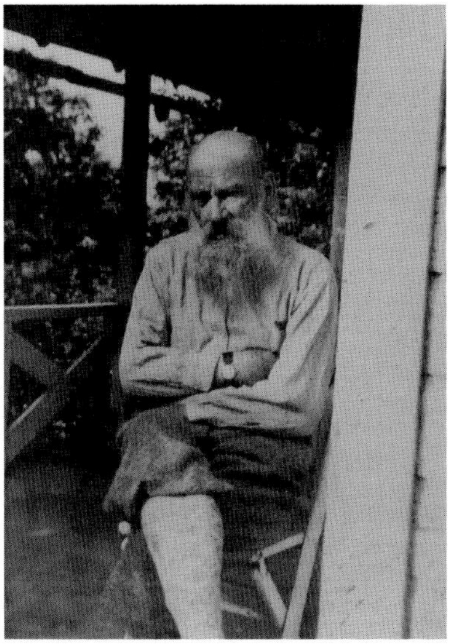

Count Ilia Tolstoy
Count Ilia Tolstoy, son of famous author Leo Tolstoy, and George Grebentschikoff founded Russian Village in the 1920s. Russian artists made Russian Village (Churaveka) their home. The village's printing press was used by Ukranian and Russian writers and scholars. Famous composer Sergei Rachmaninoff was a visitor. The site is listed in the National Register of Historic Places. (Author's collection.)

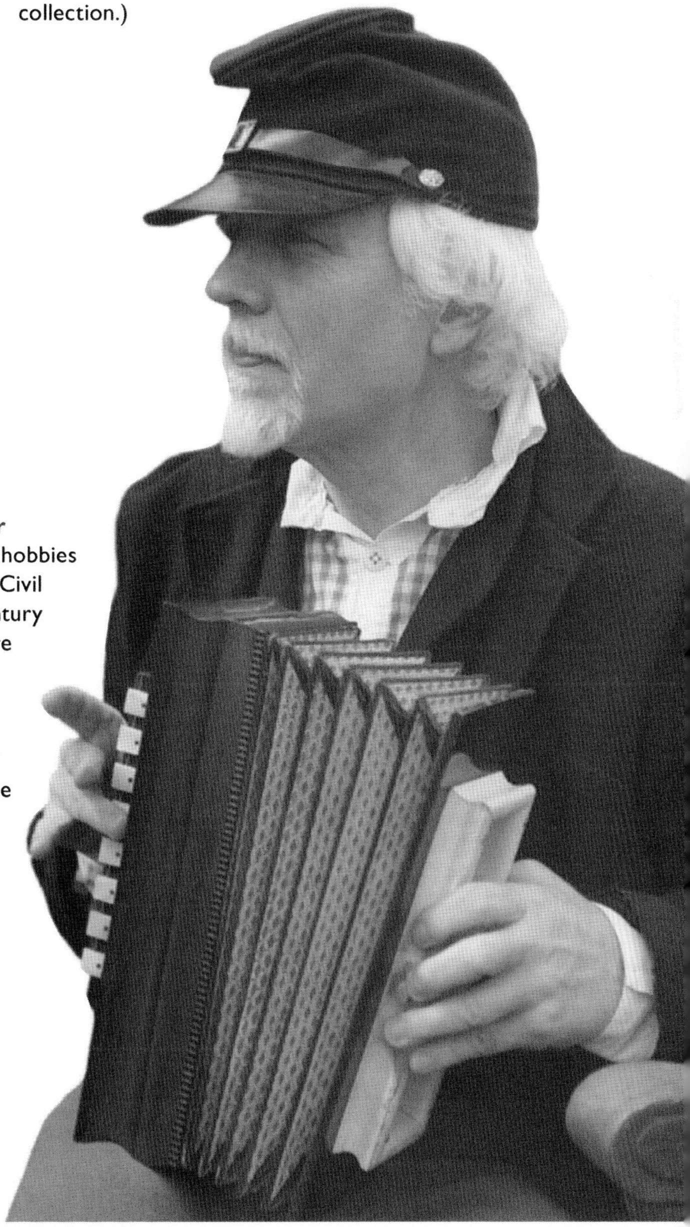

Virginia Serenader John Dwyer
John Dwyer sought to combine his hobbies of music, wood craftsmanship, and Civil War history by recreating 19th-century music. The Virginia Serenaders were formed and became one of the earliest groups of this type. To best emulate 19th-century songs, extensive research, handcrafting of musical instruments, and experience in restoration woodworking were essential. (Courtesy John Dwyer.)

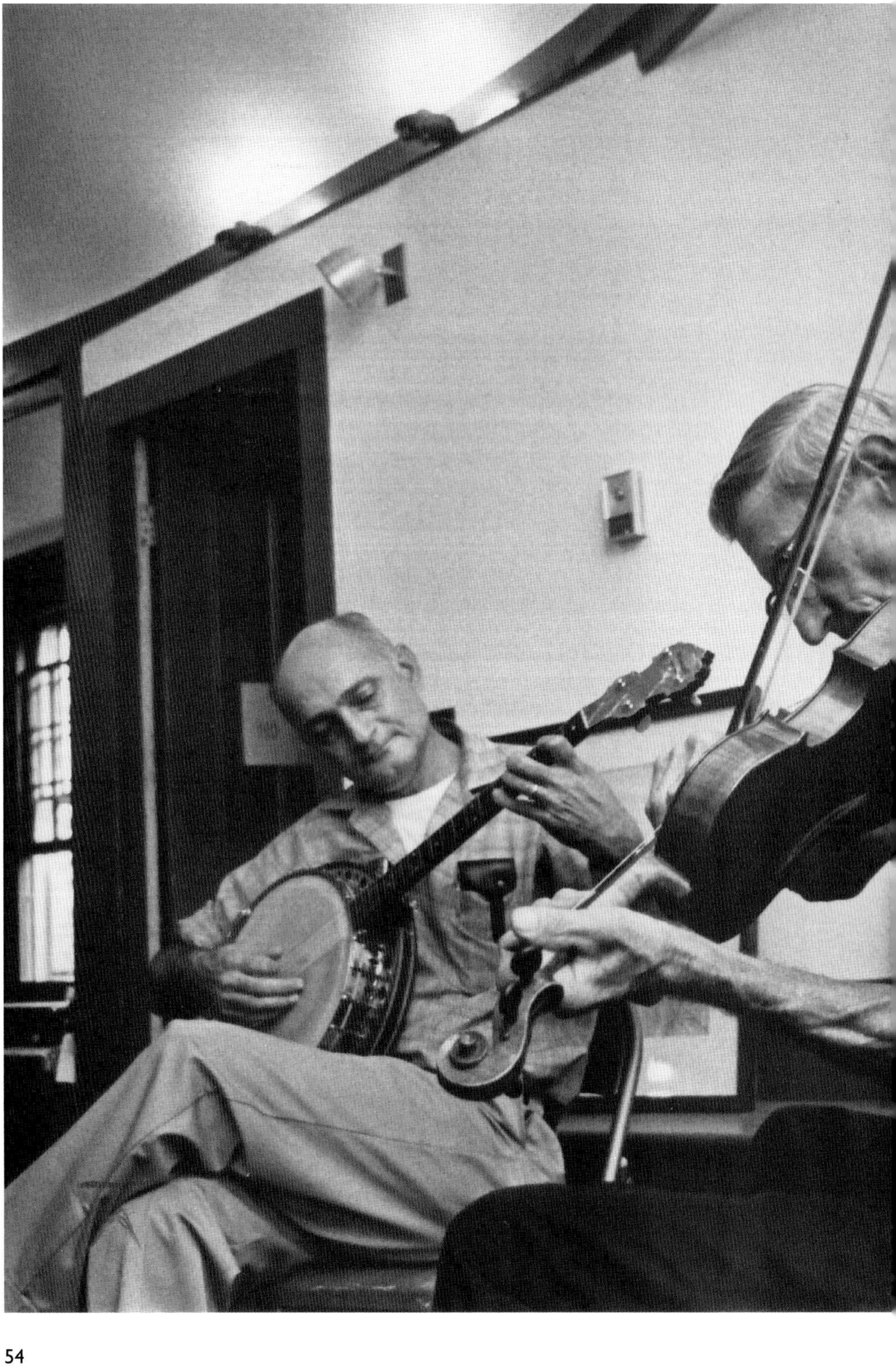

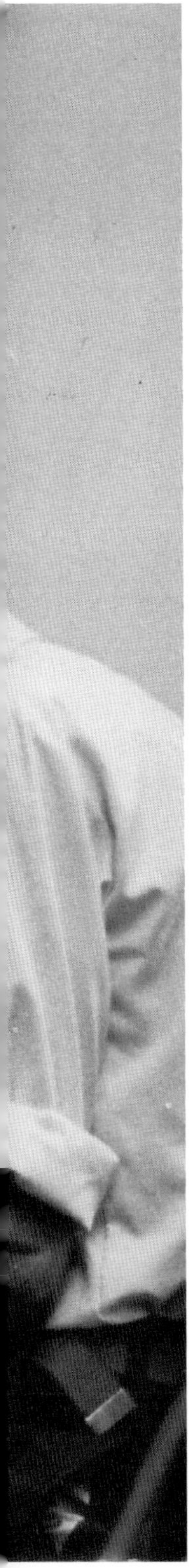

John Ludorf

John Ludorf (right) typified an early Southbury farmer. He was born in 1897 and lived on West Purchase Road where he farmed using 1890s methods. The Southbury Historical Society was given the Ludorf barn and some farmland by Marie Ludorf, his daughter, to become an agricultural museum. John served on the town's planning and zoning commissions and participated in county fiddling contests at fairs and church socials. He also was a gifted poet and kept diary accounts of his daily life. He is pictured here with Everard Graham. (Courtesy Bullet Hill School Archives.)

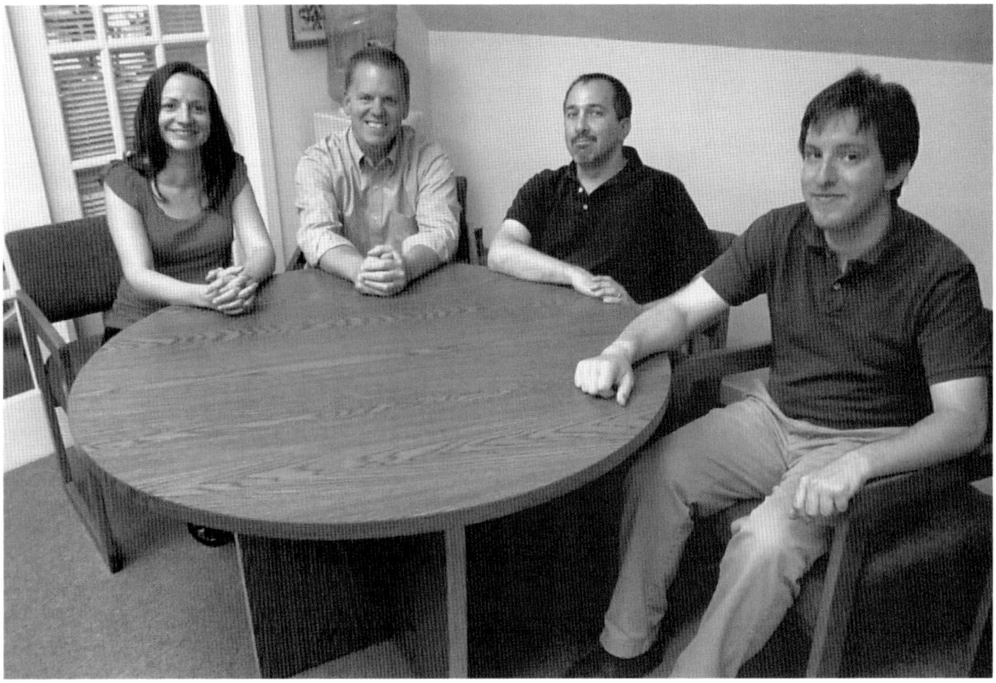

John Henry Morrow and the Republican-American Southbury Bureau
On October 29, 1881, the *Waterbury Republican* made its debut as a weekly newspaper published by John Henry Morrow. The *Republican-American*, the daily Waterbury newspaper, has had a Southbury news bureau since early 1980 and has been located in Playhouse Corner since 1998; it shares office space with the *Heritage Villager*. The staff covers community news west and south of Waterbury. The *Republican-American* Southbury bureau staff members are, from left to right, Quannah Leonard, bureau chief Chris Gardner, Rick Harrison, and Matthew O'Rourke. (Courtesy Chris Gardner.)

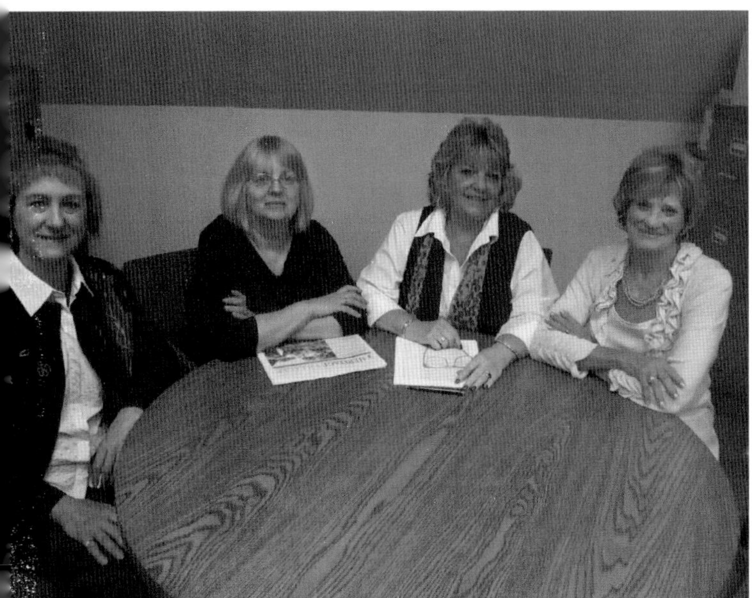

Emmett and Mildred Crozier and the *Heritage Villager*
The *Heritage Villager* recently celebrated its 45th anniversary. Founding editors Emmett and Mildred Crozier achieved their goal of reflecting the special character of Heritage Village, a community for residents over the age of 55. The Croziers met their mission for 10 years, and the popular bi-monthly newspaper was sold to John and Virginia Middleton in 1977. *Heritage Villager* staff members pictured here are, from left to right, editor Britt Goodman, Emily Mullins, Terry Lieder, and Rebecca Bowes. (Courtesy Chris Gardner.)

CHAPTER FOUR

Having Fun

All work and no play makes Jack a dull boy.

When it comes to having fun, this town knows how to do it in style. With abundant winding rivers and Lake Zoar, there is a lot of opportunity to have fun on the water, whether it is boating, fishing, or water-skiing. No one can forget the picture in local newspapers of the Jamieson boy and his barefoot water-skiing. Lynne and Stuart Wilson Jr. were very involved with the Lake Zoar Water Authority over the years and were instrumental in protecting and promoting its many assets. The opening day of fishing at the well-stocked Southford Falls always means cars parked along the roadside by many eager anglers.

Southbury has many town parks and they have provided opportunities for innumerable outdoor activities. Ballantine Park, Community House Park, Ewald, Lakeside, the Boat Launch, Settlers Park, Lake Zoar, and the Gordon Schielke Park are all sites for Little League, cheerleading, hiking, Pop Warner football, soccer, swimming, and boating. The two state parks in Southbury, Kettletown and Southford Falls, add to these unusual facilities for townspeople to enjoy. Many open space areas including Platt Park add scenic trails for hiking.

Numerous events have been sponsored by clubs, groups, and organizations throughout Southbury. Heritage Villagers can take part in multiple clubs, ranging from golf to politics. A treasured tradition of summers past was the annual firemen's carnival held at Community House Park. Many fond memories have been made at these special activities and occasions.

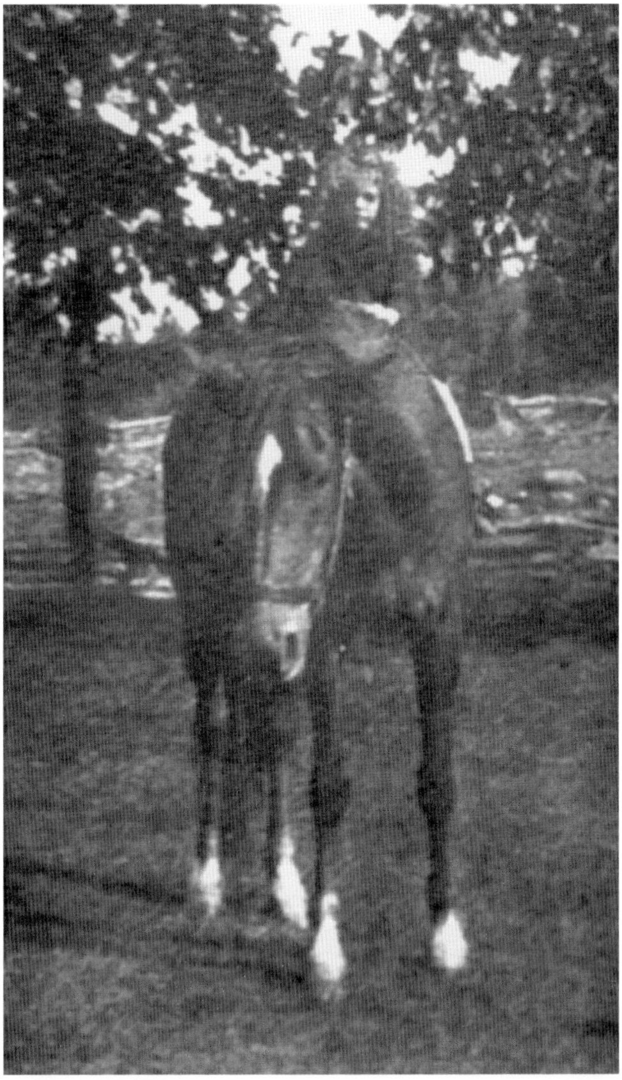

Samuel Green II
When Samuel Green II was a boy, he enjoyed going to the Southford section of town when he was bored. The reason for this was his love of horses, and in particular, racing them for money. Later in life, Samuel owned and operated Green's General Store on Main Street. (Courtesy Samuel Green III.)

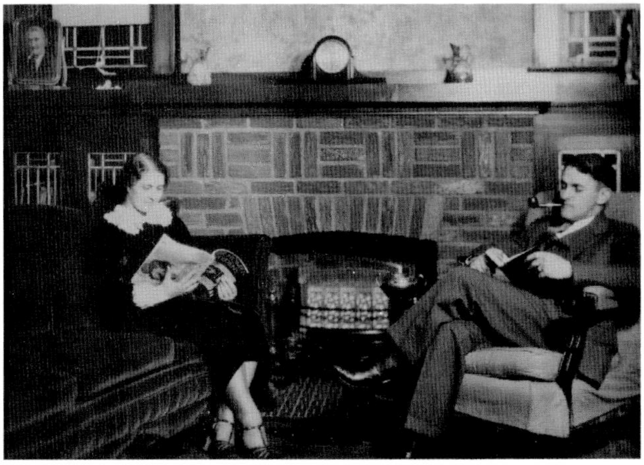

Sam Green II and Dorothy
Sam Green II and his wife, Dorothy, enjoyed their home on Main Street. Sam was born in the house that later became the Congregational Parsonage located on the corner of Main Street and Old Waterbury Road. (Courtesy Samuel Green III.)

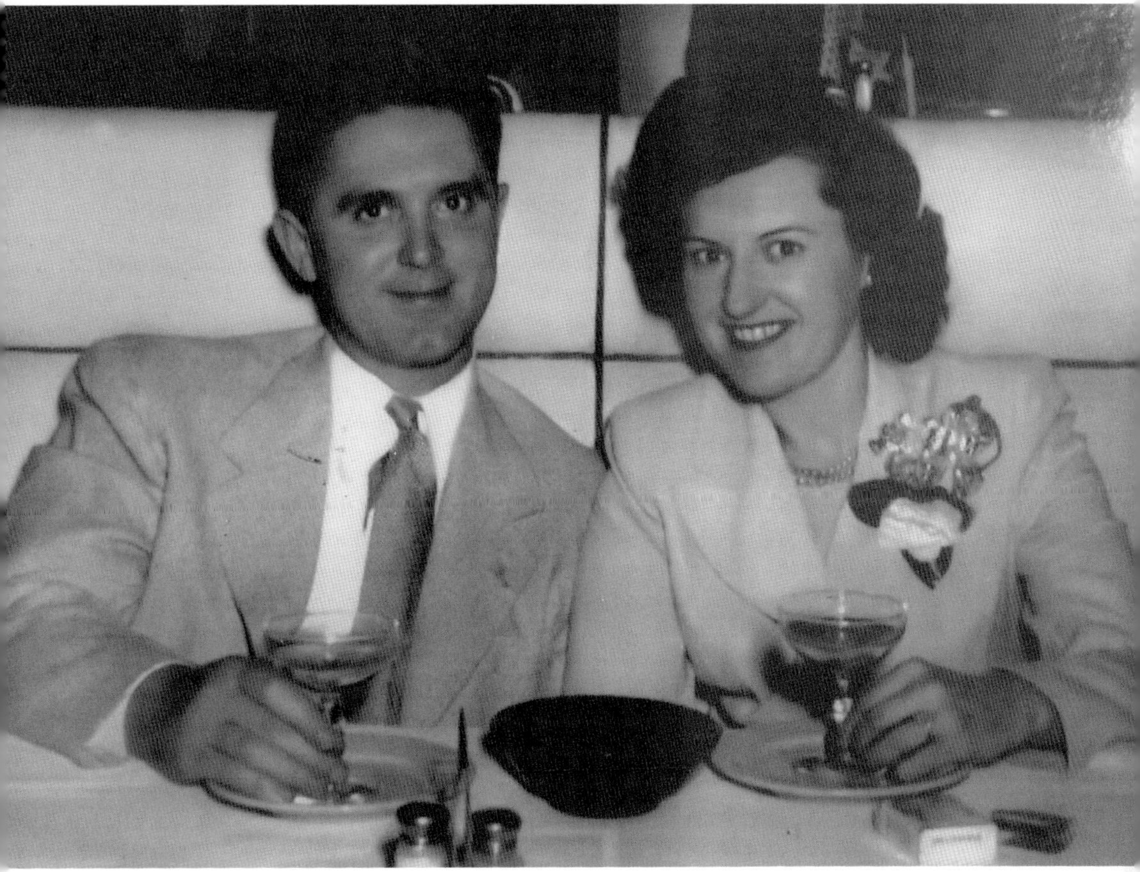

Richard J. Hine and Irene Hine

Richard and Irene Hine were lifetime Southburians. Richard was one of the original founders of the Southbury Lions Club and Southbury Ambulance Association. The couple was active in annual fundraisers such as chicken barbecues, ham and bean suppers, and bulb and broom sales. Richard and his brother James owned and operated the family business, Hine Brothers Inc., for decades. Richard is pictured here with Irene. (Courtesy Jay Hine.)

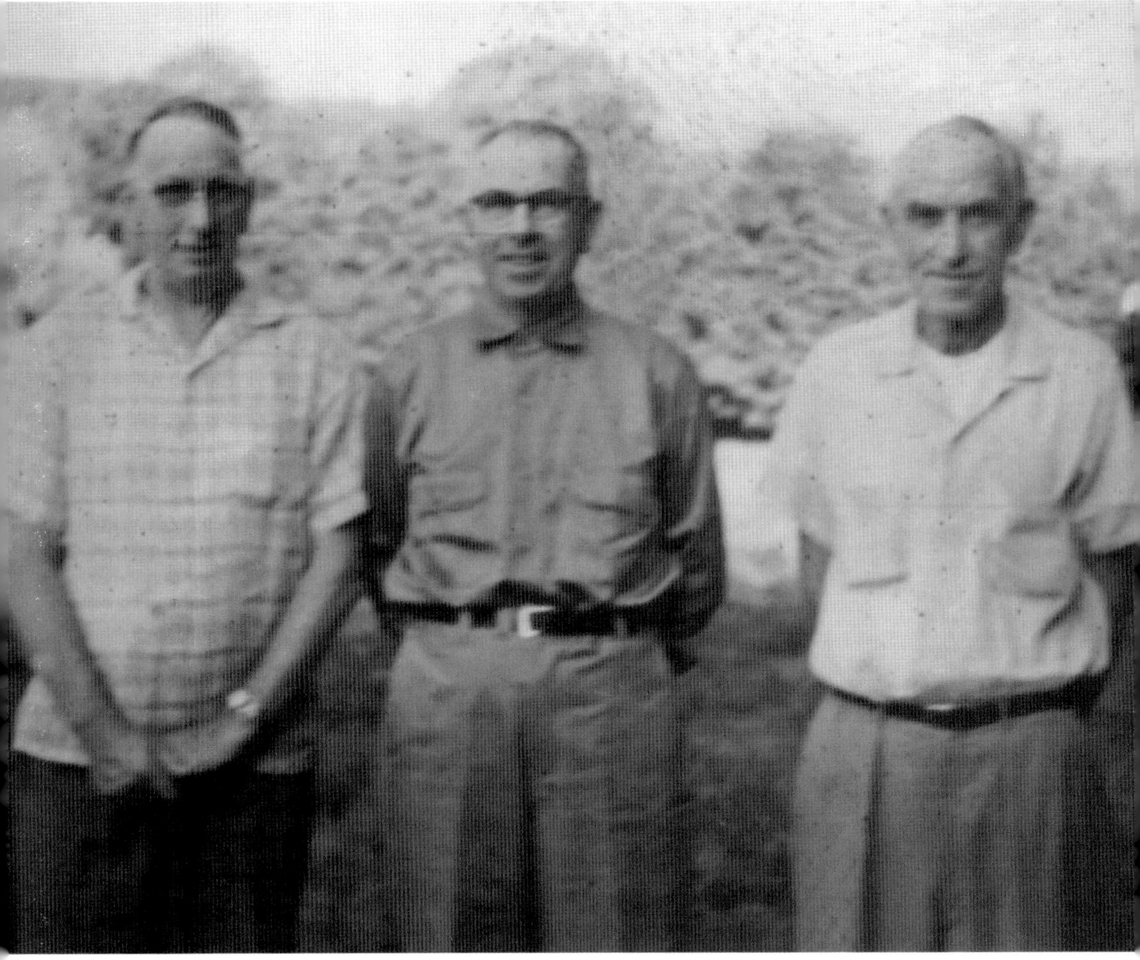

The Bennett Brothers

Pictured from left to right are Arza Bennett Sr., George Bennett, and Homer Bennett. George worked for the US Postal Service for 42 years. As Southbury Conservation Commission's chairman, he was instrumental in the town's purchase of open land. George received local and national land preservation awards and was named Southbury's "Mr. Conservation." Homer Bennett Sr. has been a successful local businessman for many years. Arza Bennett Sr. was Southbury's first Volunteer Fireman's Association chief. (Courtesy Arza Bennett Jr.)

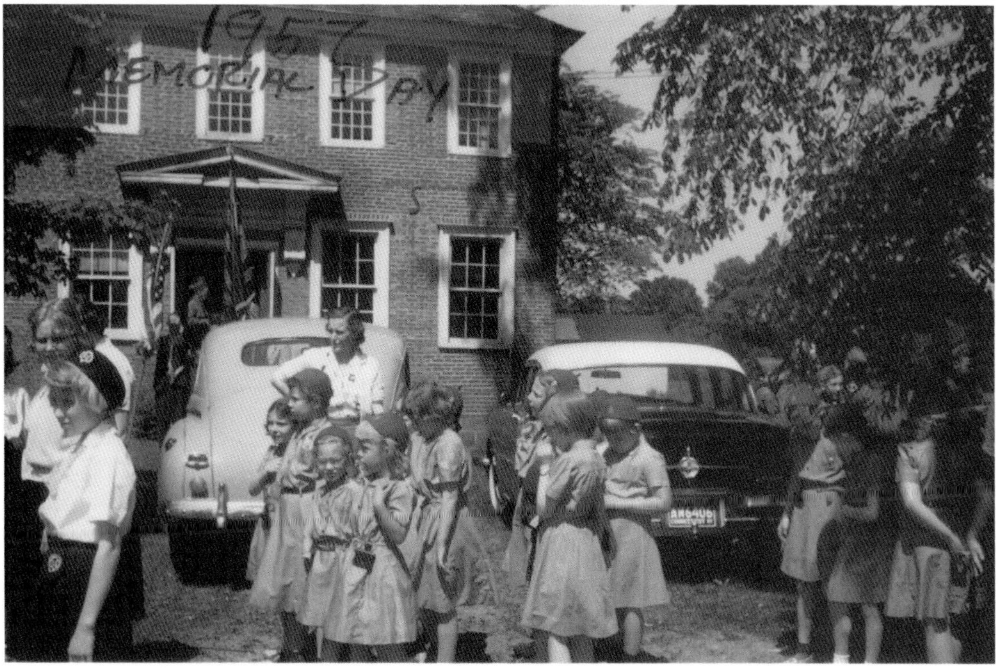

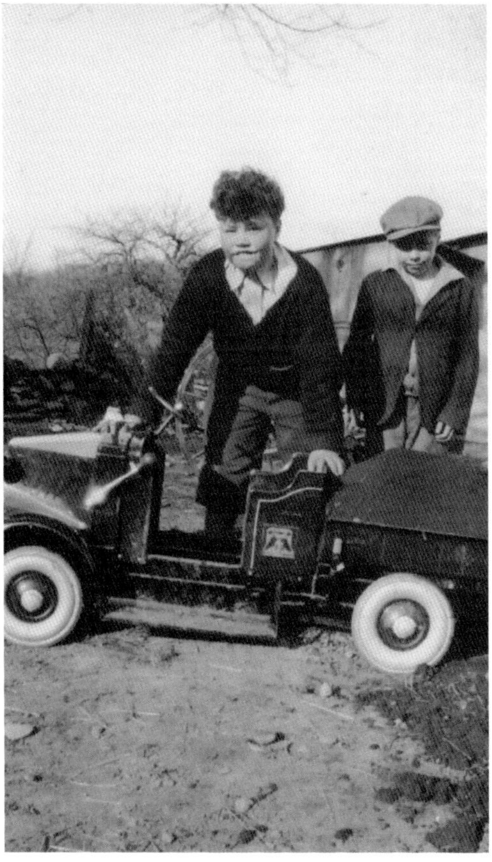

Joyce Hornbecker and the Girl Scouts
Southbury girls have been members of the Brownies and Girl Scouts since the early 1900s. Joyce Hornbecker was one of the key Girl Scout leaders for many years. She encouraged girls to develop leadership skills. She was also very involved with the Lake Zoar Authority Committee. Southbury's Memorial Day Parade features many adult and young people's organizations—including the Girl Scouts—in honoring veterans. Typical of the children's groups were these Brownies lining up at Bullet Hill School in 1957, preparing to march to the World War II monument on Old Waterbury Road. Following the parade, the Girl Scouts and Boy Scouts were taken to the churchyard and given soda. (Courtesy VFW Post 1607.)

Future Business Leader and Friend
Two Southbury youngsters illustrate childhood friendship in this 1932 picture: George Stone Sr. (left) and David Hicock. George Stone Sr. later became town fire chief and a successful owner of the H.H. Stone store. (Courtesy Mark Stone.)

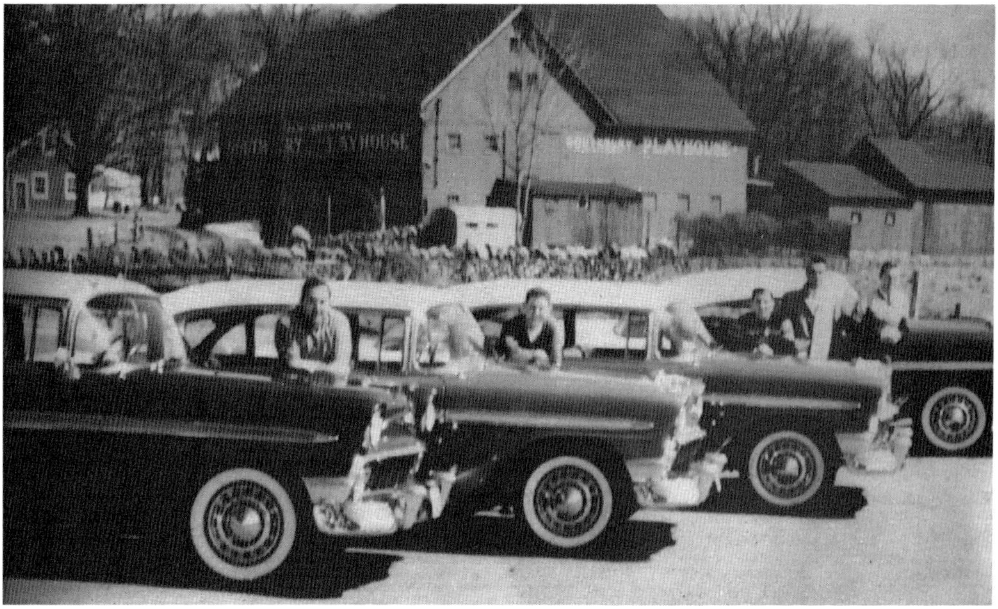

Korean War Veterans
These friends lined up with their new Chevys in front of the Southbury Playhouse. The majority of the young men were Army veterans from the Korean conflict. From left to right are Alfie Candido, Eddie Grisgraber, Dan Candido, Freddy Mackowitz, and Bob Johnson. The Candido brothers owned and operated the Southbury package store and the nearby dry-cleaning business. Freddy Mackowitz was associated with a local insurance business, and Bob Johnson worked for the local St. Pierre Oil Company. (Courtesy Dan Candido.)

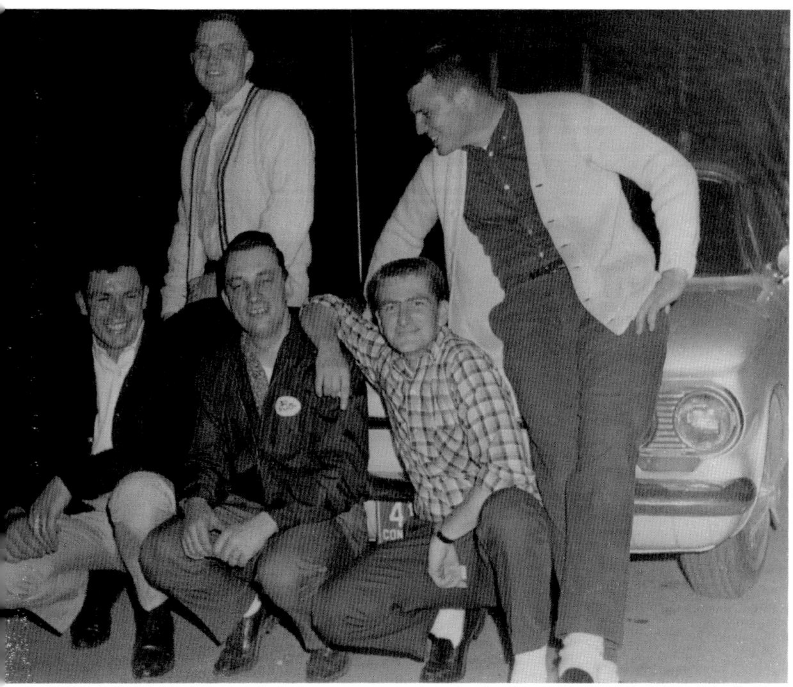

Future Town Businessmen
High school friends are pictured enjoying each other's company while wearing the cool and stylish clothes of the time. From left to right are (first row) Ed Platt, Bob Mackowitz, and Les Mitchell; (second row) Ed Wildman and Bill Bette. Ed Wildman worked for the family's Wildman Carpet business. Ed Platt owns and operates the family dairy farm. Les Mitchell operated a local insurance agency and served as president of the Southbury Historical Society. (Courtesy Ed Wildman.)

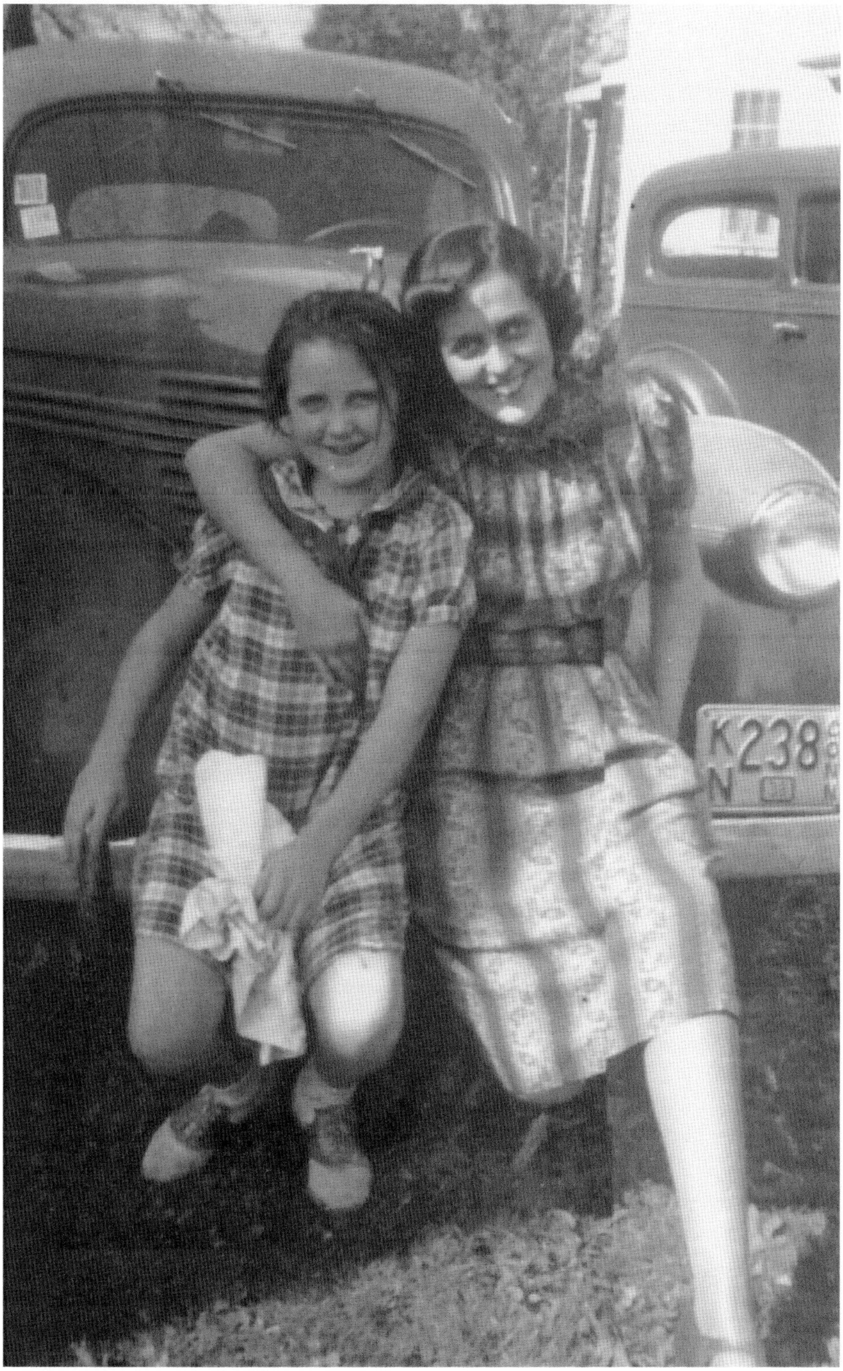

Ruth Hine Ewald

Ruth Ewald followed her family's tradition and became a schoolteacher, teaching in both the Southbury and Woodbury school systems. Her daughter also followed the same route. Here, two young Hine sisters from Main Street North are dressed in the popular gingham dresses of their youth: Jeannette Hine Chaffee (left) and Ruth Hine Ewald. (Courtesy Jane White.)

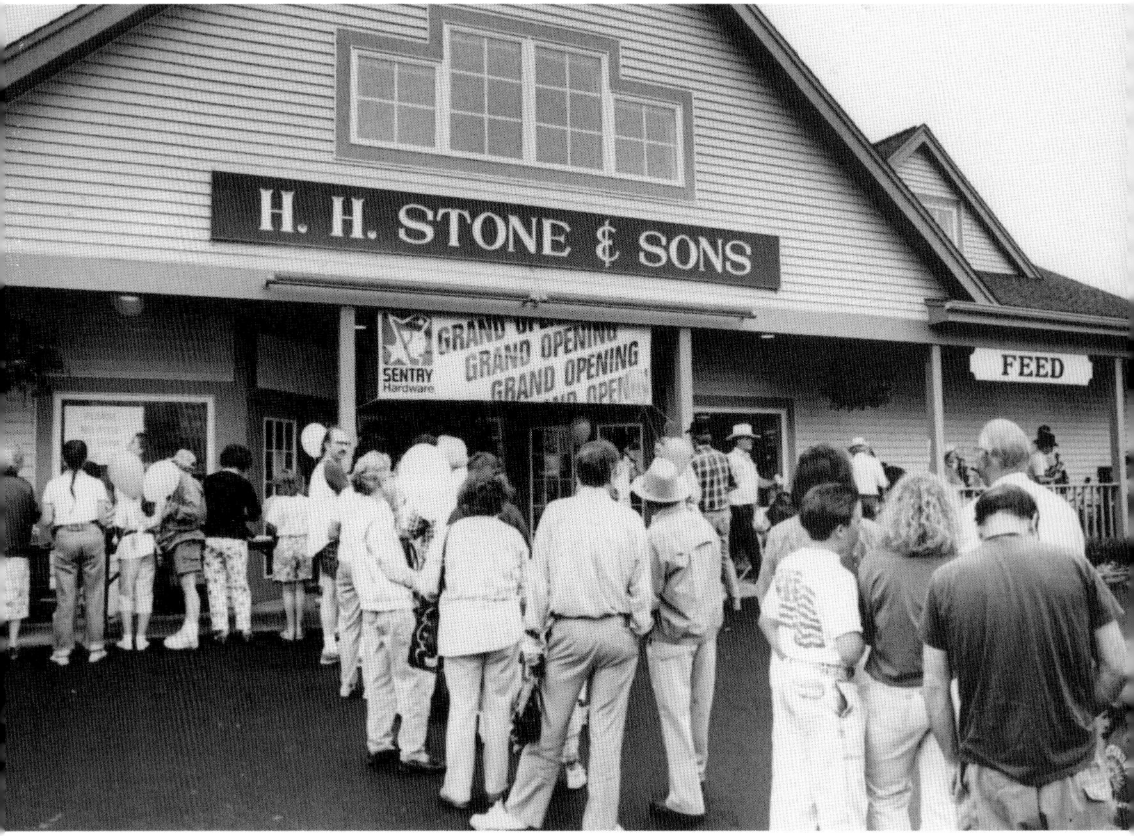

The Stone Family and H.H. Stone Inc.

The Stones have carried on the family business from generation to generation. When Mark was younger he worked part time for Leila and George Stone Sr. Now, he is the vice president of the company. This picture shows the opening-day event he organized for the new H.H. Stone building in 1991. H.H. Stone was in business long before the advent of hardware chain stores. For personal help and attention, there is nothing like a local hardware store. Hamburgers and hot dogs were served at the grand opening of the new H.H. Stone location on Main Street South in 1991. This new store was moved farther back from the original site due to widening of the road. (Courtesy Mark Stone.)

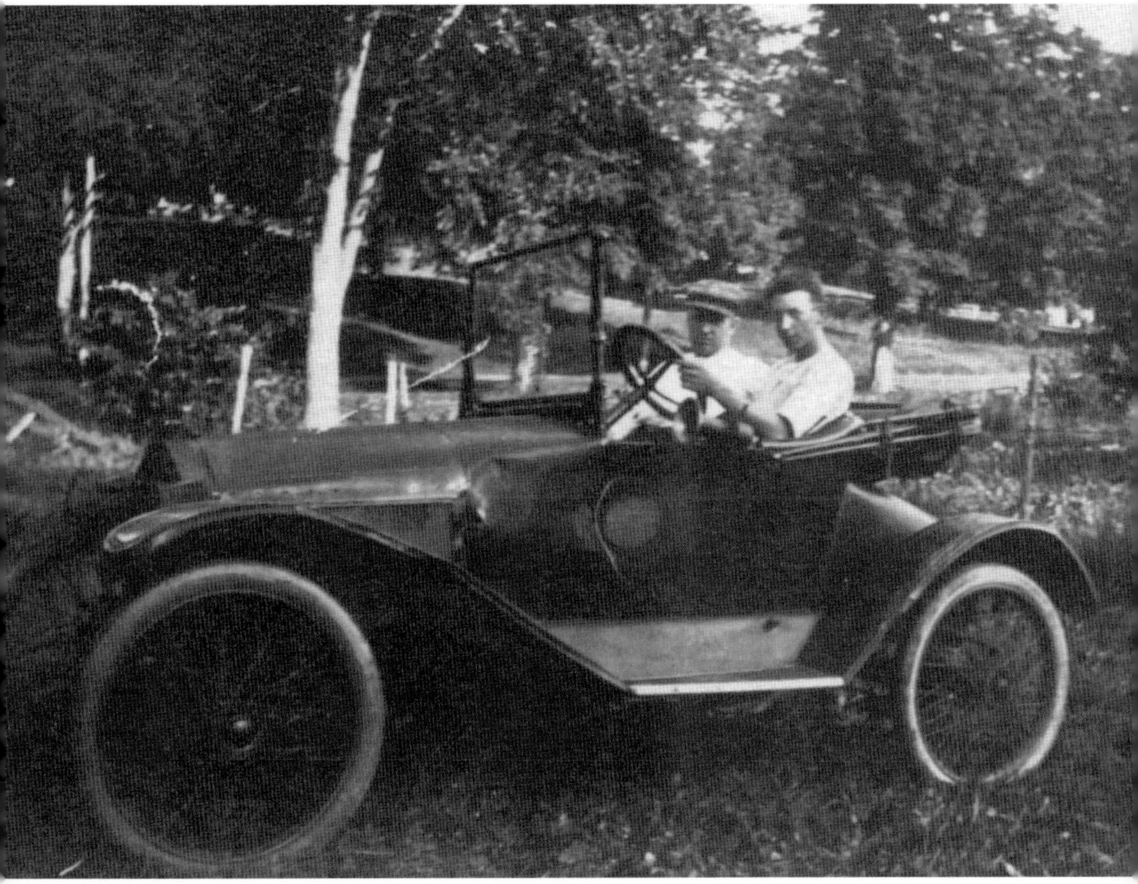

Arza Bennett
Arza Bennett Sr. (right) blended his mechanical skills with his hobby. His favorite pastime was driving his Metz sports car. Bennett had a talent for mechanics at an early age, and Paul Bronson, a Woodbury businessman, was so impressed with Bennett's skills that he sent him to mechanics school. Metz cars were built in Waltham, Massachusetts, and were in production as early as 1898. Louis Kolb is pictured with Bennett. (Courtesy Arza Bennett Jr.)

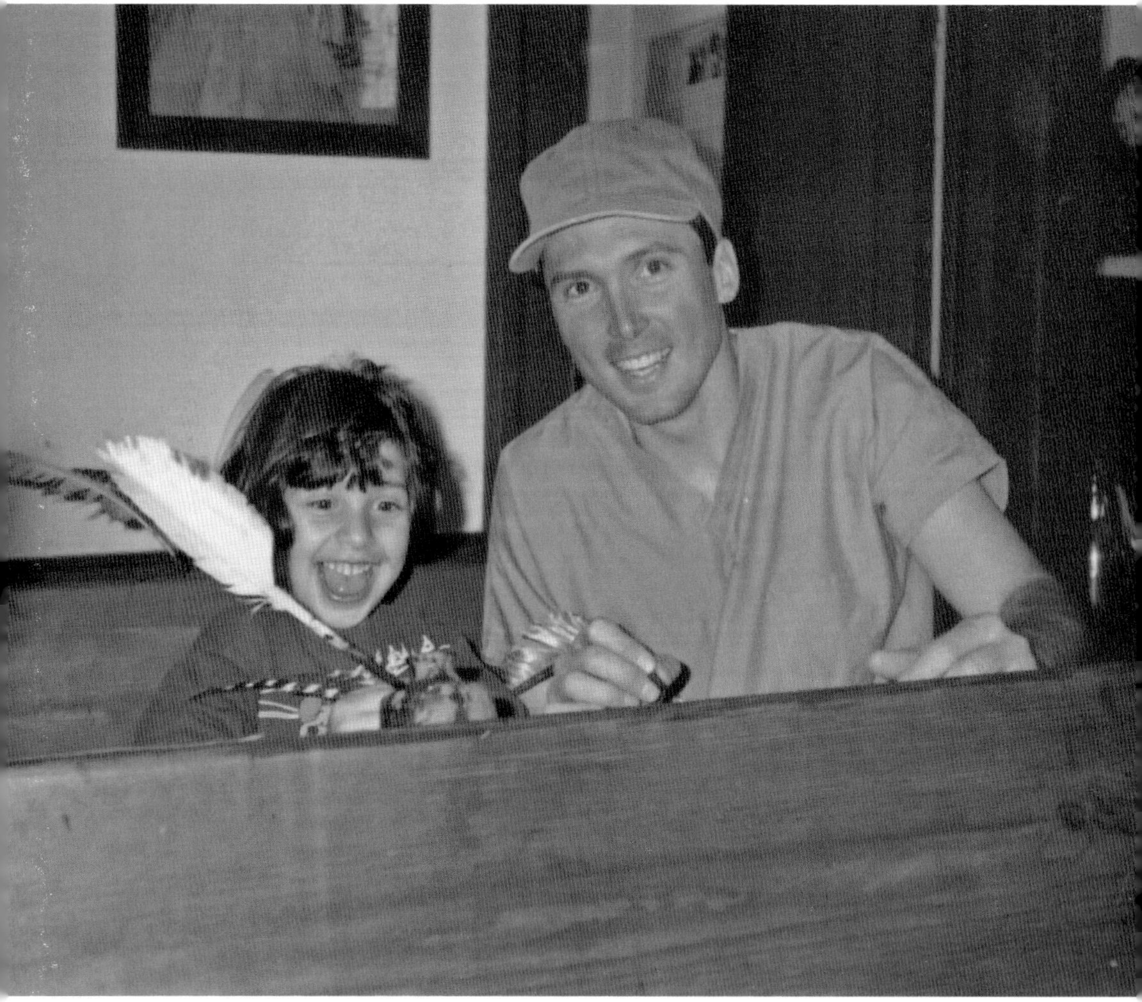

Dr. Charles Guck

Charles Guck has operated the successful Southbury General Dentistry Practice at Dr. Samuel Green's former house, next door to Bullet Hill School, for over 20 years. As longtime chairman of the Southbury Parks and Recreation Commission, he worked with the administration in establishing Settlers Park. Here, Grace (left) and Dr. Charles Guck enjoy a Bullet Hill School Days Open House. (Courtesy Catherine Palmer.)

CHAPTER FIVE

Getting Down to Business

I put all my genius into my life; I put only my talent into my works.

—Oscar Wilde

For over a century, Southbury was an agrarian community. The natural resources of the town were valuable to the citizens, but most important was the abundance of waterpower. The advent of small manufacturing plants and mills began Southbury's industrial revolution in the 1800s, as residents employed powering their machinery with energy from the many rivers and streams throughout our area. The South Britain section of town in particular produced many businesses including saw, grist, textile, and cider mills. Tanneries, clothiers, and several hat shops opened. Brick kilns were present in sections of town including the area on Main Street North near the Perry Farm. Distilleries and trap factories added to the array of water-powered factories. A number of products were manufactured, such as shingles, tacks, buttons, brads, wagon wheels, shears, knives, silver spoons, thimbles, hoop skirts, and bustles. At one time, in the mid-1900s, local accounts referenced more than 60 small factories and shops in Southbury. The Southford section was home to the Diamond Match company and Southford Paper company, both of which employed many residents in the 1800s.

The 1900s brought improved transportation in the form of more bridges and ferries, improved roads, and the railroad system. Trains brought a whole new way of life to communities along the rails. Goods and services improved as they could be sent via train to various destinations. All components of the railroad system provided jobs and, in Southbury, many men were employed by building tracks and the station house, serving as train masters, and providing manpower to load and unload products. Agricultural jobs used to be the predominant source of living, but that was now shifting to manufacturing jobs related to the railroad.

The road system expanded with improved surfacing materials and evolved from the impassable mud ruts caused by spring and fall rains to dependable ways of getting from place to place. Residents were employed by the quarries that provided road materials; men built machinery to grind the stone and worked as pavers in the new paving businesses. In 1963, when Interstate 84 was built, Southbury became connected to Connecticut and New York and business continued to flourish.

Improved commerce brought an expansion and diversity to the shopping community and to the availability of products for the consumer. From the necessary presence of general stores in the Southbury, Southford, and South Britain sections of town, additional little stores and services appeared. Over the years, clusters and plazas of stores and shops sprung up to meet the needs of the ever-growing population that occurred when this rural community became a rural residential community. The highways brought convenient access for residents to travel to work outside of Southbury, and new neighborhoods appeared throughout the town's vast mileage.

Getting down to business is a commitment that Southbury citizens have made throughout history. Southburians have adapted to changing times and have taken advantage of the many innovative uses of natural resources to enhance and enrich their way of life.

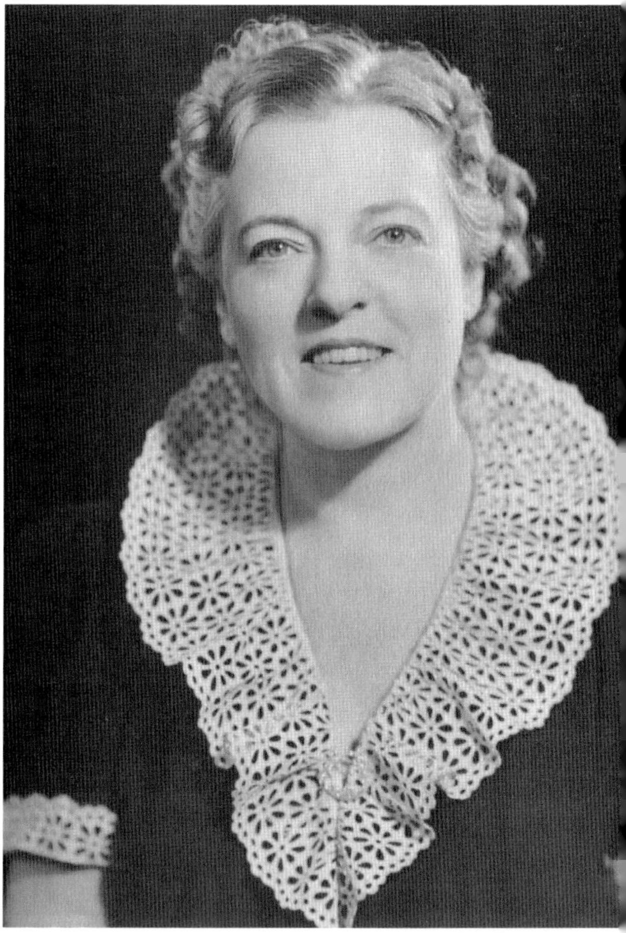

Nellie Brown and the Old Hundred Inn
When a good Yankee dinner was desired there was no better place to go than Nellie Brown's. Nellie opened the restaurant in 1933 in her family's summer home. Advertisements promoted the inn as a place of unusual merit, serving lunch, tea, and dinner. In addition to running the inn, which was named after a church hymn, Nellie also wrote a cookbook in 1939 featuring 200 years of New England cooking. (Courtesy Samuel Green II.)

Samuel Green II and Boxed Iced Cream
Buying ice cream from a grocery store was not always possible. In 1940, Samuel Green II started the Old Hundred Ice Cream business and sold to local inns, ice cream parlors, and drugstores. He expanded by selling the first prepackaged "boxed" ice cream to 400 northeast groceries. Baskin Robbins acquired the business, followed by a British conglomerate that closed in 1998. The facility had employed many locals. (Courtesy Samuel Green III.)

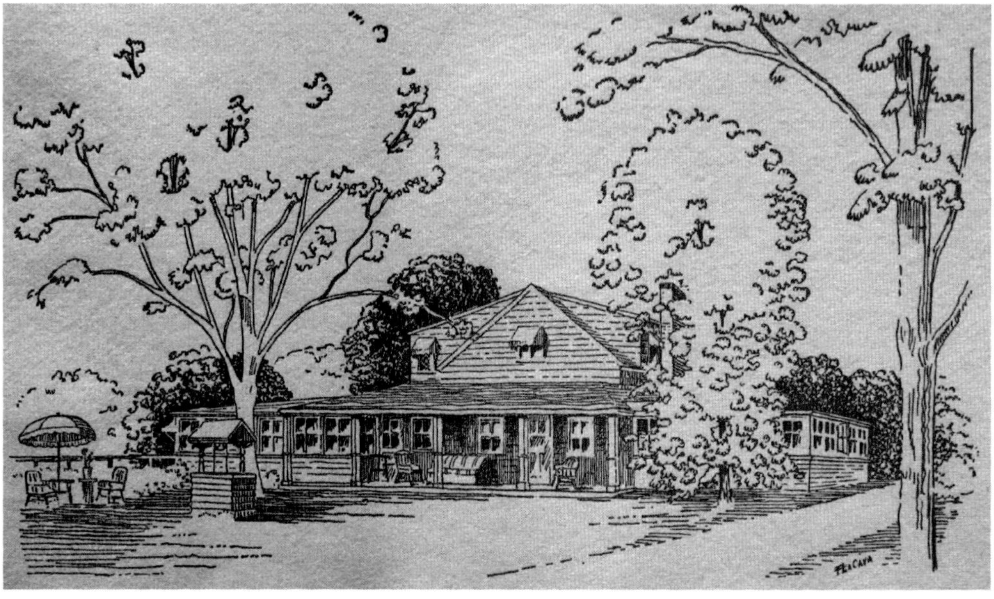

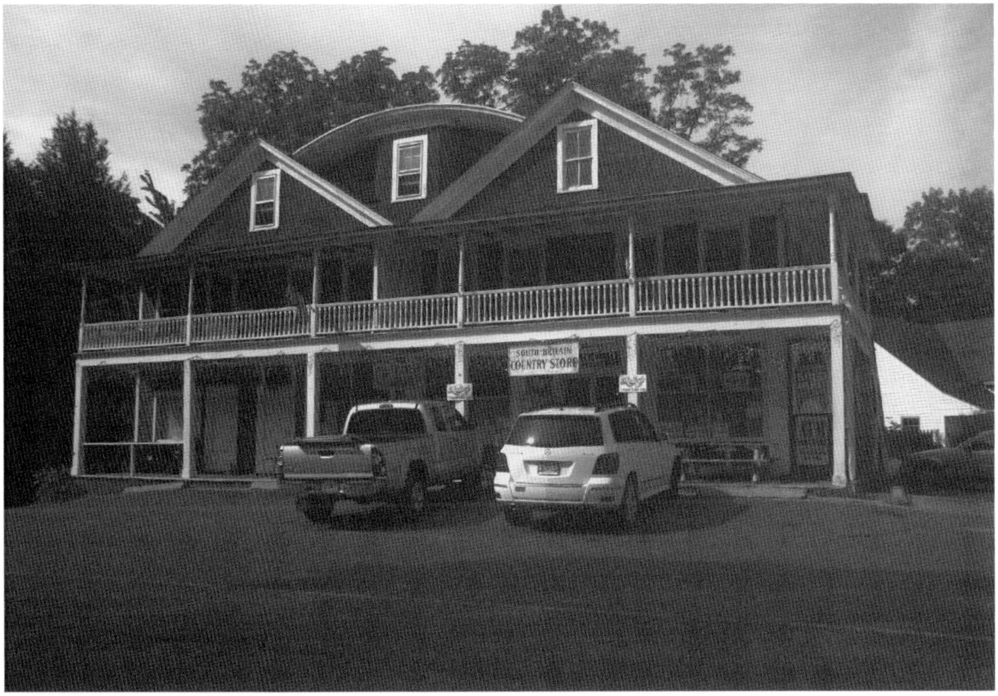

South Britain General Store
This general store originally was called Mitchell and Williams and burned down in 1905. A.H. Wilson replaced it with a three-story building. The store has had several owners; the most recent was Anthony Scheessele, who bought it in 1983. He donated the original Mitchell Store sign to the local historical society. The age of a person can determine what they call the store. Old-timers refer to it as "Mitchells" or "Pritchards." Younger generations call it "Tony's." (Courtesy Andrew Skok.)

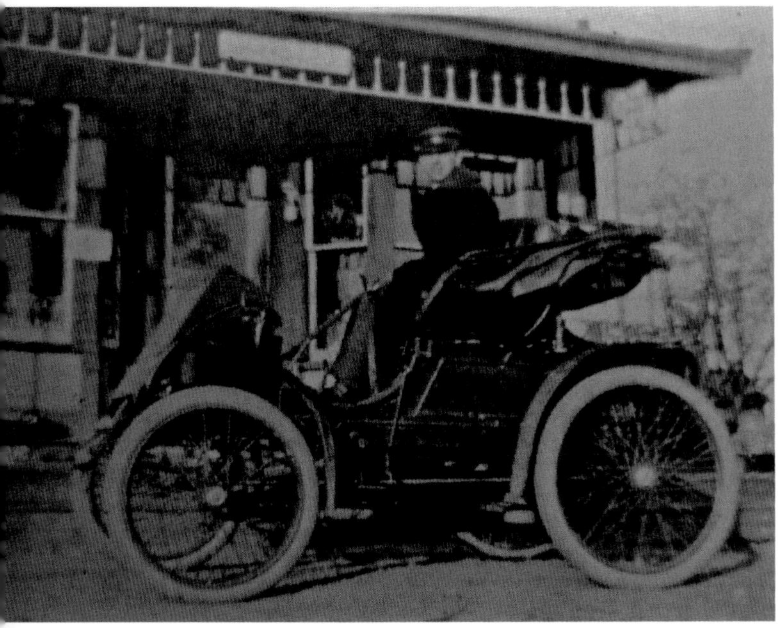

Harry Brown
Harry Brown had the oldest Cadillac dealership at the time in the United States. He ran it in the 1930s and 1940s. It covered all of Western Connecticut. His wife, Nellie Brown, ran the Old Hundred Inn. Harry served as postmaster for 12 years and also represented the area as a state legislator. (Courtesy Samuel Green III.)

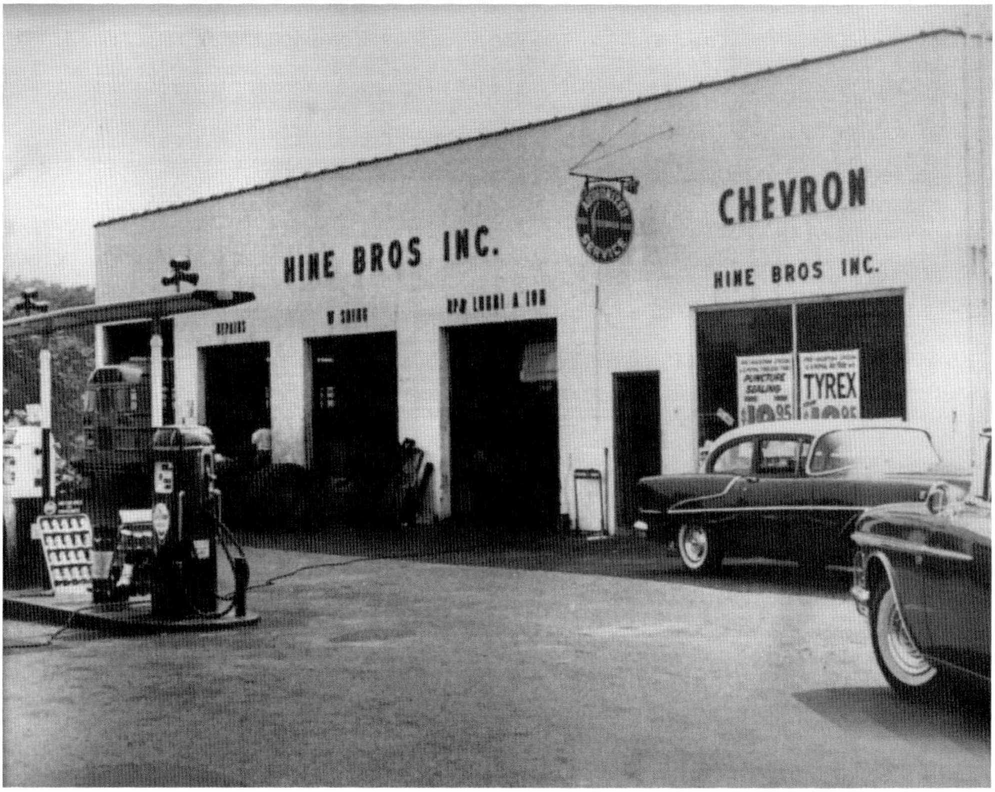

Hine Brothers
Richard and Jim Hine opened their garage in 1946, and it still serves many locals today. They serviced trucks from the Old Hundred Ice Cream business during the night hours so it wouldn't affect the business's workday schedule. When I-84 was built, the Hine brothers repaired big mixers and sharpened monster drills. Currently, the business is operated by Ken and Jay Hine and Jay's wife, Laura. Richard Hine remembers comedic pianist Victor Borge once trying to barter his bill with his Rock Cornish game hens. (Courtesy Jay Hine.)

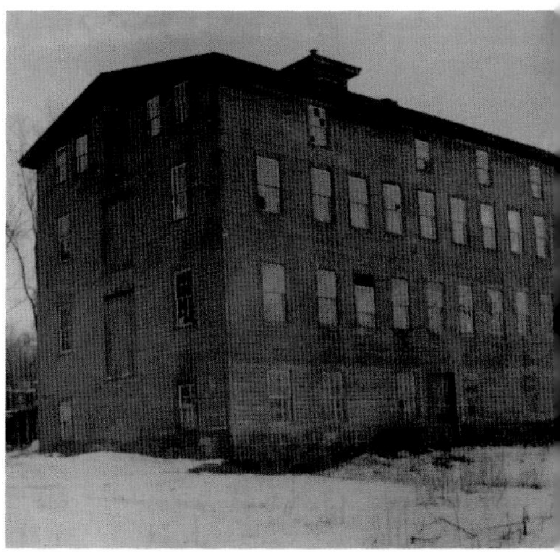

Ira Hawkins and the Hawkins Company
In 1900, Ira Hawkins took over the Bradley and Hoyt mill and started the Hawkins Company to manufacture animal traps. Aside from traps, numerous other items were produced in the building, including woolens, tacks, buttons, and plastic assemblies. Factory operations stopped in the 1960s. Hawkins was very generous and supported local projects, including a library. He also installed an electric light at the corner of Main Street, as well as a pump that brought water down from the springs on the hill and served three houses in town. He started a community club that met in extra space at the factory for dances, banquets, and other activities including one of the favorites, a bowling alley. (Courtesy Althea McGahie.)

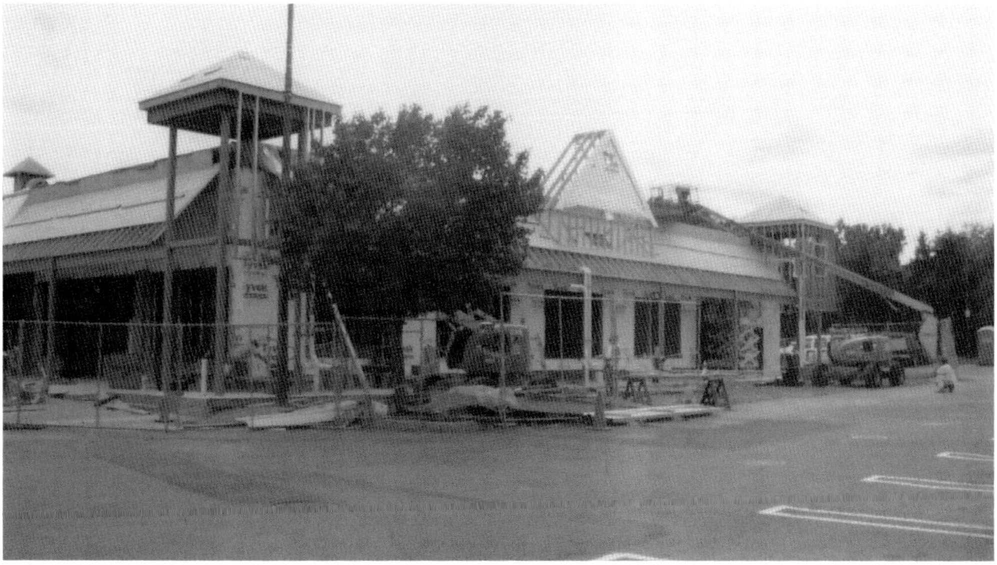

Rudy Gatto and the Southbury Plaza

Contractor Rudy Gatto built the Southbury Plaza in the 1970s. Previously, the land was part of the Perry Farm. Prior to the plaza being built, residents had to go to Danbury or Waterbury to shop at a department store. Southbury has a wealth of retail space, which is consolidated into a few plazas located around Main Street. Before the land was developed into Southbury Plaza, it was owned by the Perry family. The present-day McDonald's restaurant is located at the site of the former Perry barn. The Bennett children enjoyed the open fields in their play. Shown here in 1942 are, from left to right, Arza "Bud" Bennett Jr., Kathy Bennett, and May Bennett. (Above, courtesy VFW Post No. 1607; below, courtesy Arza Bennett Jr.)

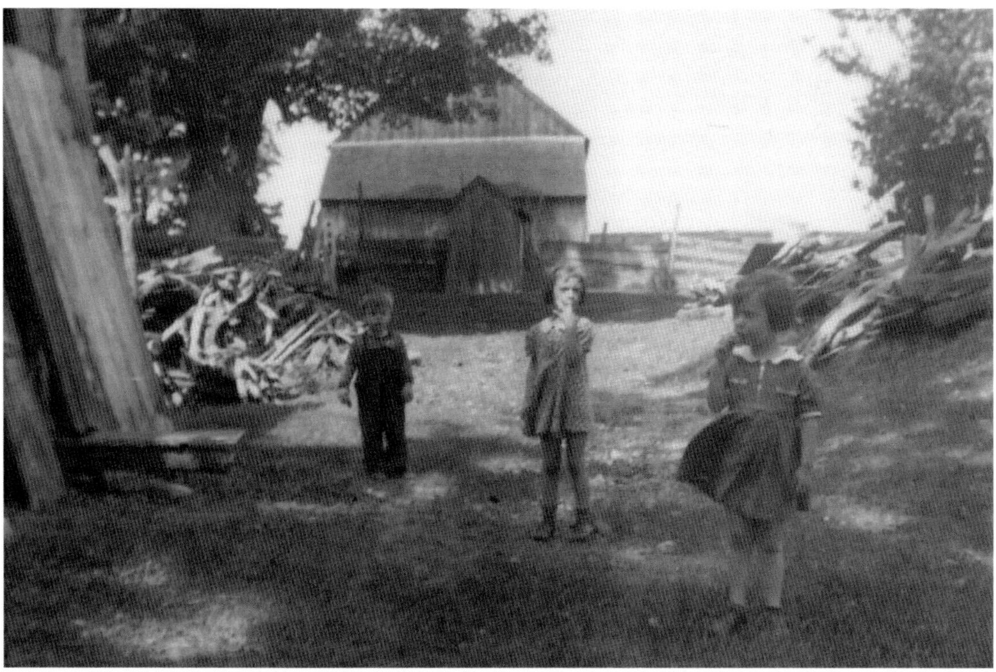

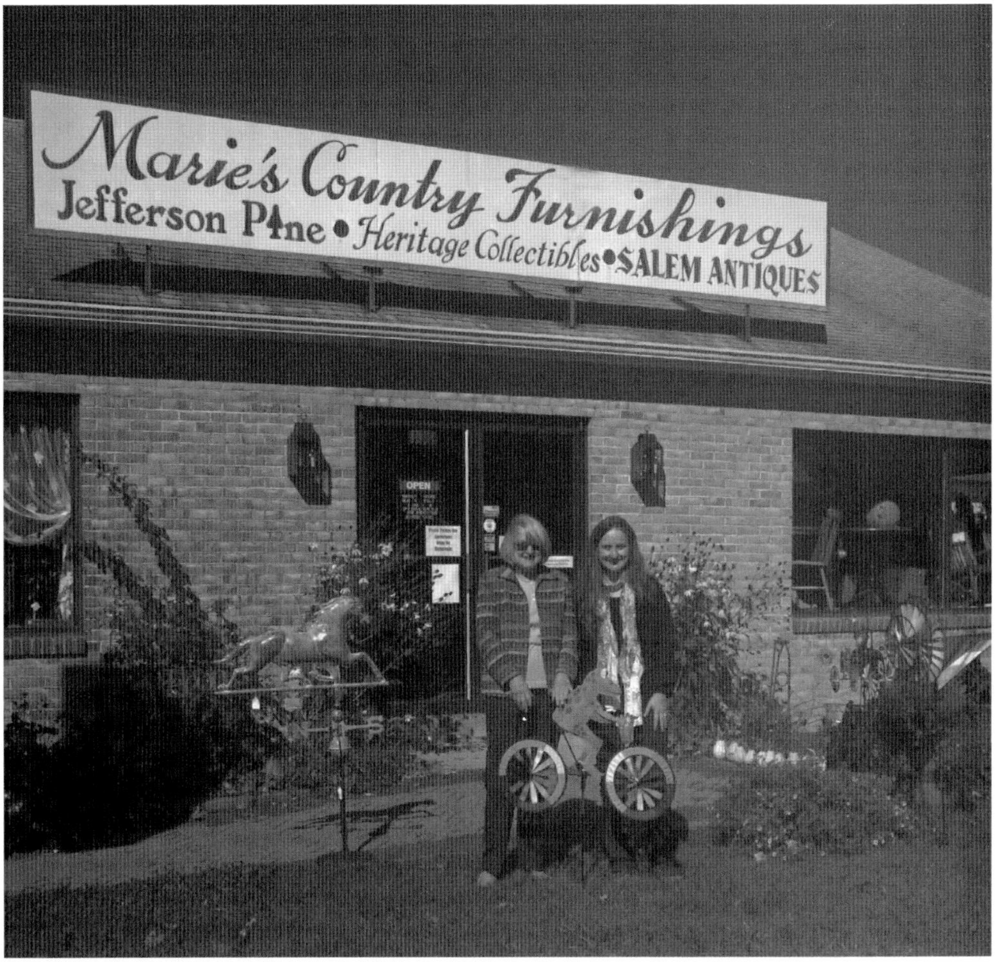

Marie Anctil and Therese Dostie
Marie Anctil and her daughter Therese are pictured in front of Marie's Country Furnishings. The store was in the Heritage Village Bazaar for more than 20 years, and stayed there until the end as one of the last tenants. The business was moved from Heritage Village to Main Street South and has been there for 13 years. Marie has loved doing business in Southbury over the years. Therese and her husband, Donald Dostie, run the business today. (Courtesy Andrew Skok.)

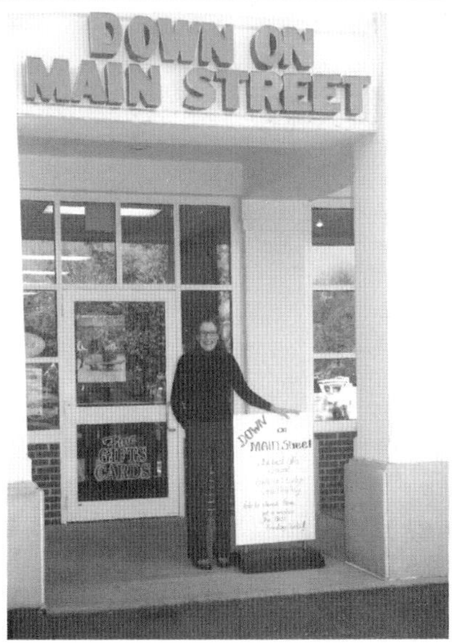

Down on Main Street
Kristin Pardee is pictured in front of the Down on Main Street store, a popular store that has been located for 15 years at its present location at the Southbury Green. Kristen has worked for the owner, Larry Schneider, and his business for 18 years. (Courtesy Andrew Skok.)

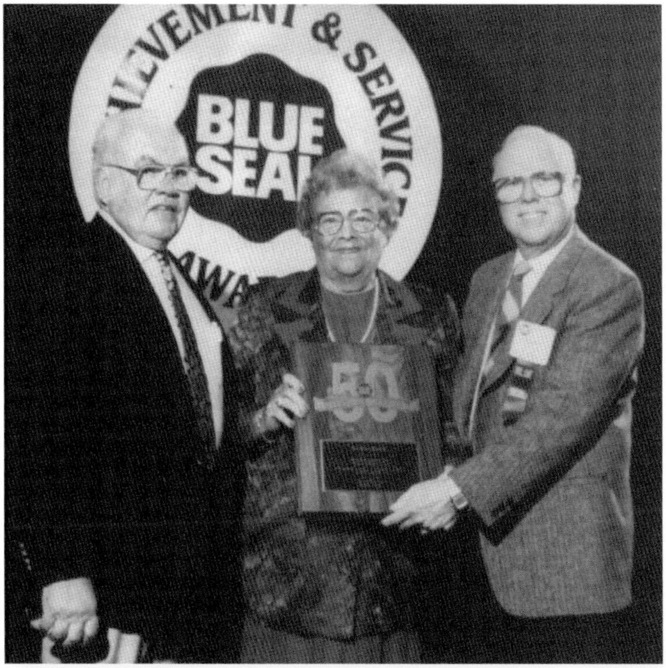

George and Leila Stone
George (left) and Leila Stone (center) are pictured receiving an award for selling Blue Seal animal and farm products in their store for 50 years from a company representative. George was a dedicated fire marshal. He and his son George Jr. were both past presidents of the Lions Club. Leila and George's wedding anniversary was on Flag Day (June 14) as was George's birthday. The couple enjoyed a Friday date at Woodbury's Constantine restaurant. George met with fellow birthday friends Harold W. Davis and Bob Johnson to smoke birthday cigars. (Courtesy Mark Stone.)

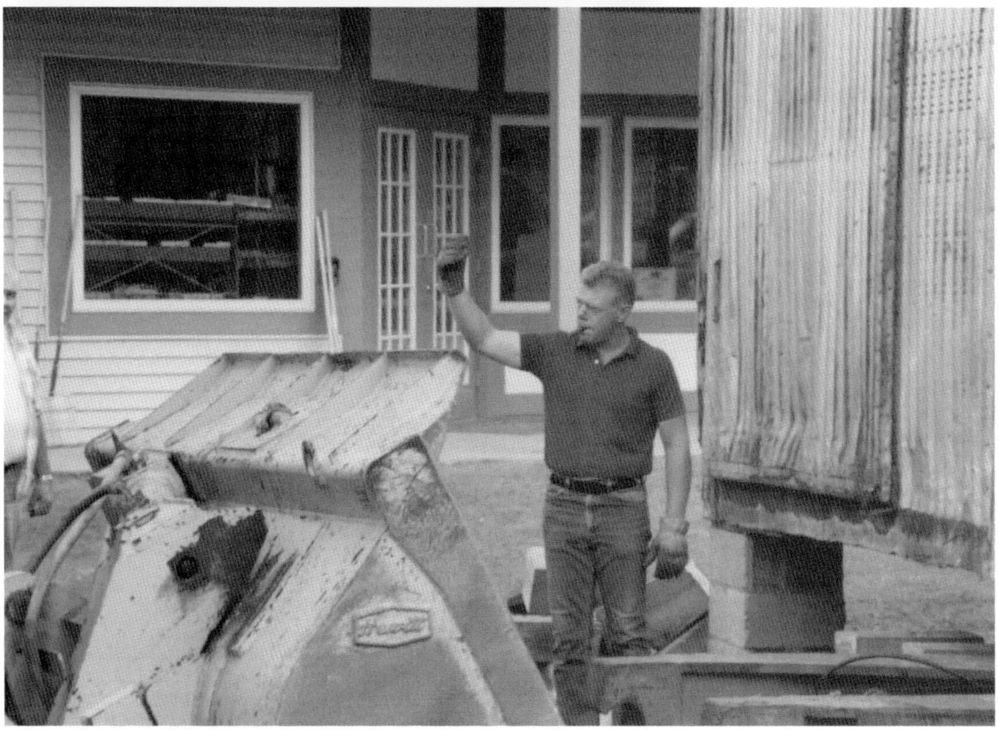

George Stone Jr.
George Stone Jr. is pictured while helping direct the relocation of a building. This is a rare photograph as George Jr., a past president of the Lions Club, is camera shy. George is the owner of Stone's Construction Company. (Courtesy Mark Stone.)

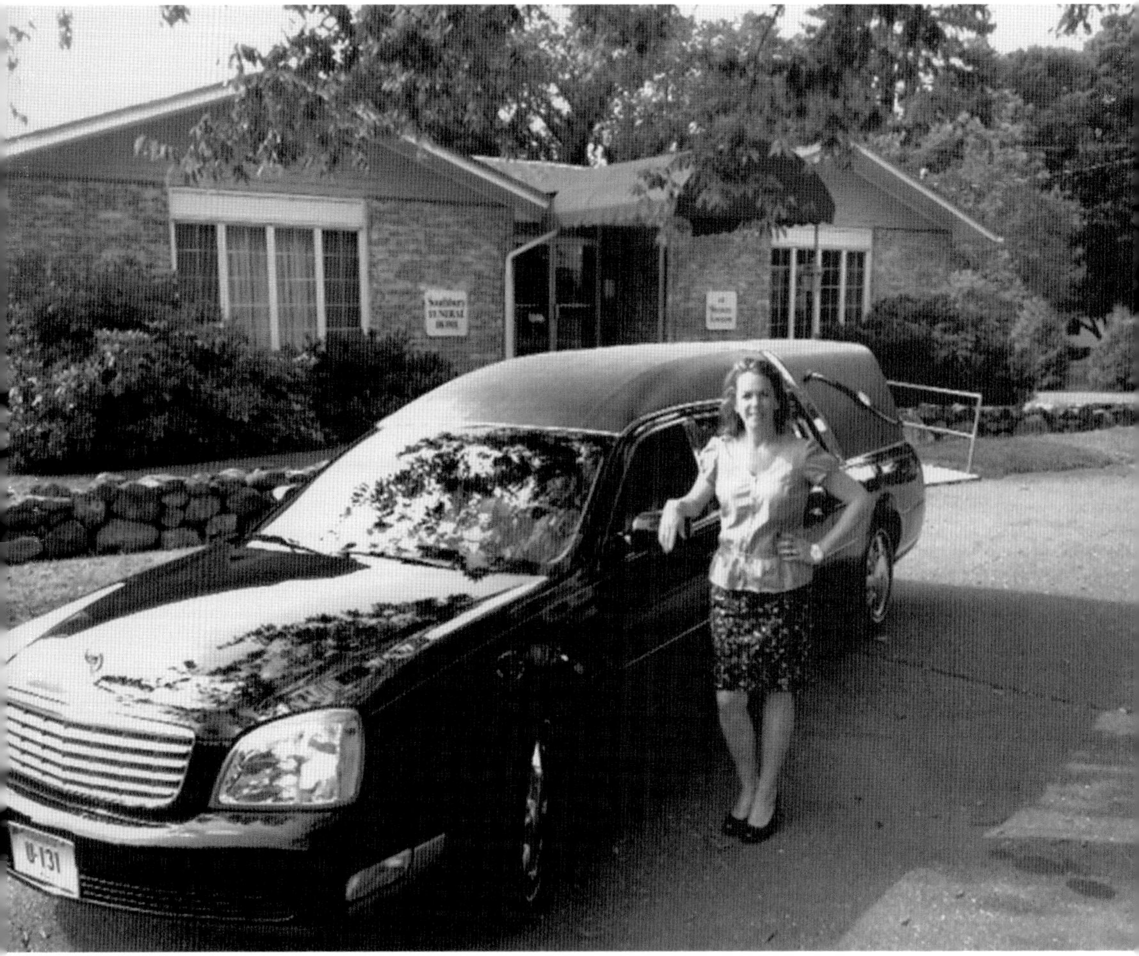

Liisa Lovetere-Stone

Liisa operates Southbury's Lovetere Funeral Home, built in the 1960s. It is the Southbury division of the main business in Woodbury, which was built in the 1800s and has always been in the family. Liisa is a third-generation Lovetere working at the funeral home. Her late uncle Joe Lovetere was partners with Earle Munson, who was one of the founders of the Woodbury Telephone Company. Joe passed away unexpectedly at a young age while she was in college, so it was natural for her to switch to mortuary school to continue the family business. Dave Munson, who has worked for the company since the early 1980s, is the late Earle Munson's nephew. They both pride themselves on operating a truly family-owned business.

When Liisa attended mortuary school more than 25 years ago, there were only three other girls in the class. Today, 60 percent of mortuary students are women. She likes to think that she helped promote women into the funeral service business. Liisa and her husband, Mark, have two young children who are no strangers to the family business. At ages seven and nine, they are taken to work with her and when appropriate, they help with tasks. There are many funny, sad, heart-warming, and tragic lessons learned along the way. During a funeral for a young man who was killed while piloting a plane at Sikorsky, a flyover occurred during the cemetery service. Every time a plane flies over her head to this day, Liisa remembers that day with a feeling of awe. (Courtesy Liisa Lovetere Stone.)

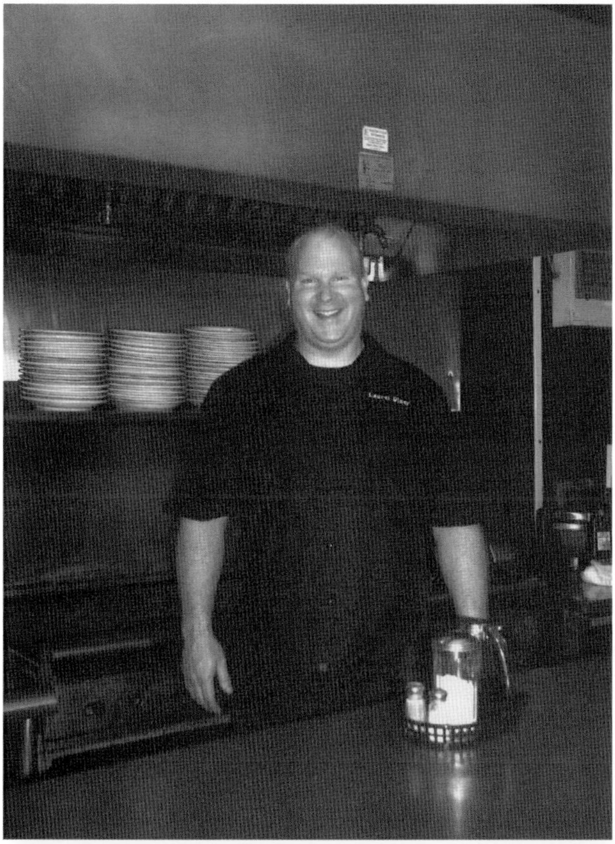

Peter Homick
Peter Homick always wanted to run his own business and raise his family in a nice town like Southbury. He bought the Laurel Diner in 1997. It was there that he met his wife, Stephanie. The diner has been mentioned in *The New Yorker*, *US News and World Report*, *Yankee* magazine, and roadfood.com. People hungry for good food and conversation have been coming to this local eatery for many years. Patrons are also attracted to Peter's custom of listing menu items on the walls. Television personality David Letterman frequented the restaurant in the early 1990s. (Courtesy Andrew Skok.)

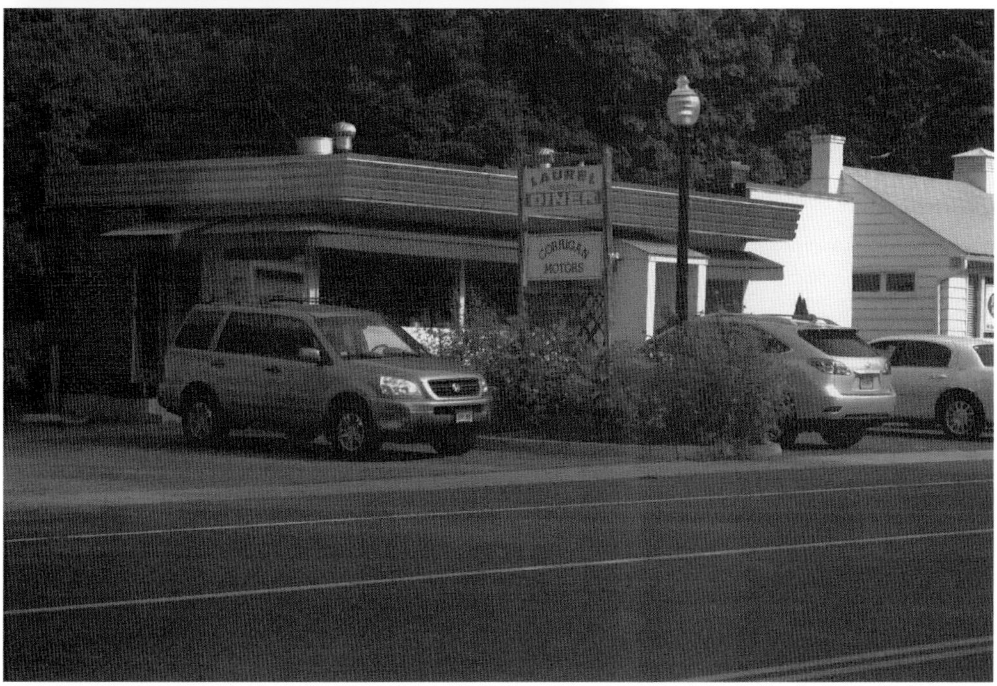

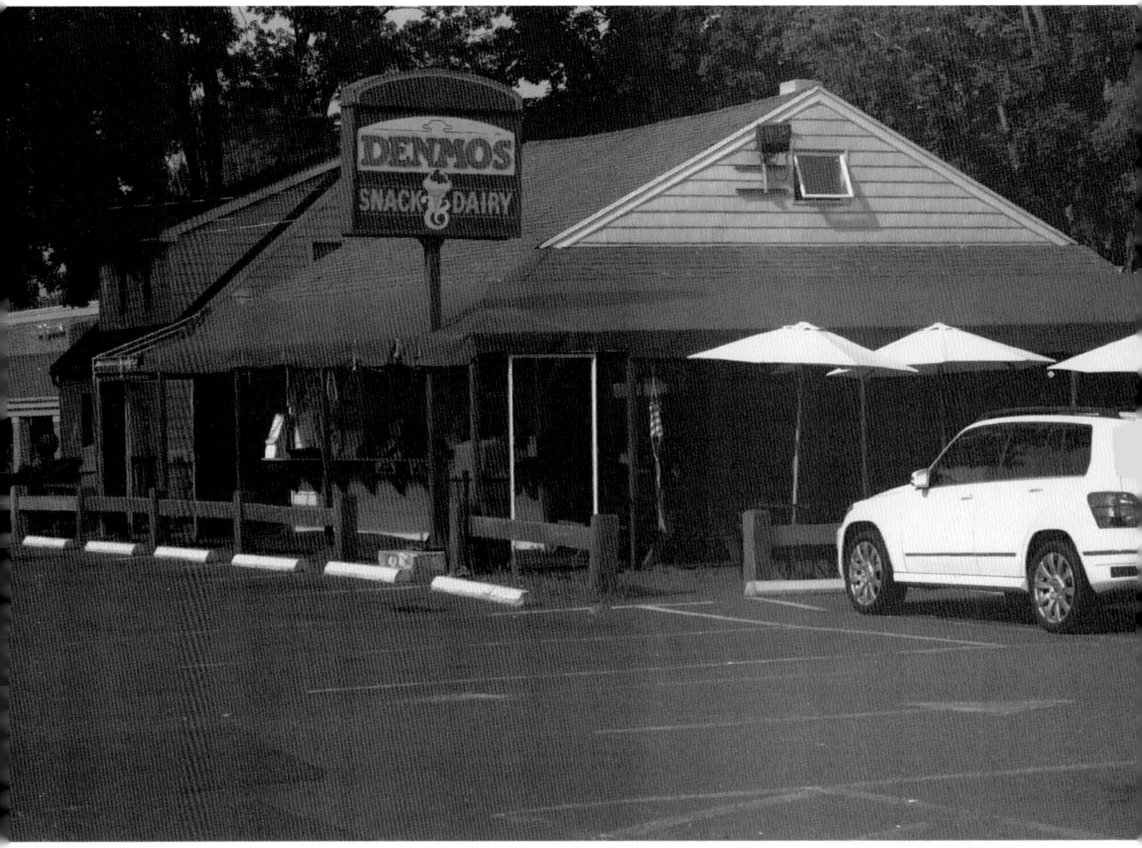

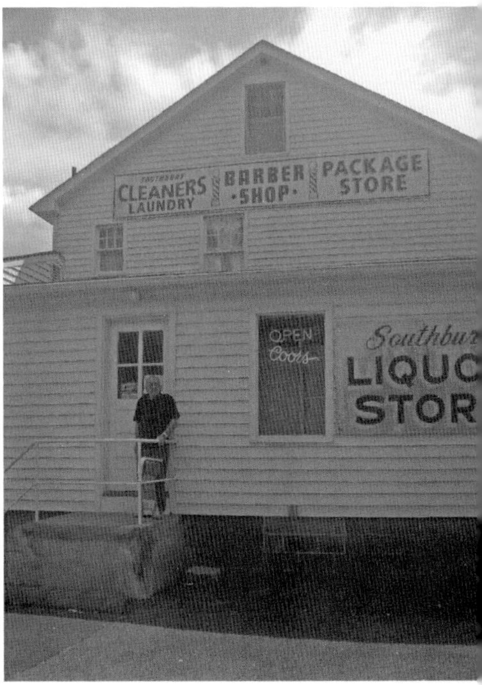

Dennis and Marilyn Luccarelli

Dennis and Marilyn Luccarelli bought the restaurant formerly called Cedar Hollow Snack and Dairy in 1978. The restaurant's name, Denmos, was created by combining the couple's nicknames, Den and Mo. Dennis always opens at 8:00 a.m., but on the opening day of fishing season, he makes grinders for anglers starting at 4:00 a.m. Their daughter Chloe is learning to manage the business. Culinary customs have changed since the 1970s, and the once-popular slushies have been replaced with 20 ice cream varieties. (Courtesy Andrew Skok.)

Dan Candido

Dan Candido stands in front of the package store that was started after Prohibition with his brother, former First Selectman Alfio Candido. Candido's widow, Mary Ann, is now a partner in the business with Dan. In 1929, Dan's father ran the first barbershop in what is now the back room. It was later moved to the end of the building. (Courtesy Andrew Skok.)

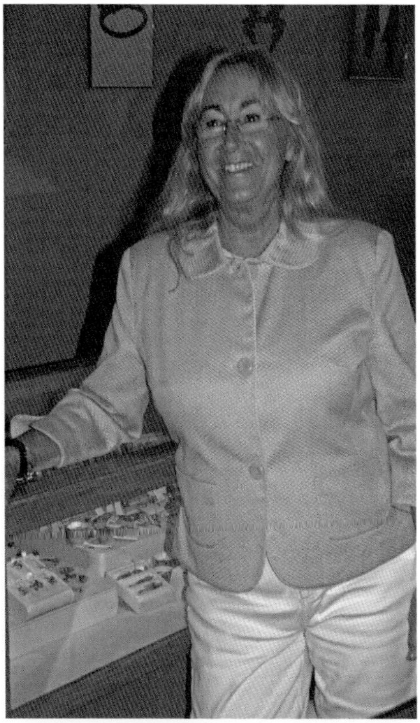

Gayle O'Neill, Antique and Fine Jewelry
Gayle recalled a Christmas Eve when, after she had put the jewelry in the safe, a snowplow operator knocked at the door. He was looking for a gold chain to give as a Christmas gift. Gayle brought out some necklaces, and he selected a very fine one. When she inquired about his budget, she realized it was much less than the necklace's cost. Gayle smiled and accepted the amount he had, wrapped up the gift, and wished him a Merry Christmas. When Gayle is not working at her store, which has been a part of the community for more than 25 years, she loves to relax on her boat. She has owned a jewelry store in Southbury since November 1984 and has been in the business since 1979. She started out buying gold and silver, but was attracted to vintage pieces and beautiful handmade settings. She has an appreciation for beautiful craftsmanship and high-quality, one-of-a-kind pieces. (Courtesy Andrew Skok.)

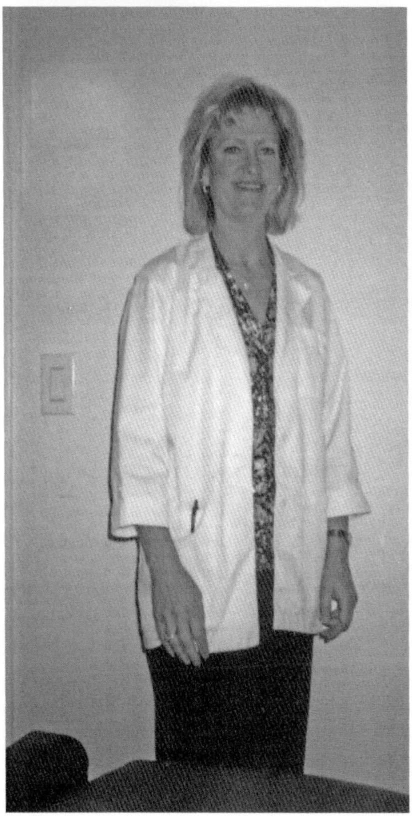

Dr. Carol Mancini, Chiropractor
Carol Mancini became a chiropractor to help people with their health and wellness. Mancini Chiropractic is located on Main Street South. She provides both treatment and current education about the maintenance of a healthy skeletal system and its importance for harmony with the entire body and optimum health. (Courtesy Catherine Palmer.)

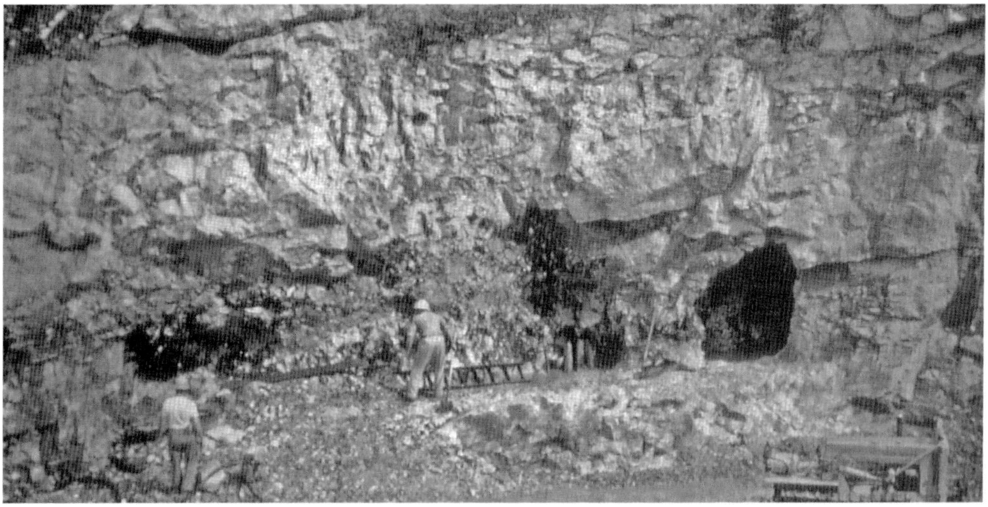

Curtis Men at Work in the Southford Quarry
Burritt C. Curtis and his wife, DeLoris Stone Curtis, owned the Curtis Quarry on Hulls Hill Road. The quarry was used from 1800 to 1950. During World War II, the silica it produced was used to manufacture periscopes. The quarry was worked by the Bridgeport Finishing Company, which mined quartz for wood filler. The Curtis family home next to the quarry was built around 1800. (Courtesy DeLoris Curtis.)

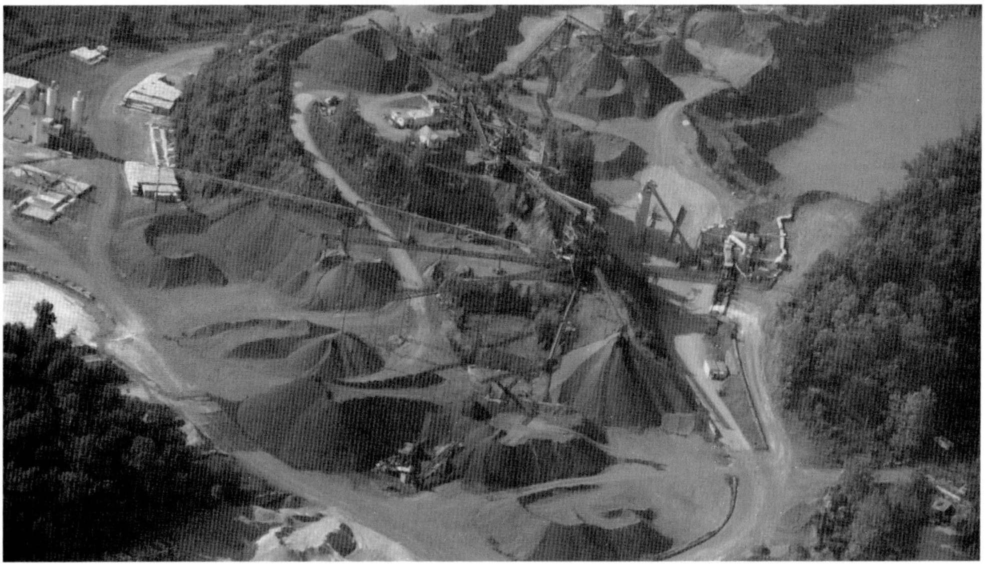

O&G Quarry
In 1923, Andrew Oneglia and his partner, Flaviano Gervasini, opened a road-building business in Torrington, Connecticut. As O&G began to build more roads, securing a reliable source of high-quality materials was necessary. O&G developed a network of quarries throughout Connecticut and New York. The Southbury quarry was opened in the 1930s. There are more than one dozen company facilities. This O&G quarry has been referred to as the Southbury Quarry to differentiate it from the one farther north in Woodbury. It is well known for three varieties of Prehnite: green, rare yellow, and rare white that is almost free of iron impurities. Sphalerite crystals including calcite, agate, apophyllite, and zeolite were mined. (Courtesy Carol Haskins.)

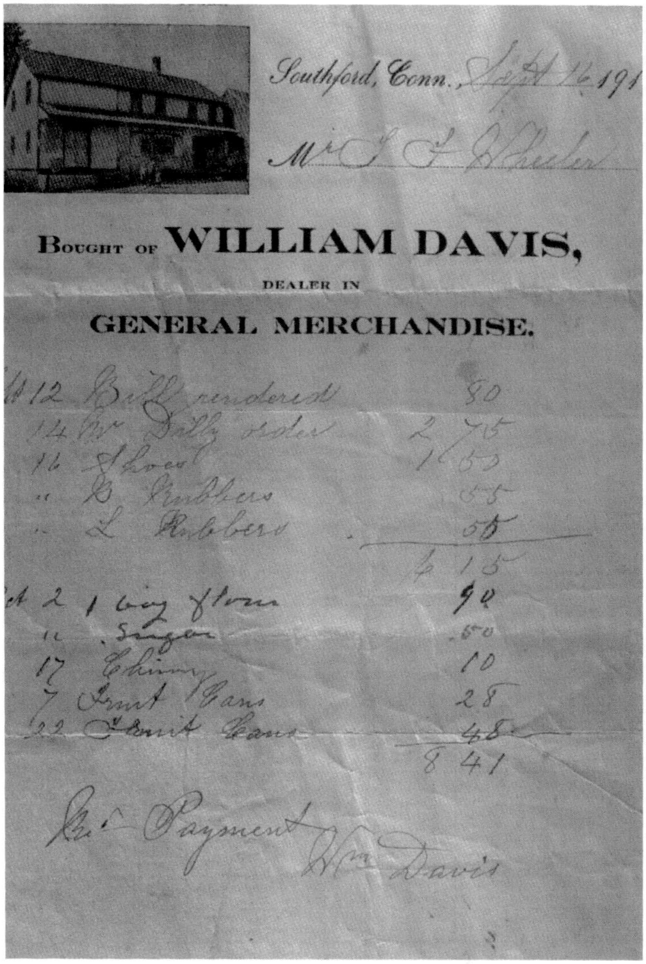

Southford, Conn., Sept 16 191

Bought of WILLIAM DAVIS,

DEALER IN

GENERAL MERCHANDISE.

12	Bill rendered	80
14	Mr Dally order	2 75
16	Shoes	1 50
"	B Rubbers	55
"	L Rubbers	55
		6 15
2	1 bag flour	90
"	Sugar	50
17	Chimney	10
	7 Fruit Jars	28
	12 Fruit Cans	48
		8 41

Rec. Payment Wm Davis

H. William Davis, Southford General Store
H. William Davis and his wife, Kayanne, currently run the Southford General Store. He served as the Planning Commission chairman for the town of Southbury. He became a selectman and then progressed to first selectman. A post office once operated for many years out of the store, which also housed a livery. Pictured is a bill from the Southford General Store. (Courtesy H. William Davis.)

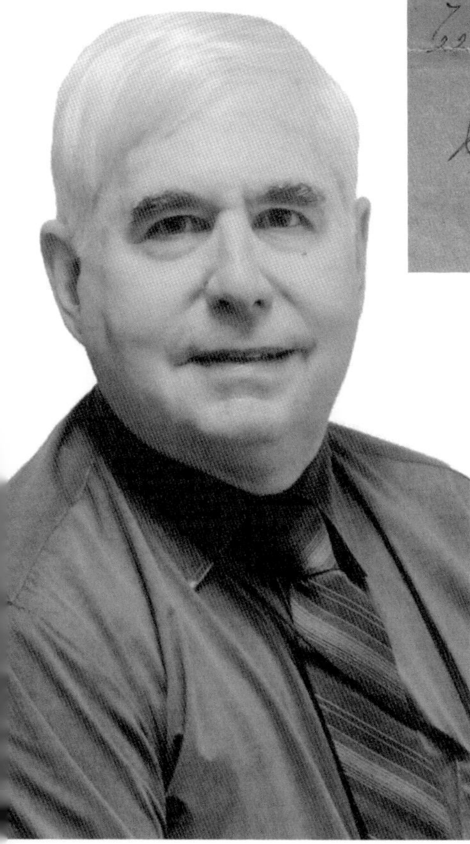

Dr. John Purcell
John Purcell was considering where to establish his dentistry practice while he was still a Georgetown University senior. He knew Southbury was rural and wanted to begin practicing in a small town. He opened his office in 1975 and was the fifth general practice in the area. He moved to Playhouse Corner in 1989. John is a past president of the Tribury Rotary and has been the Historic Buildings Commission treasurer for more than a decade. (Courtesy John Purcell.)

Mark Stone

Mark Stone stands in front of the H.H. Stone Hardware Store, which was named after Harvey Harry Stone. Mark is the secretary, treasurer, and vice president of the corporation. The business began in the 1890s and incorporated in the 1950s. Mark started working as a helper to his grandparents. He is married to Liisa Lovetere Stone, who runs the Lovetere Funeral Home. The new 1991 building replaced a smaller 1953 building, and houses the hardware store and business offices. The prior building housed a milk-hauling and dairy provision business; the business also provided equipment for about 50 farms at the time. (Courtesy Andrew Skok.)

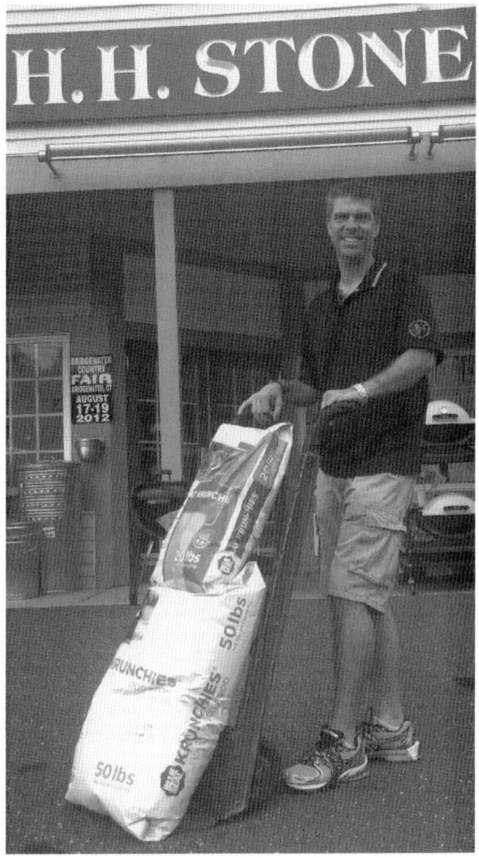

Harvey Raymond Stone and Milk Truck, 1938

Harvey Raymond Stone's son Harry had a feed and grain store on Depot Hill that was later moved to Main Street. His son Harvey owned a trucking business, Harvey I. Stone & Son. Pictured is an early milk delivery truck used in 1938. (Courtesy Mark Stone.)

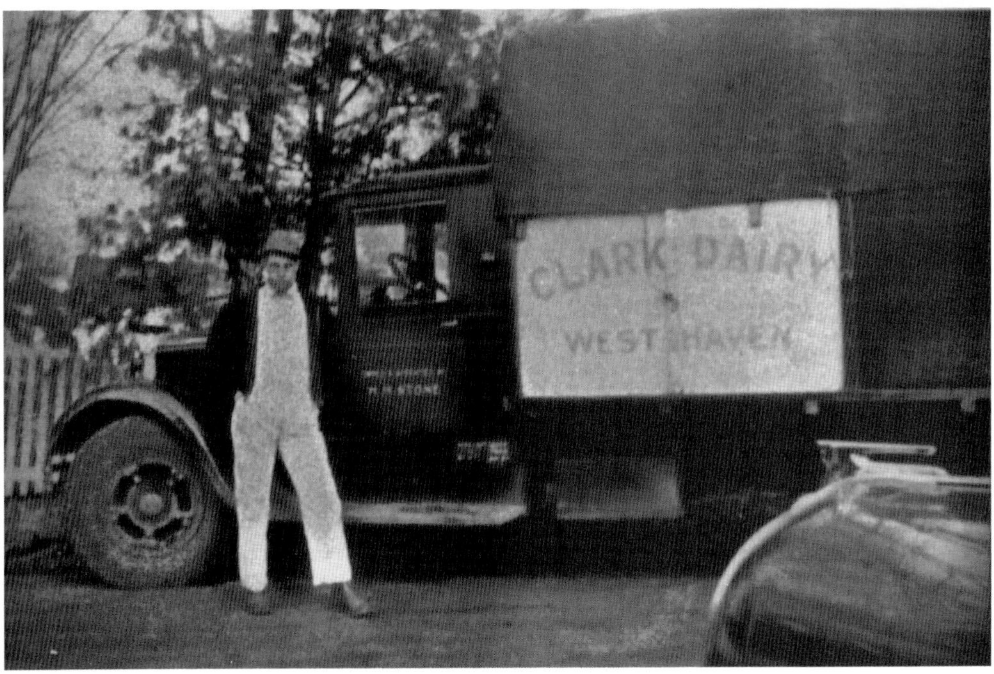

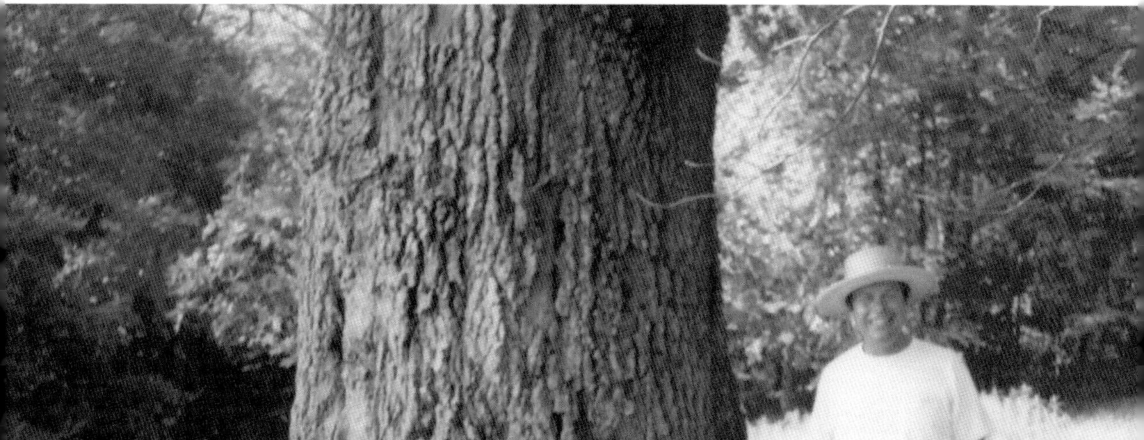

Edward A. Platt, Preservationist

Ed Platt, seventh-generation dairy farmer, stands by a magnificent black oak tree in the 1783 family farm pasture. He and his wife, Jeannine, their children Matthew, Sarah, and Benjamin, and their grandchildren have long enjoyed this tree, which has been named a Southbury Heritage Tree. Ed has held membership and leadership positions in many organizations promoting economic vitality and advocacy for the preservation of agriculture and farmland. He was the state chairman of the US Department of Agriculture Farm Service Agency for eight years, a Central Connecticut Farmer's Cooperative Board of Directors member, and a member of the Southbury Rural Preservation Commission. He is proud of giving many teenagers the opportunity to work with cattle and operate farm equipment while experiencing nature close at hand. Several former employees are now farm owners, including sons Matthew in New York state and Benjamin on the Platt family farm. (Courtesy Catherine Palmer.)

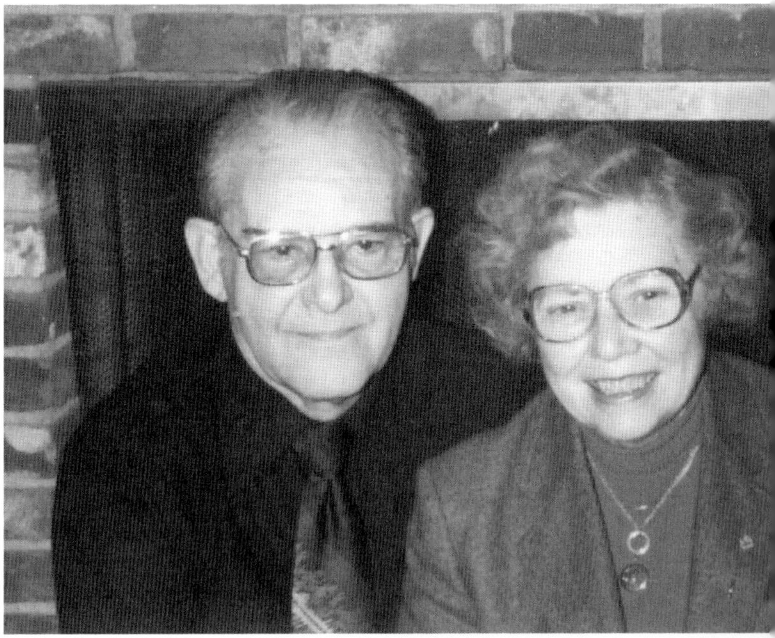

Dorothy and Wesley Rouse
Dorothy and Wesley Rouse were sometimes the first people one would meet when looking for a house in Southbury. They ran Rouse Realty off Old Field Road. Son Wesley Jr. is a famous landscape designer who was featured on television, while daughter Betsey followed in her parent's footsteps as a realtor for many years. (Courtesy Betsey Rouse Bette.)

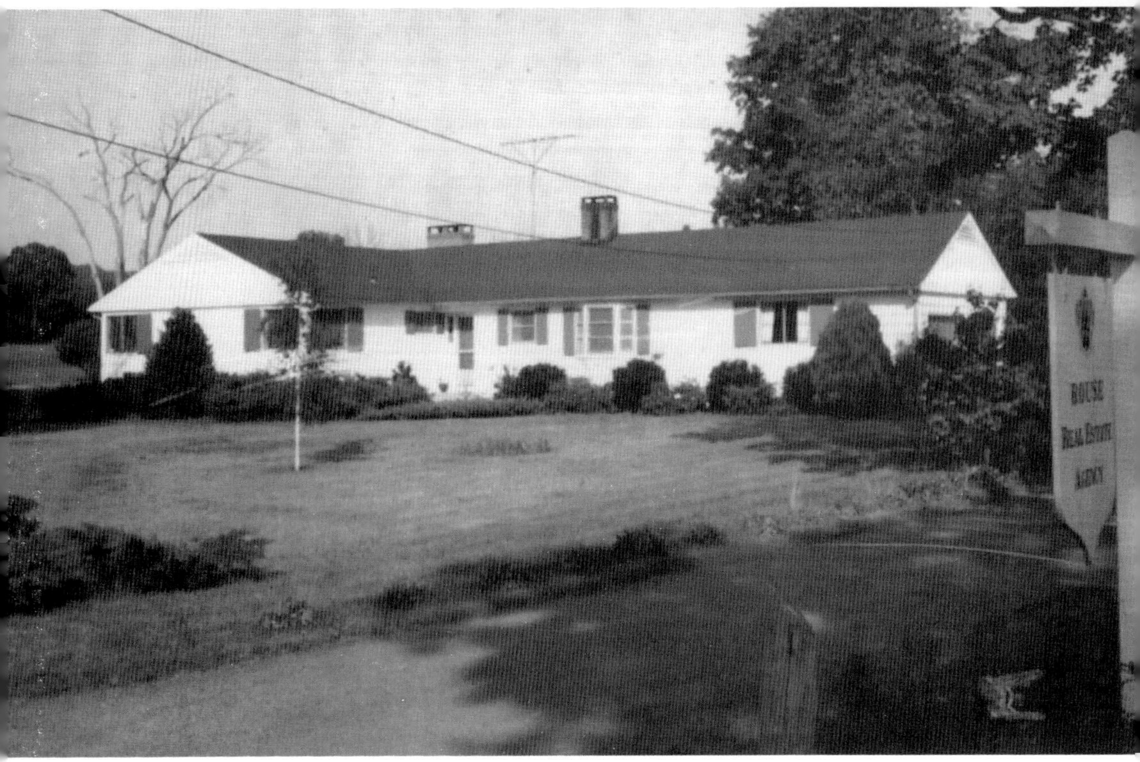

Rouse Realty
Dorothy and Wesley's Rouse Realty business flourished for many years, and they were always helpful in every aspect of the realty business. Many residents today remember the professional attention the Rouses gave to every detail of property transactions. (Courtesy Betsey Rouse Bette.)

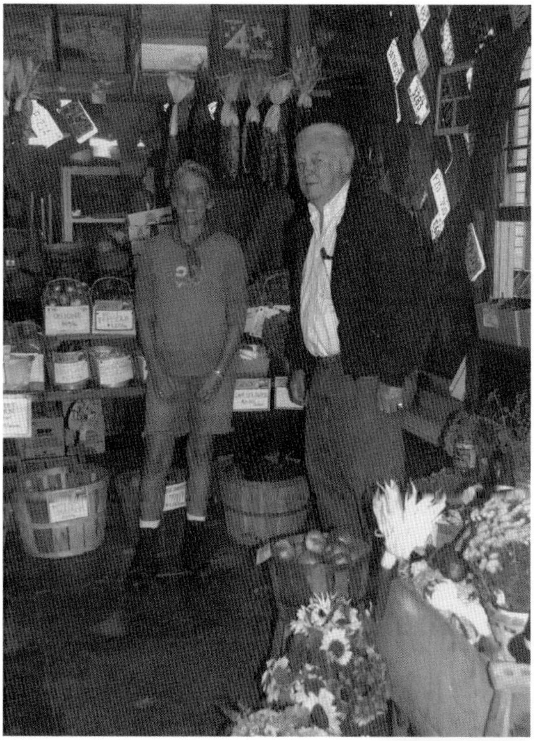

The Starchaks and their Farm Stand
Pictured are Robin Starchak and her father, William Starchak. Southburians have purchased sweet corn for many years at the Starchaks' farm stand, known as Pete's Produce. Robin named the business after her great-uncle Peter Fleming. William Starchak remembers selling ears of corn on the driveway corner for 35¢ a dozen more than 60 years ago. (Courtesy Andrew Skok.)

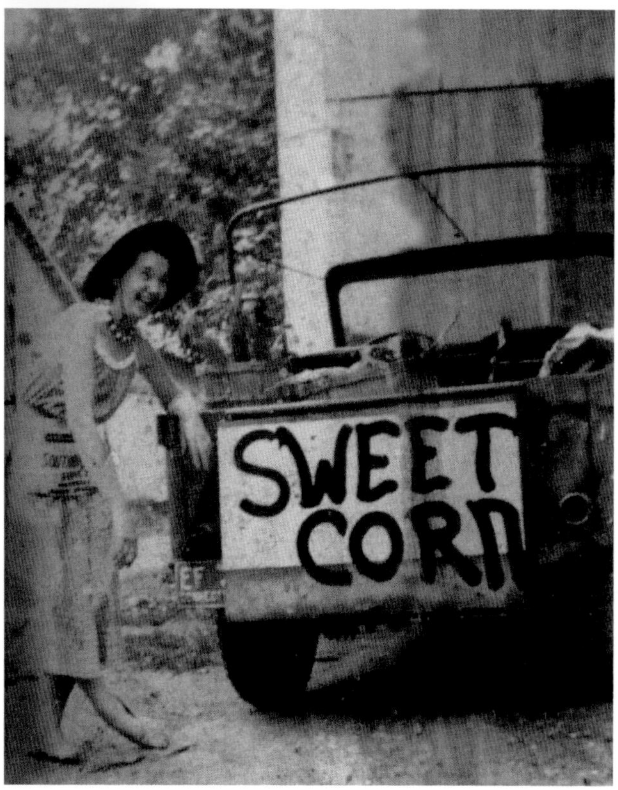

The Starchak Home in Earlier Times
William and his wife greeted Southburians for many years while working at the post office. The home on the property is the old Fleming-Stachak house, a deep bay cape built in 1800. This family farm was originally owned by the Guthrie family in the 1800s. (Courtesy Robin Starchak.)

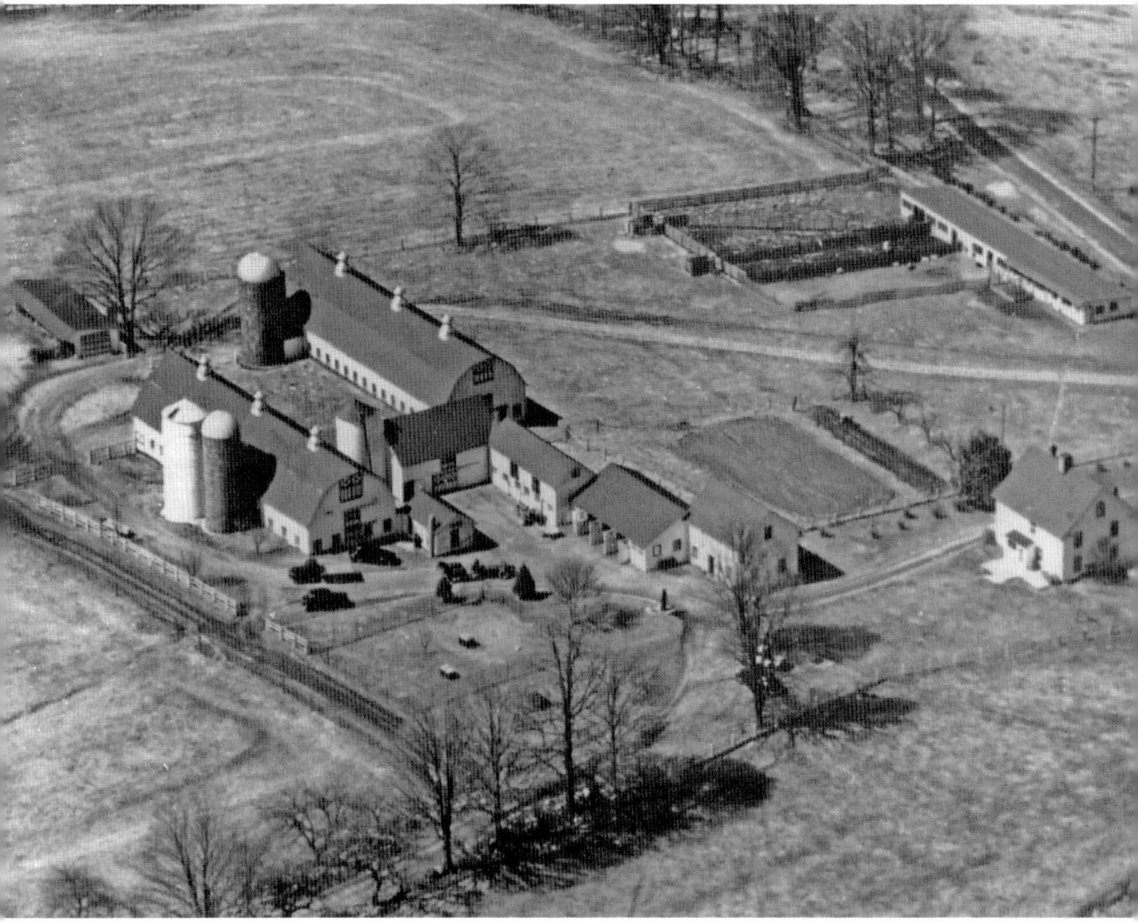

Housatonic Farm

Many future farmers started working at this farm as youngsters. Families also worked there as tenant farmers. Housatonic Farm was located on West Flat Hill Road across from the present Schielke Park Town Tree Nursery. Jeannine Robert Platt's family, the Hutter and Malumphy families, and Ed Wildman worked there. It was owned by the Graupner family, and they raised Guernsey cows. The Welch family subsequently bought the farm, followed by Uniroyal, then Ralph Crozier razed it for development. (Courtesy Jeannine Robert Platt.)

CHAPTER SIX

Community Spirit

No man is an island, entire of itself; every man is a piece of the continent, a part of the main.

—John Donne

Community spirit has thrived in Southbury since the early settlers joined together to start afresh in a new setting. They entered an environment with ample natural resources, and in true community spirit, both the resident Pootatuck Indians and the new arrivals developed a congenial and sharing relationship of those resources.

That spirit has continued throughout the years of Southbury's growth as both a town and a caring community. The settlers and their descendants have helped their neighbors in building homes, roads, bridges, churches, schools, and an enduring government. Residents have been there for their neighbors when illness and tragedies have occurred.

Individuals and organizations alike have contributed their time, their knowledge, and their commitment to the town they love and to those less fortunate to make Southbury a true example of a community working together.

From those volunteering and working together to preserve the natural and historical heritage, to the progress in providing new resources for the present and future, citizens of Southbury have demonstrated that community spirit has and will prevail.

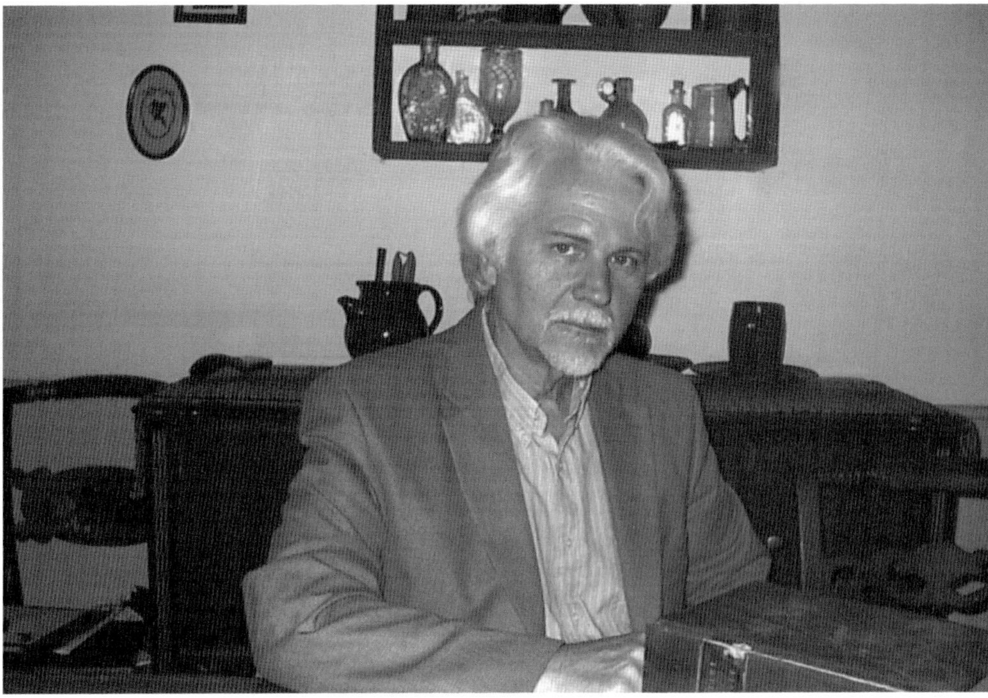

John Dwyer, Town Co-historian
John and Lynn Dwyer's children are the eighth consecutive generation to be raised in their Southford home. Deacon Adin Wheeler, Lynn's great-grandfather five times removed, built this historic home. John's interest in local history was spurred while restoring family property. John has been a member of the Southbury Historic Buildings Commission since the 1980s. (Courtesy John Dwyer.)

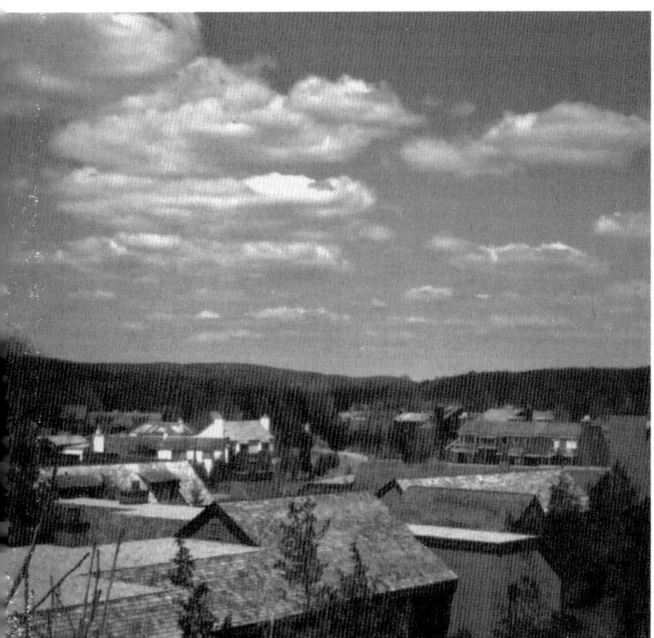

Henry Paparazzo and Heritage Village
Henry Paparazzo and his brothers created a 1,000-acre village by combining three tracts of land: two farms and the former estate of Victor Borge. This retirement village in a northern climate was considered groundbreaking since it was thought that New Englanders would want to retire in warmer climates. Heritage Village residents have contributed their talents to the community over the years, serving in town government as elected and appointed officials and volunteering in a multitude of positions in the community. Heritage Village was built in 1967 as an active community for those 55 and older. It celebrated the 45th anniversary of the Paparazzo brothers' innovative project in 2012. (Courtesy VFW Post 1607.)

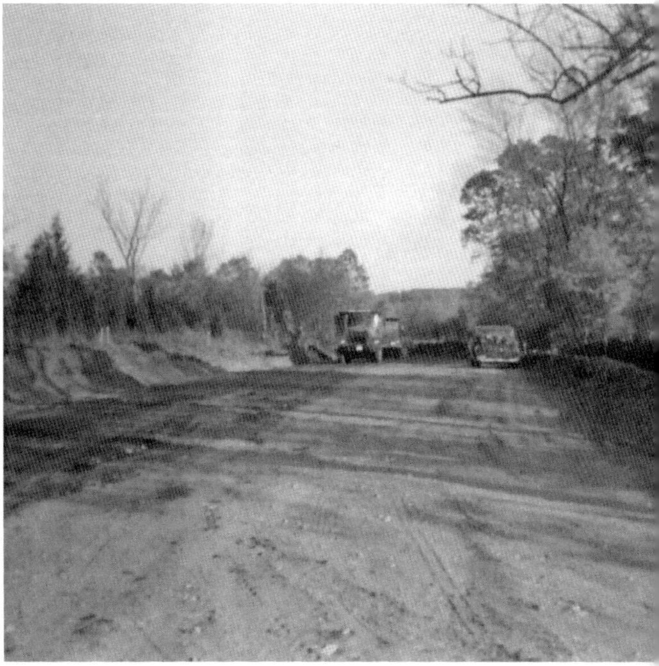

Growing the Town and Diversity
In addition to Heritage Village, which increased the town's portion of older residents, other construction was done around town. A diverse group of people with many skills and backgrounds brought needed diversity to the town. The East West Road is shown to the right as it was photographed in 1971. The Richard and Irene Hine home was moved prior to construction of Heritage Road in 1972. According to Betsey Bette, the town of Southbury bought the Hine house, moved it, then sold it back to the Hine family. Currently, Jay and Laura Hine and their children live in the family home. The complexion of the town has changed with the many different people who moved into the community. (Both, courtesy Betsey Rouse Bette.)

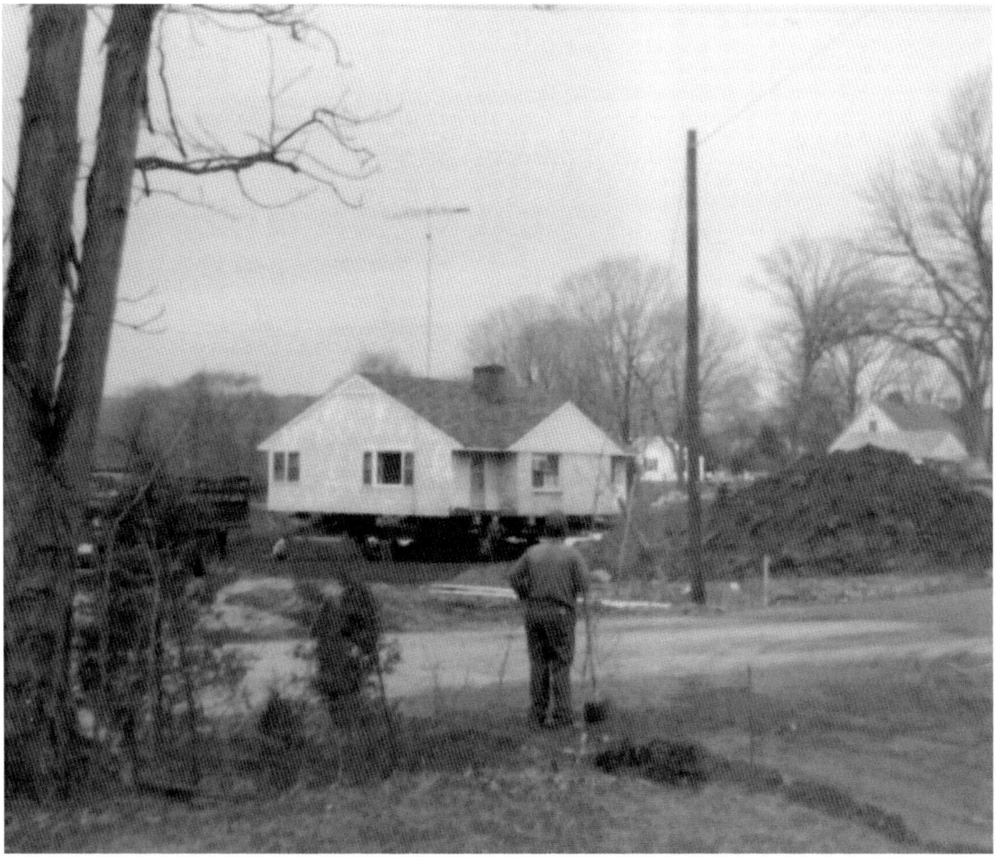

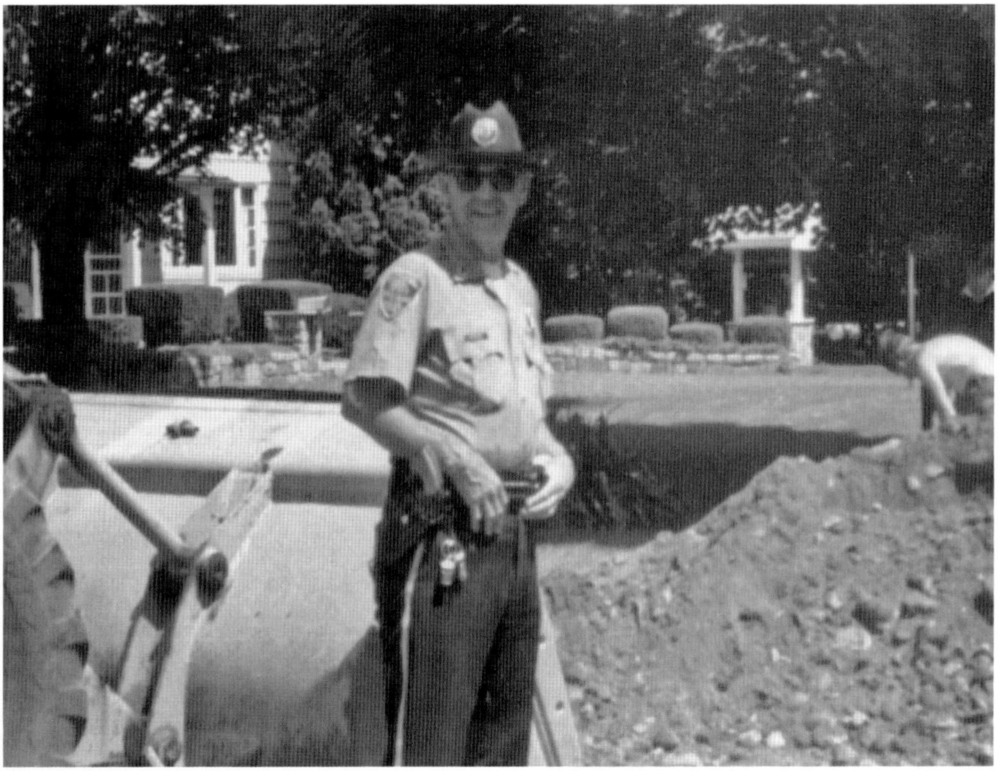

George Hitzegard

Town constable George Hitzegard directs traffic for public safety during the installation of the water line on Old Field Road in June 1985. George was a local constable for many years. He also served his community as a lifetime member of the Southbury Volunteer Fire Department. George was a professional carpenter in Southbury and a World War II veteran. He was a member of the ancient Sacred Heart Church No. 1 located in the White Oak section of Southbury and was married there. He was also a longtime member of the Knights of Columbus. (Courtesy Betsey Rouse Bette.)

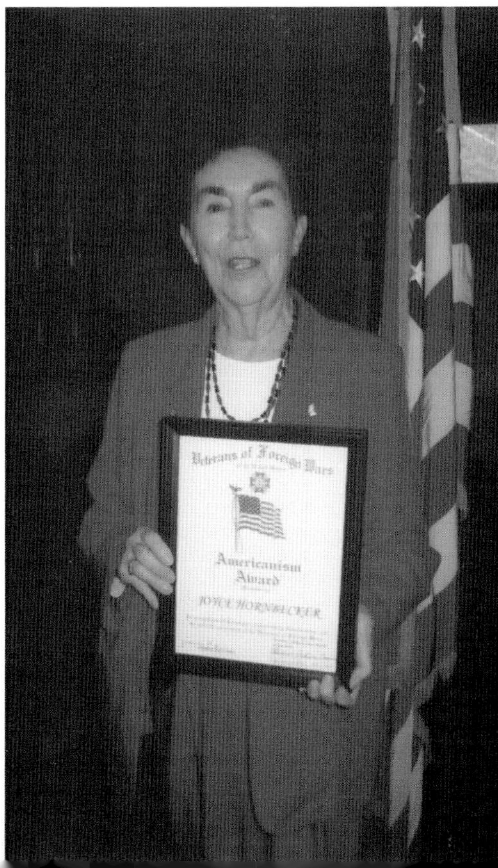

Joyce Hornbecker, Town Co-Historian

Joyce's community spirit includes leadership in the Lake Zoar Authority, Girl Scouts, Southbury Ambulance Association, Pomperaug River Watershed Coalition, and Bent of the River Audubon Center. Joyce served as Southbury's assistant town clerk and Southbury town clerk for a total of 33 years and received the 1997 Connecticut Secretary of State Award. She is pictured here receiving a citizenship award from VFW Post 1607. (Courtesy VFW Post 1607.)

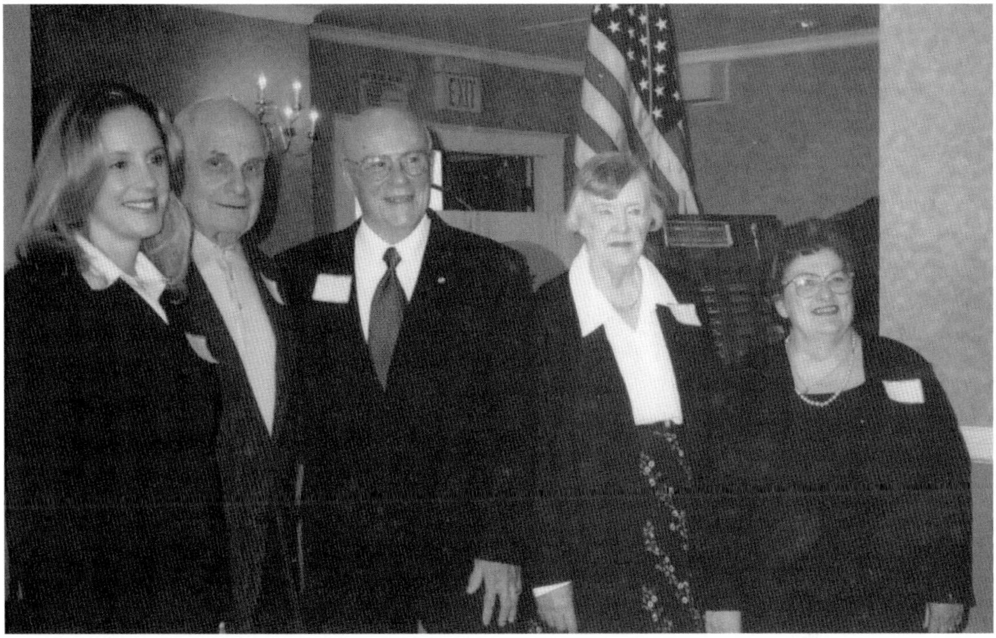

People Who Have Made a Difference, 2003
Many residents believe it is important to give back to the community, and recipients of the Southbury Historical Society Community Service Award exemplify this quality. Pictured are the 2003 recipients of the award, from left to right: Debbie Rising, Garden Club civic chair; Edmund Schade, Southbury Historic Buildings Commission and Scenic Road chair; Paul Palmer, Inland Wetlands Commission chair, Tree Committee cofounder, Rural Preservation Commission member, and selectman; Frances Voss, League of Women Voters and co-editor of the Booklet of Southbury's Boards and Commissions Committee; and Dorothy Green Manville, Southbury Historical Society president. (Author's collection.)

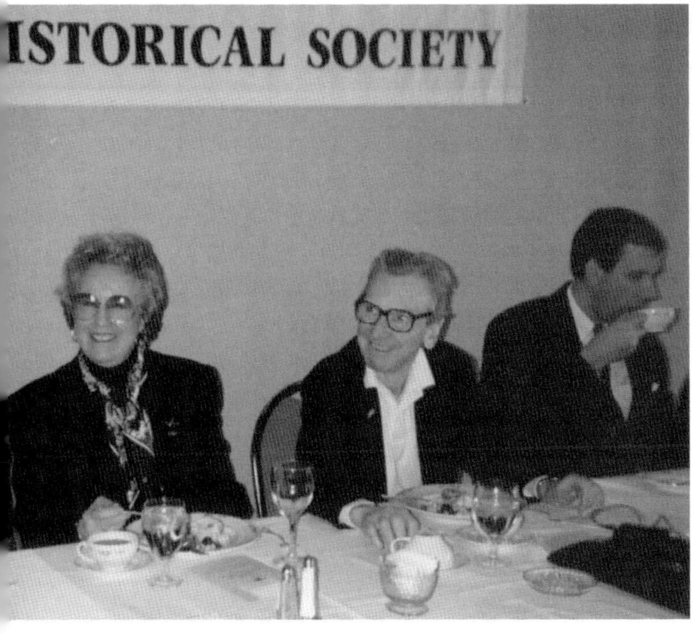

People Who Have Made a Difference, 1993
The 1993 Southbury Historical Society Community Service Award was presented to, from left to right, Catherine A. Palmer, chair of the Southbury Historic Buildings Commission, cofounder and chair of the Historical Tree Restoration Committee, and founder and director of the Bullet Hill School Days Living Museum Program; Richard C. Perry, president of the Southbury Historical Society; and attorney David A. Clough, Southbury Historical Society board member. Catherine and Richard were past recipients of the Connecticut League of Historical Societies Awards for preserving local history. (Author's collection.)

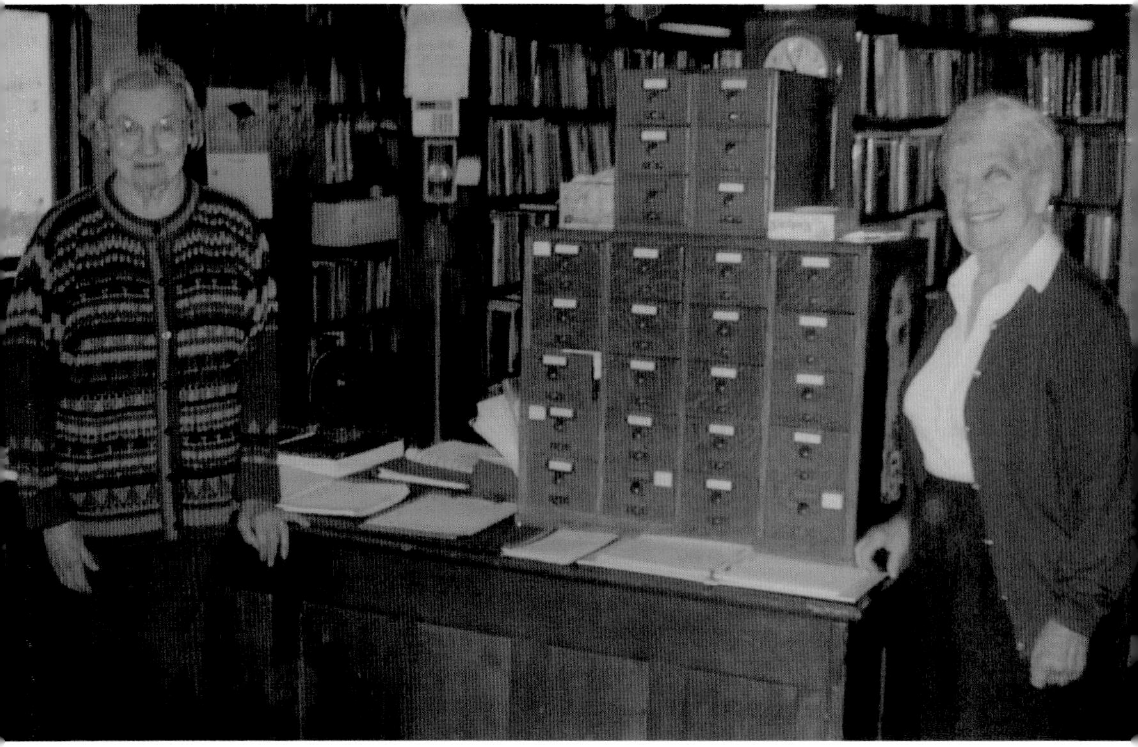

Kay Thorpe and Mary Perry, Ladies at the Library

Pictured are longtime Southbury Historical Society volunteer librarians Kay Thorpe (left) and Mary Perry. Kay had a career as a librarian long before she was a volunteer and was very gifted in book repair. She restored a large number of historic books that had been damaged and that added greatly to the collection. Mary was a historian and genealogist and started the genealogy section of the South Britain Library. The green-shingled library at the corner of Middle Road in South Britain was built in 1904. It closed in 1969 but reopened in 1972 and is maintained and preserved by the Southbury Historic Buildings Commission. The historical society preserves the books and makes them available for the public to borrow. (Courtesy Catherine Palmer.)

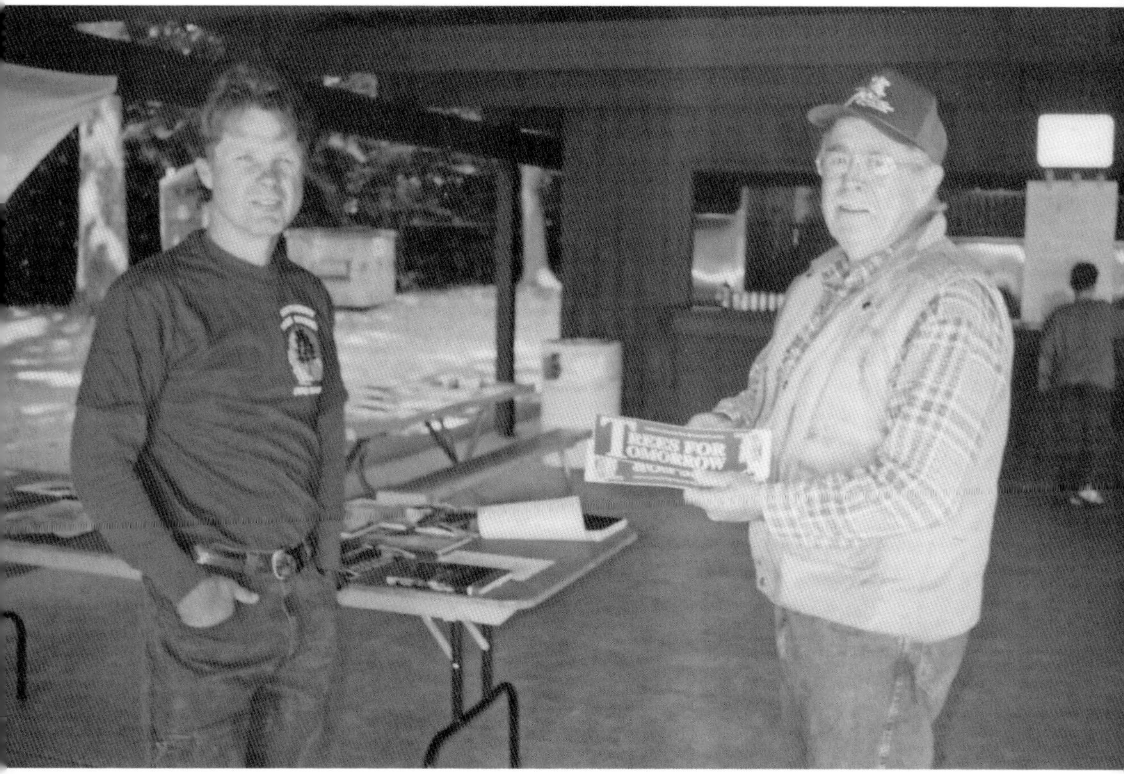

Patrick Kearns and Sidney Smith

Patrick Kearns is a certified arborist who just recently won an urban forestry award for his many contributions. Sidney Smith is a local farmer who has served on many committees and boards. Environmental Awareness Day, planned by Southbury Historical Tree Restoration Committee members, offered appropriate tree maintenance and public safety presentations. Patrick Kearns (left) is pictured sharing a discussion about tree pests and diseases with Sidney Smith. (Courtesy Catherine Palmer.)

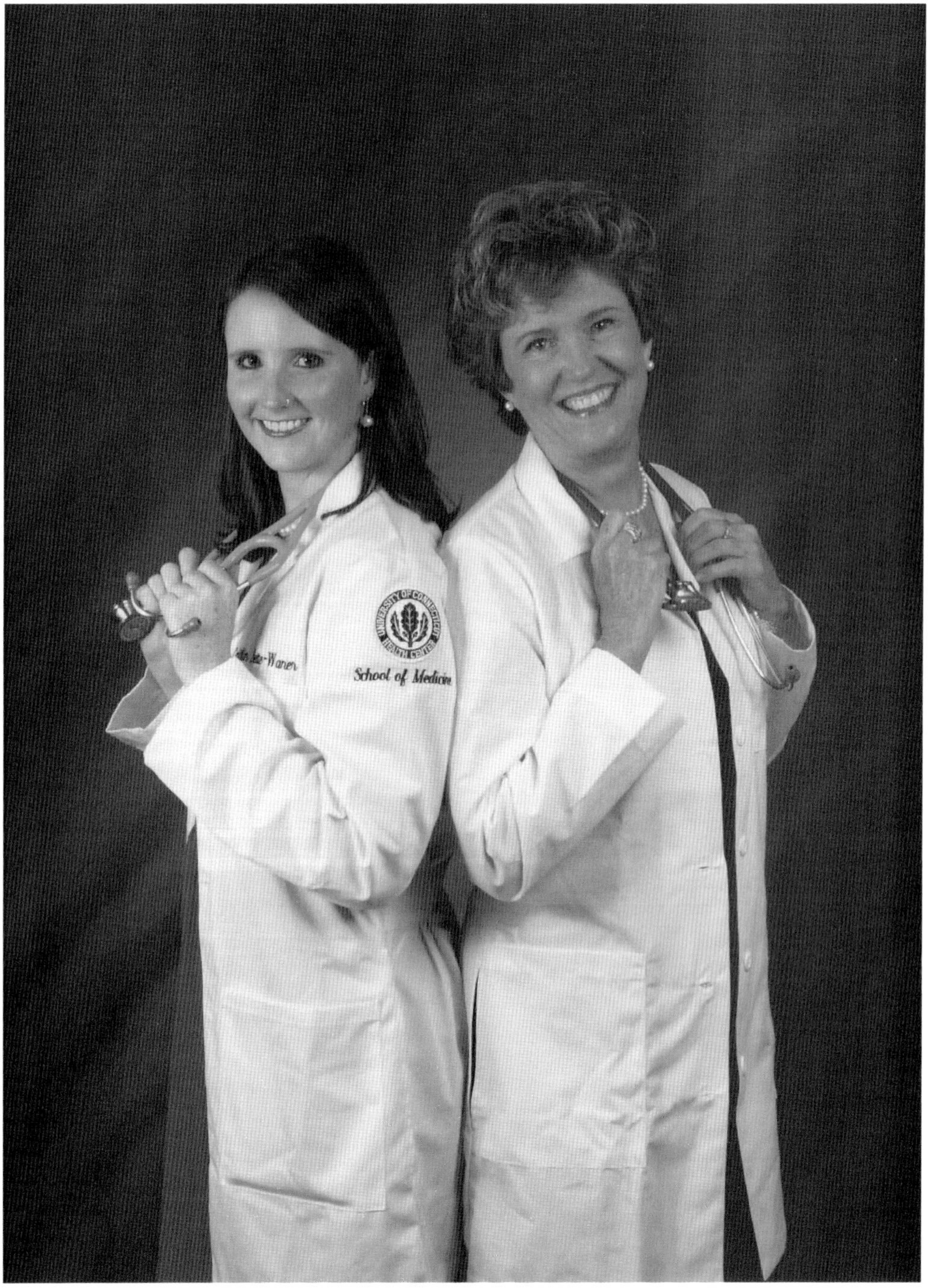

Dr. Marianne Bette and Caitlin Bette-Waner
After Dr. Marianne Bette (right) completed her nursing degree, she decided to continue on and become a doctor. Her daughter Caitlin wishes to follow in her mother's footsteps and also become a doctor of medicine and then an associate at her mother's medical practice at Playhouse Corner. Caitlin is currently attending the University of Connecticut Medical School. (Courtesy Caitlin Bette-Waner.)

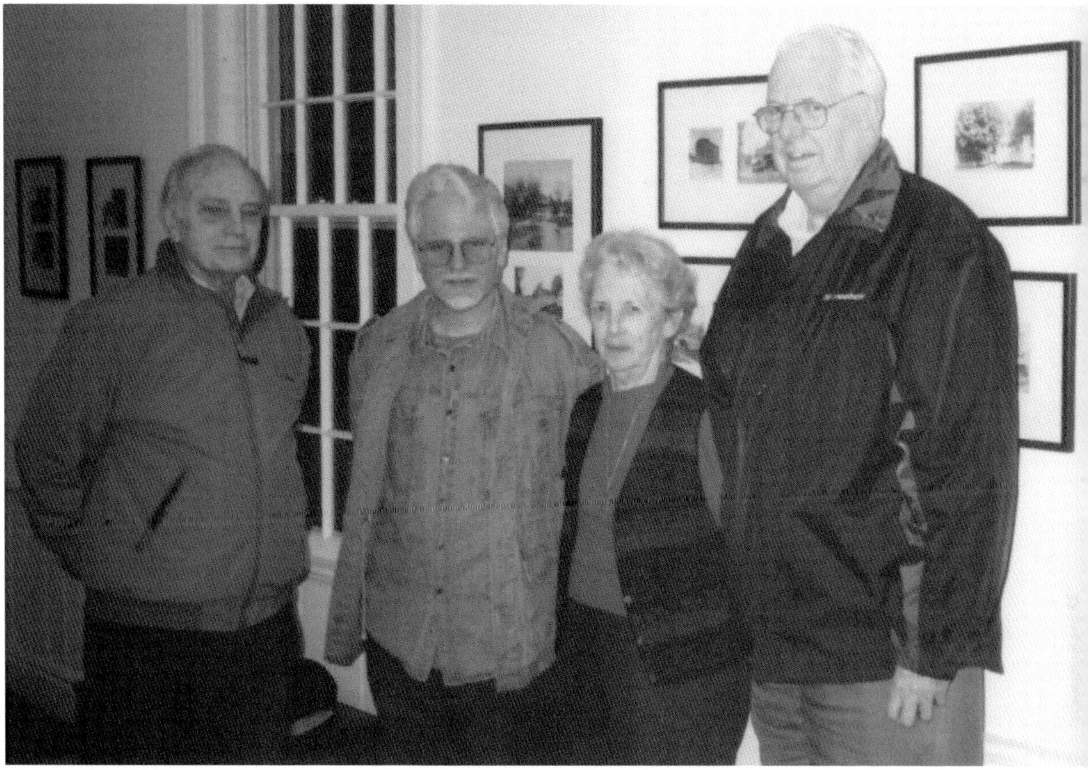

Shirley McIlroy

A tribute to Shirley McIlroy was held on the occasion of her 1994 retirement from the Historic Buildings Commission. Shirley was a founder and chair of three historical organizations: the Historic Buildings Commission, Friends of Bullet Hill School, and the Southbury Historical Society. From left to right are members Robert Klein, John Dwyer, Shirley McIlroy, and James Mattoon. (Courtesy Catherine Palmer.)

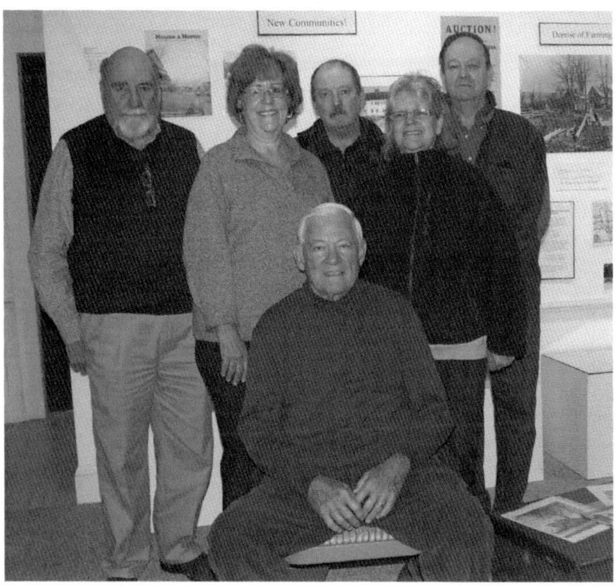

Southbury Historical Society

The Southbury Historical Society, headquartered at the Old Town Hall Museum, was organized in 1983 and collects and displays artifacts. It also operates historical programs in the Old Town Hall Museum, South Britain Library, and Bullet Hill School, which is preserved and maintained by the Southbury Historic Buildings Commission. Pictured from left to right are treasurer Bill Wilhelms, president Joyce James, George Smith (seated), Mark Manville, Leigh Graham, and Don Meyer. (Courtesy Bill Wilhelms.)

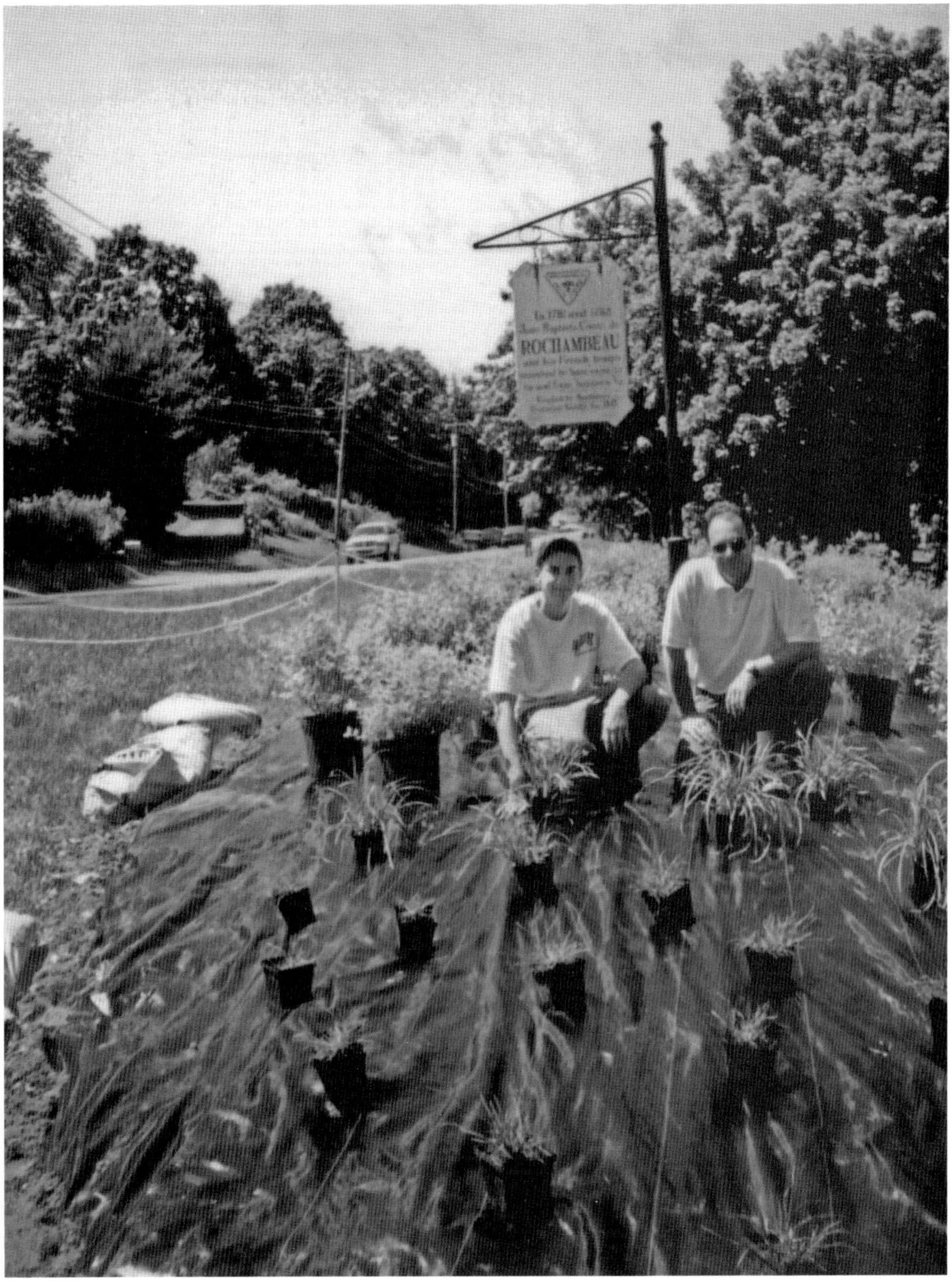

Adopt-a-Spot Garden at Historic Kingsland

Tom Mariano earned his Eagle Scout badge for planning, planting, and maintaining an Adopt-A-Spot garden at the historic Kingsland site with mentorship from project advisor Tom Gaipa, a horticulturist and treasurer of the Southbury Historical Tree Restoration Committee. This site is one of 11 gardens maintained by local businesses. Currently Wesley Rouse Jr., owner of Pine Meadow Gardens, maintains the site. (Courtesy Catherine Palmer.)

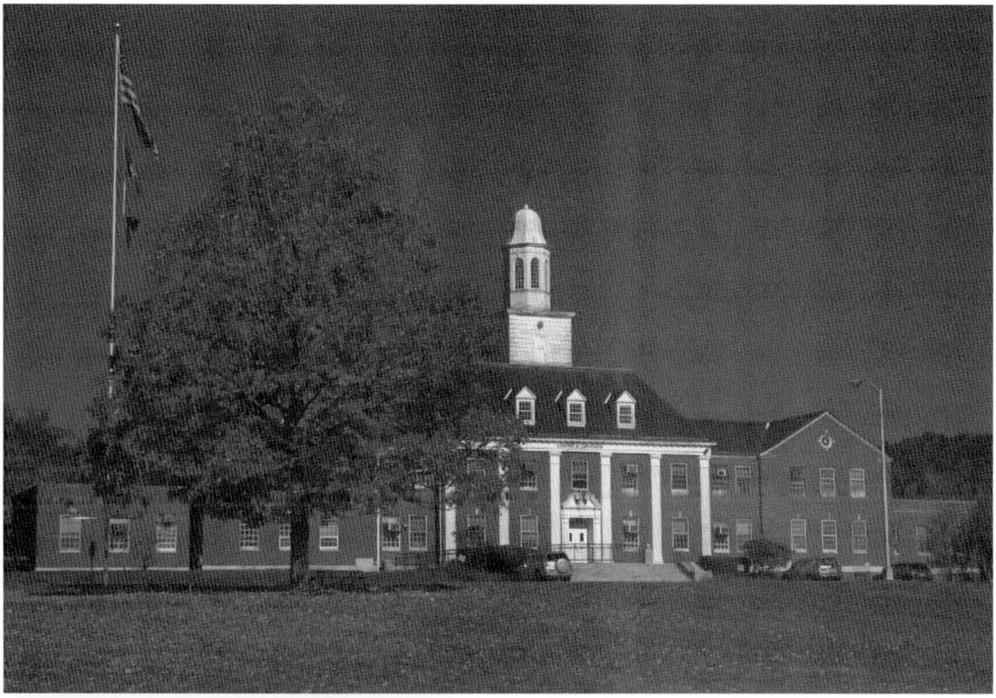

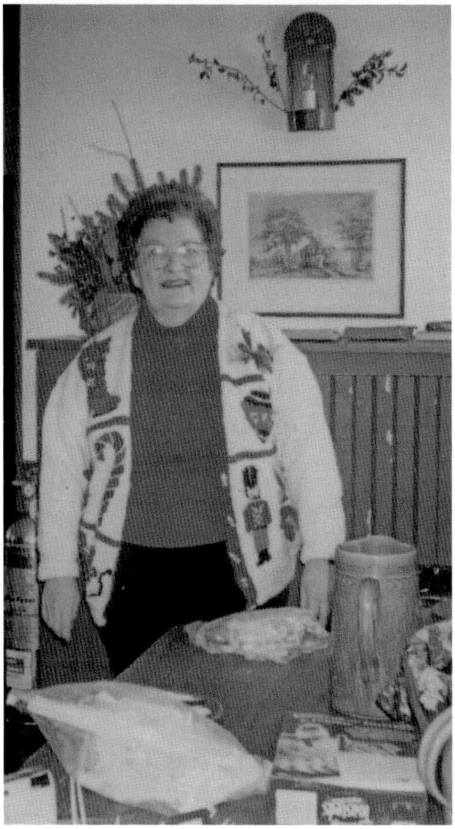

Eugene Harvey and the Southbury Training School
The Southbury Training School is directed by Eugene Harvey. Many locals have worked at the school built in the 1930s as a home for the mentally challenged. In 1986, admissions were closed and the Connecticut Department of Mental Retardation was directed to attempt to place residents elsewhere. The school still operates for remaining clients in care of the staff. (Courtesy Andrew Skok.)

Dorothy Green Manville
Dorothy worked as director of nurses for many years at the Southbury Training School. She was a Southbury native and was dedicated to the town and served as Southbury Historical Society president. As an avid collector of Wallace Nutting photographs, she had a vast knowledge about him and his collection of work that was frequently shown at museums. She is pictured at a holiday open house for Southbury Historical Society. (Courtesy Catherine Palmer.)

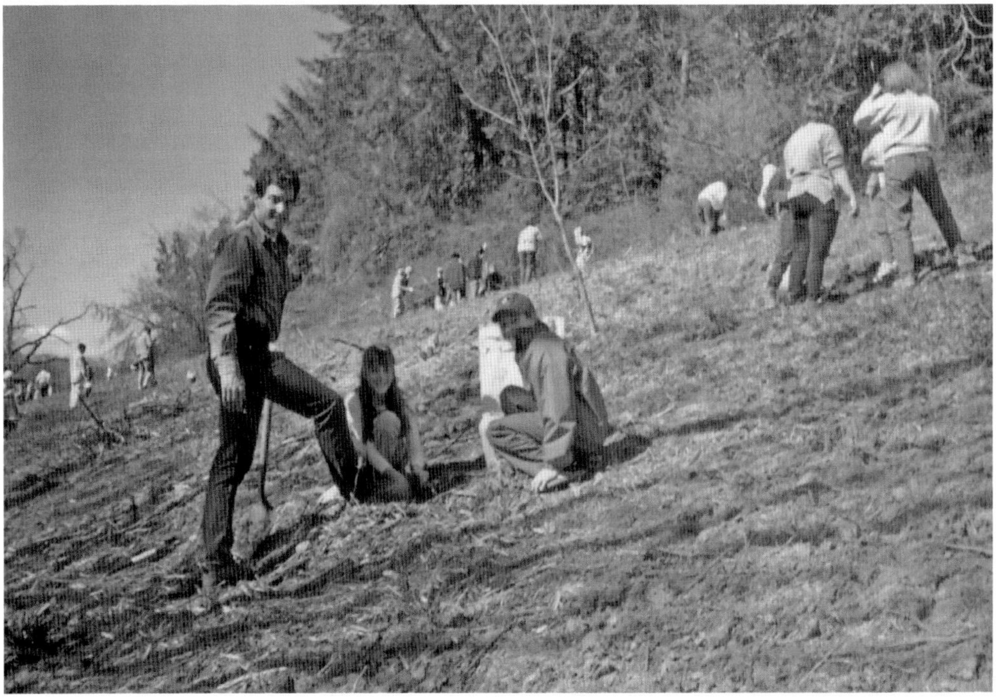

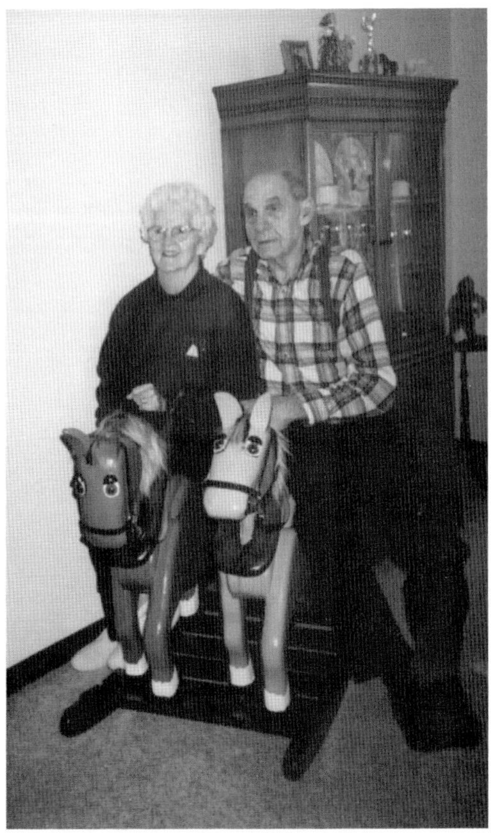

Platt Park Volunteers

Paul and Catherine Palmer were appointed by the Board of Selectmen and were founders of the Historical Tree Restoration Committee. Platt Park was the scene for volunteers and tree committee members to plant 500 spruce and fir trees to enhance the hillside entrance trail into the park. A large number of trees flourish today and add to the natural beauty. Pictured are volunteers Mark and Hannah Burzynski and Sharon Cieply. (Courtesy Catherine Palmer.)

Theresa and Frank Bette

Frank Bette, a talented wood craftsman, created hobby horses. He and his brother Joseph Bette Sr. owned the A.J. Bette Heating and Plumbing Company in South Britain. They were well-known copper and brass artisans and highly respected for their expertise in that field, as well as in heating and plumbing. Theresa and Frank Bette are pictured rocking away on their hobby horses. (Courtesy Betsey Rouse Bette.)

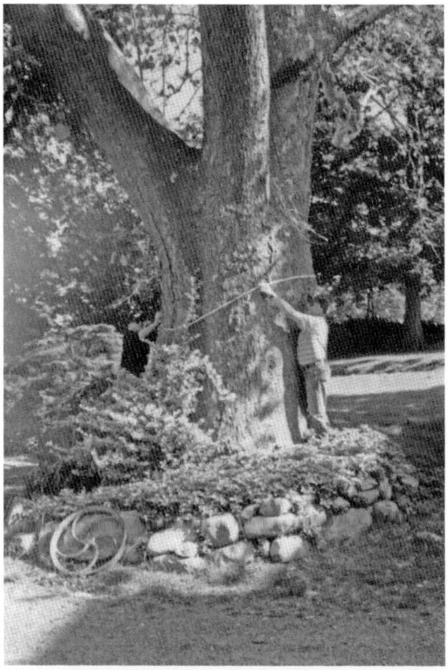

William McAllister and Paul Palmer
William McAllister was an active member of the local horse community. He ran the Rolling M Horse Ranch and was a member of the Connecticut Farm Bureau and the Southbury Fire Department. Paul Palmer has been a true community member. He was the chairman of the Inland Wetlands Commission for more than 25 years, on the Board of Selectmen, and a member of the Rural Preservation Commission. The ancient sycamore tree on the McAllister farm on Main Street North was standing in front of the McAllister barn when church bells rang throughout the land at the time of President Lincoln's funeral. It is listed as a Southbury Notable Tree and also on the Connecticut Notable Tree Register. Pictured are William McAllister (left) and Paul Palmer. (Courtesy Catherine Palmer.)

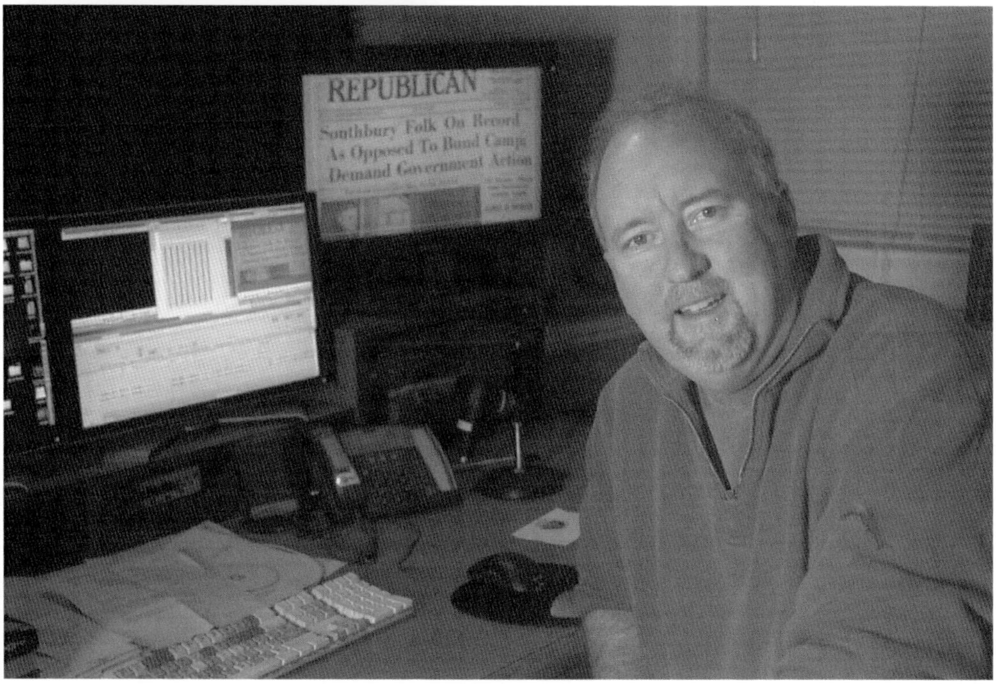

Filmmaker Scott Sniffen
Scott has been in the film and television business and communications industry for more than 25 years. He created a German American Bund award winning documentary. Interviewees included Lillian Hicock Wentworth and her 1938 college thesis about the German American Bund. Scott's goal in producing the film was to paint a picture of 1937 Southbury townspeople and their sheer patriotism in ridding the community of the Nazi youth camp sponsored by the German American Bund. (Courtesy Scott Sniffen.)

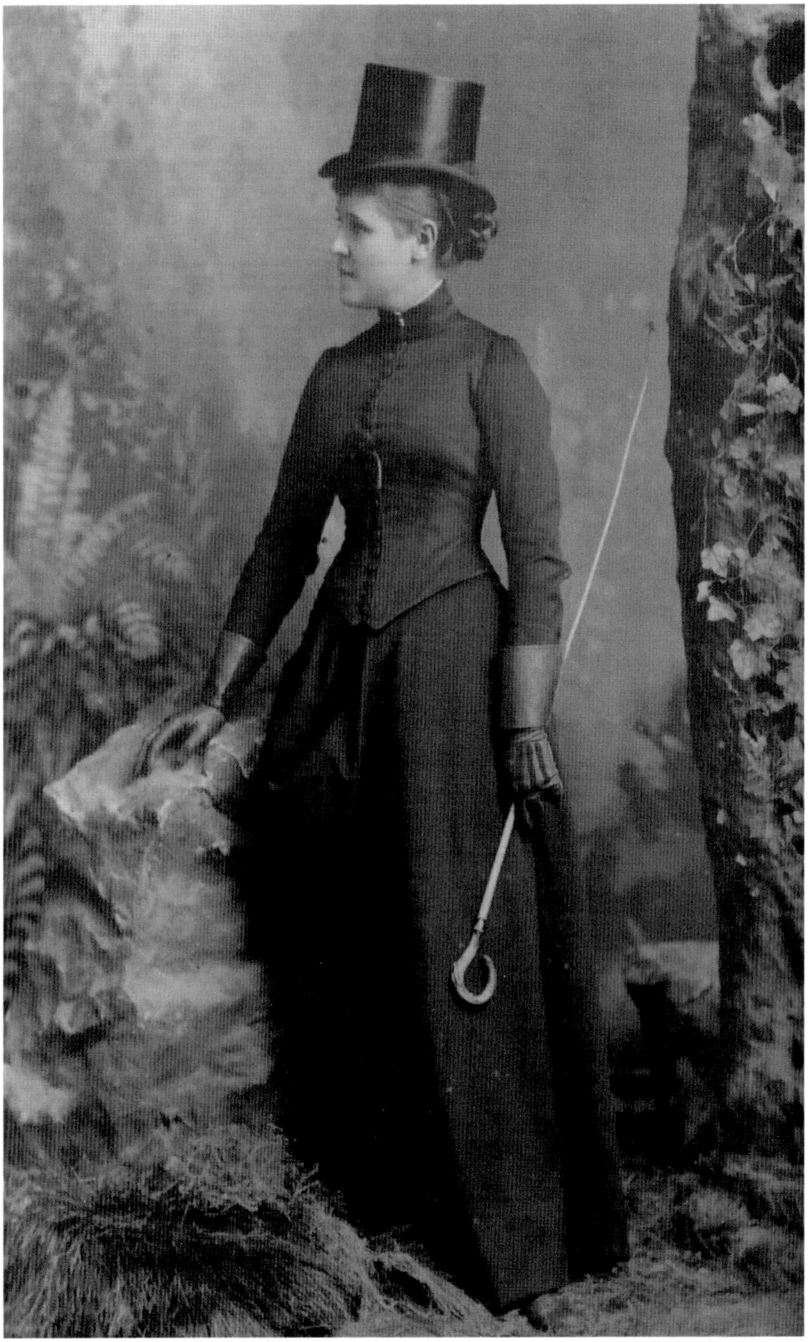

Jennie Hinman and the Bund
In 1937, the German American Bund tried to establish a Nazi training camp in Southbury. Hinman spoke out forcefully and eloquently to reject the Bund. Many German Americans sent letters to townspeople warning of the atrocities in Germany and the truth about Nazi intentions. Southburians took a stand and appointed a zoning commission that prevented the Nazi presence in Southbury. Other communities in the nation were not able to stop similar camps. (Courtesy Ann Hinman Lilley.)

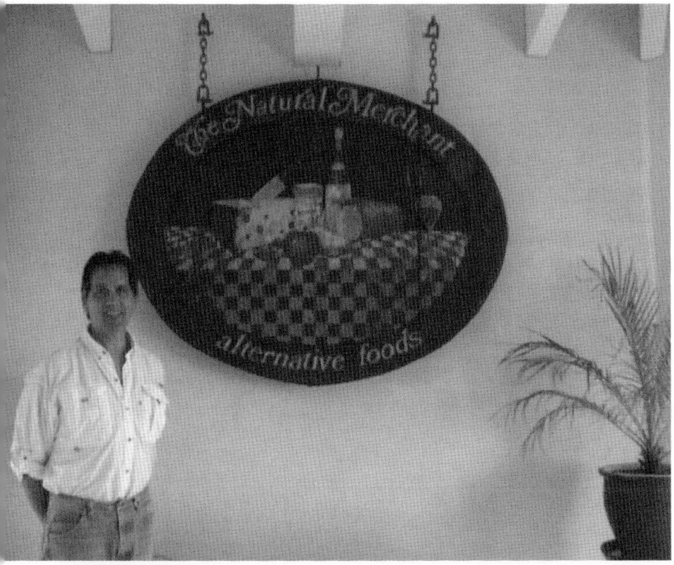

Stephen LeFebvre and New Morning Natural Foods
Stephen LeFebvre founded Woodbury's New Morning Natural Foods in 1969 and Southbury's Natural Merchant in 1977. The stores were based on sustainable living and community principles and became hubs for those interested in organic foods, healthy living, and spiritual wellness. A café and wellness center offered nutrition, meditation, and other healing arts. Stephen and Sherry LeFebvre sold the store in 2004 and embarked on a new journey to New Zealand. (Courtesy Steve LeFebvre.)

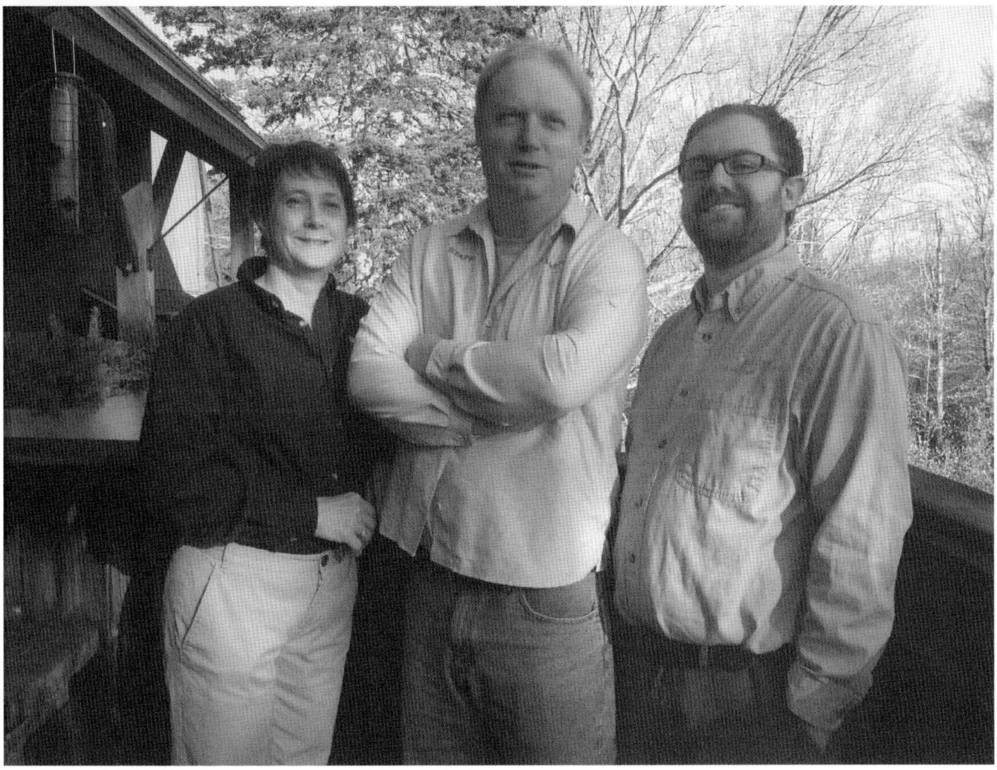

Howard and Althea Clark
The Audubon Center at Bent of the River was a gift to the National Audubon Society from Howard and Althea Clark. Their intention was for it to be a sanctuary for birds and other wildlife and an environmental education center for Southbury residents. The property has more than 100 acres of shrubs and grasslands and 15 miles of hiking trails. Audubon staff members, from left to right, are Director Leslie Kane, James Drennan, and Ken Elkins. (Courtesy of Leslie Kane.)

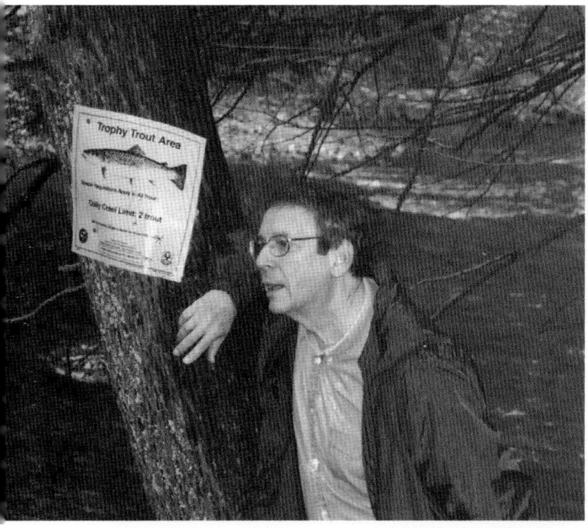

Dr. Marc Taylor
Dr. Marc Taylor, a physician and the 1999 founder and longtime director of the Pomperaug River Watershed Coalition, is shown measuring the water quality of the Pomperaug River. Marc became an advocate for compromised rivers and helped restore, maintain, and preserve this essential resource. His mission extended from studying the quality and quantity of the Pomperaug River to the national movement to protect all waterways. Marc once said, "The problem is that too many people think good only comes from above, rather than understanding that we can create good." And so he decided—after already having done a world of good as a doctor—to become a committed environmentalist. (Courtesy Carol Haskins.)

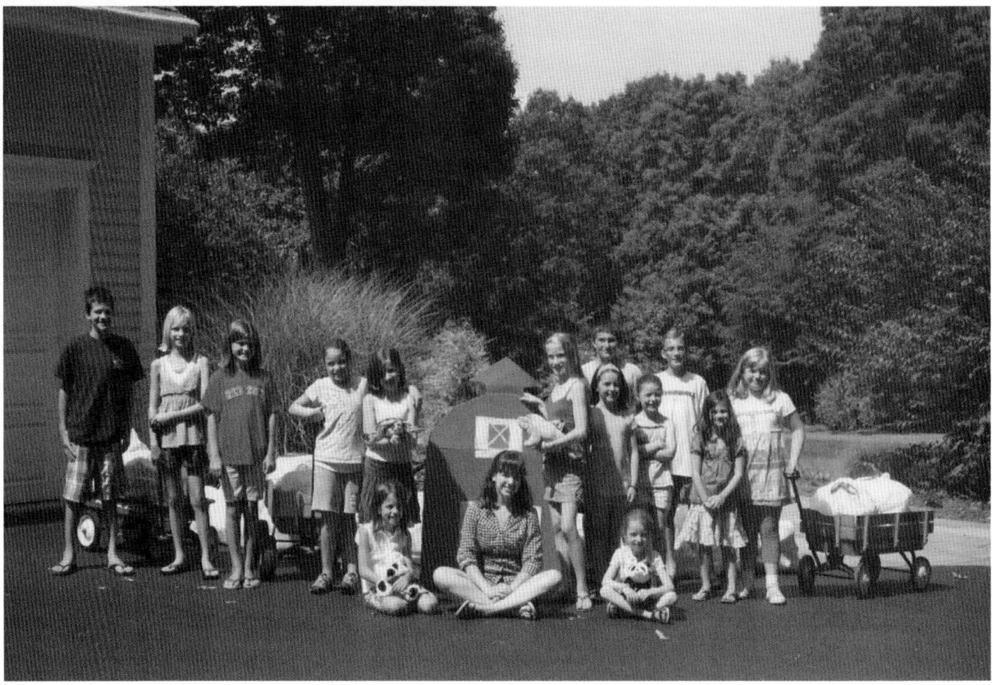

Anna Bower
Anna Bower felt that, as a young person, it was a necessity to conserve natural resources and preserve the environment. The Youth Wildlife and Recycling Foundation (YWARF) was founded in 2012 by Anna Bower Richardson and a group of children. They are making a difference in the community by recycling and utilizing funds to aid endangered animals and the local Audubon society. Their efforts include educating the public about the necessity to recycle and preserve the environment. The Southbury Board of Selectmen has designated the foundation members as youth ambassadors for their sustained efforts to promote recycling. YWARF members, from left to right, are (first row) Grace Bower Richardson, Kate Kaminski, and Carolyn Bonomo; (second row) Hayden Frisbee, Julie Bilchek, Jacqueline Pugliese, Katie Roberts, Julia Bower Richardson, founder Anna Bower Richardson, Joe Alvord, Katherine Bonomo, Lauren Bonomo, Christopher Bilchek, Eleanor Frisbee, and Emily Matson. (Courtesy Kathy Bower Richardson.)

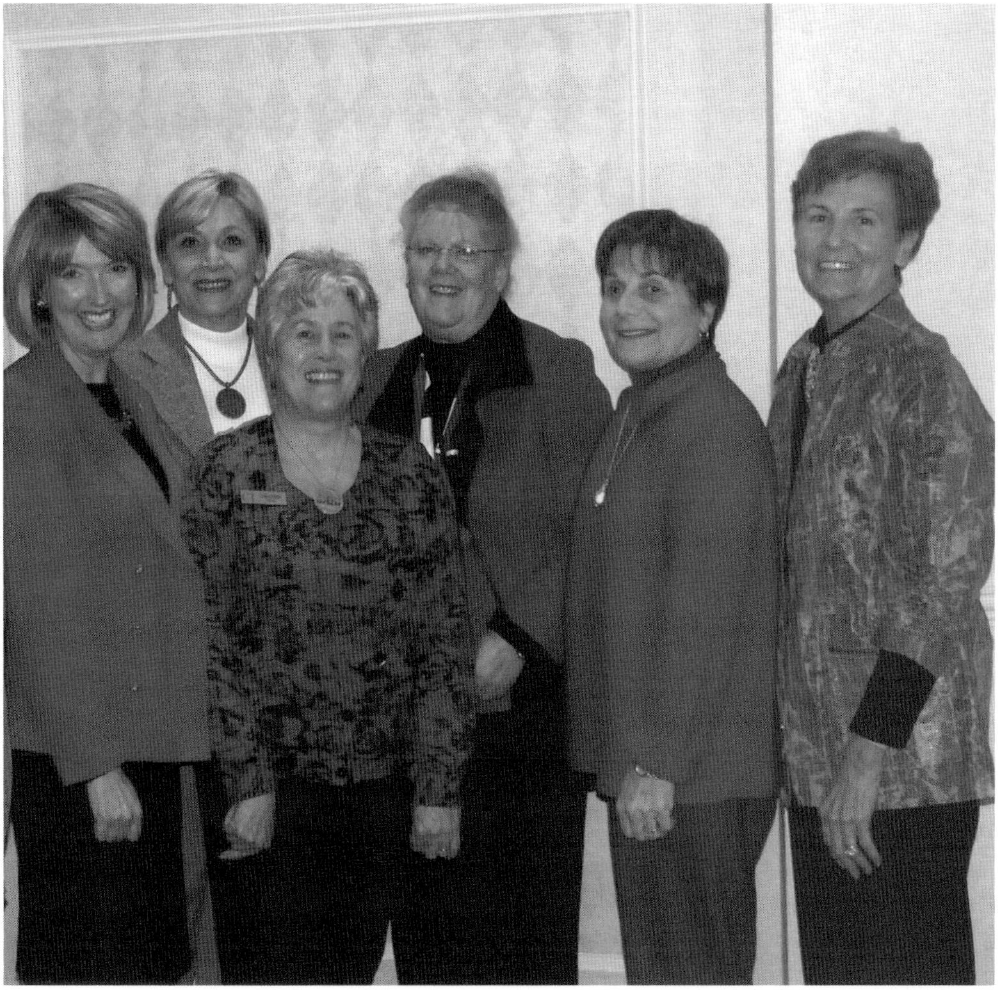

Southbury Garden Club

Southbury is a prettier place thanks to the Southbury Garden Club. The Southbury Garden Club is both an educational and civic organization. Members maintain the herb garden at the Bent of the River Audubon Center, four gardens at two community parks, and the colonial garden at the historic Bullet Hill School. Special events include holiday decorations for all of the public buildings, floral and horticultural exhibits at the library, and maintenance of the flower barrels around town buildings. There is an annual children's sunflower contest, and civic awards are presented to local businesses that contribute aesthetic plantings that enrich Southbury's environment. Fundraisers include flower shows and a spring plant sale. These funds are used for the mentioned activities as well as for gift baskets for shut-ins. It was founded in 1959. Southbury Garden Club's goals are to promote knowledge and activities in horticulture, conserve natural resources, learn and teach artistic use of plant materials, and participate in civic programs for children and adults. Currently, this includes a landscaping project at Ballantine Park, gardens for the food bank, holiday baskets for Safe Haven and nursing homes, and holiday wreaths for Southbury's buildings. Garden club officers pictured here from left to right are president Lynne Ramsden-Calabrese; first vice president Peggy Fainelli; Donna Nowak, president of the Federated Garden Clubs of Connecticut; second vice president Claire McRae; treasurer Stephanie Fischer; and corresponding secretary Elena Maclean. (Courtesy Maureen Nichols.)

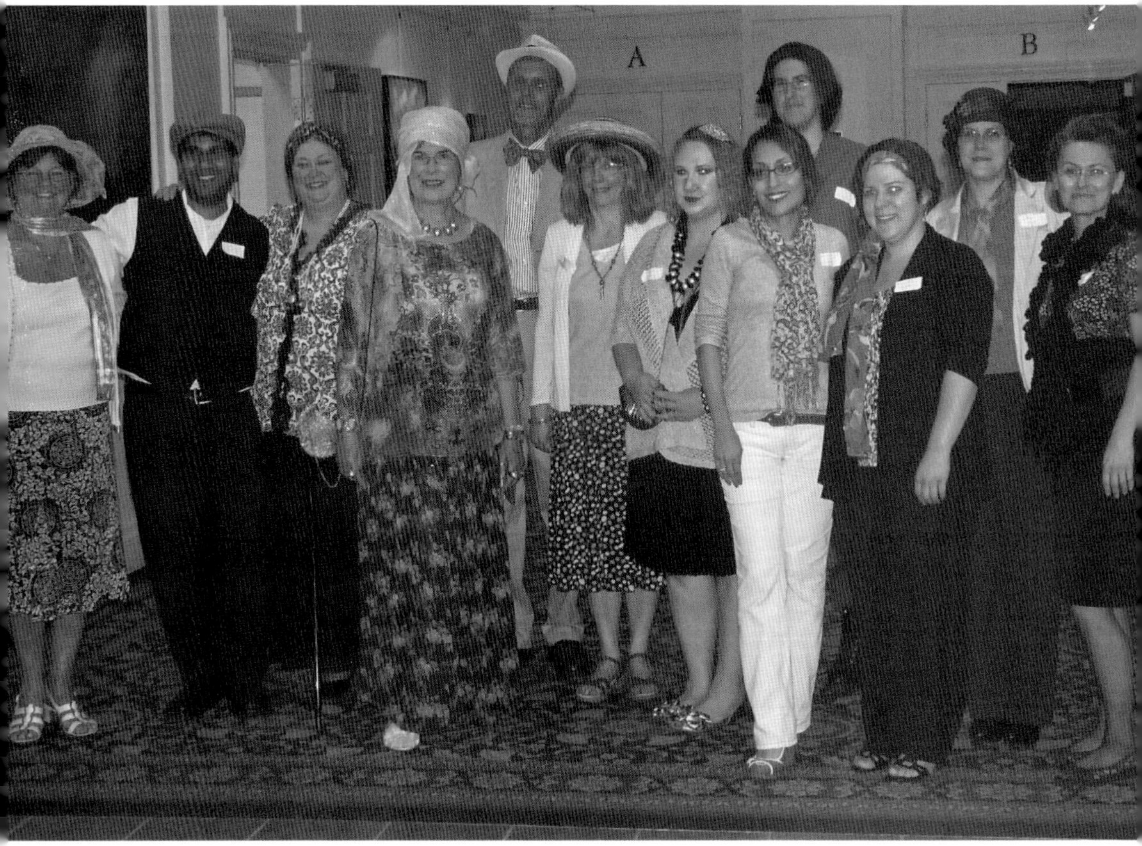

Shirley Thorson

Shirley Thorson has worked in the Southbury Public Library system since completing her master's degree in library science. The Southbury library outgrew its building on Main Street South while Shirley worked there, and a new library was built on Old Field Road six years ago. Shirley has been the head librarian for many years. Her leadership and expertise have provided enormous growth for the library as a valuable resource for lifelong education. She has worked closely with the Southbury Library Board of Directors and the volunteer group Friends of the Library to enhance and enrich all of the many services the library offers to the public. Under her directorship, close to 100,000 current and classic books, large-print and audio books, CDs, DVDs, e-book readers, magazines, and newspapers are available with summer reading programs for children, book clubs, free wireless access, an e-mail newsletter advising readers of new items, a website, and a variety of diverse programs for all age groups and interests. Shirley, her colleagues, and the library board have implemented a strategic plan to continue upgrading the library resources for the community.

In 2010, late resident Lu Burke, a book lover and former copyeditor for *Life* magazine and *The New Yorker*, left more than $1 million to the library. These funds will be directed—by head librarian Shirley Thorson, her staff, and the Southbury Library Board—toward enhancing and enriching the Southbury Public Library collections. The library team makes it possible for residents to have access to information and entertainment in many forms. This picture shows a 1920s skit acted by library staff that was part of "Murder in the Library: A Mystery Event" by teen librarian Heather Aronson. Pictured from left to right are Caroline Bernard, Joseph Capella, assistant head librarian and children's librarian Joan Stokes, Irene Sudol, Tom Stokes, head librarian Shirley Thorson, teen and reference librarian Heather Szaley Aronson, reference librarian Katherine Mostacero, Amy Schupack, reference librarian Kari Burgess, Dawn Bennett, and Kathleen McGowan. (Courtesy Shirley Thorson.)

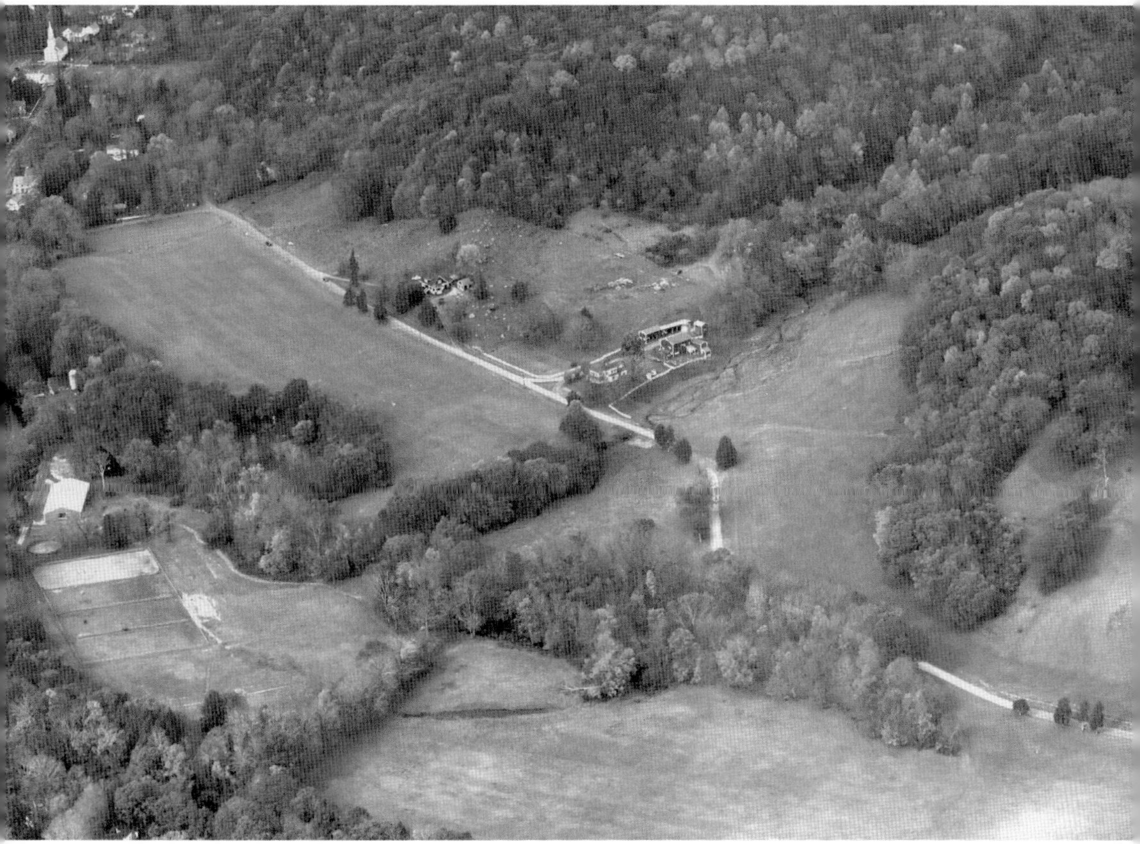

Southbury Land Trust

Tom Crider has been the president of the Southbury Land Trust since 2008. The Southbury Land Trust was founded in 1978 as a private nonprofit conservation organization dedicated to the preservation of Southbury's natural resources for the enjoyment and benefit of all residents. Tom has been instrumental in getting support from more than 600 member households and businesses. Supporters take pride in the fact that helping protect Southbury's natural beauty gives a lasting gift to future generations. Much of Southbury's agricultural heritage and historic landscapes remain intact within the more than 1,000 acres that Southbury Land Trust has preserved. This photograph shows the Platt farm, one of the preserved land trust areas. (Courtesy Don Antilla.)

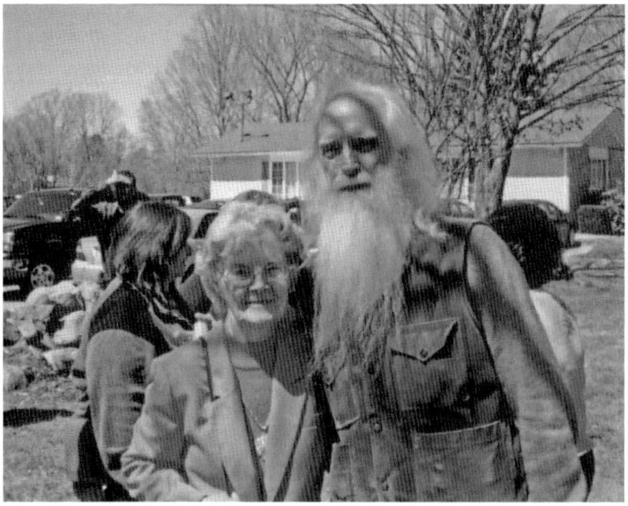

Renee Blum and Mac McEvoy
A dedication ceremony honoring the late First Selectman Alfio Candido brought community members to the site. Renee Blum (left) was a 20-year Southbury Town Hall office manager and Commission for the Elderly member, and Thomas O. "Mac" McEvoy is a 15-year Bullet Hill School Days board member and Friendly Visitor Organization member. Mac models for Dan Troani's Civil War portraits as Gen. Robert E. Lee. (Courtesy Catherine Palmer.)

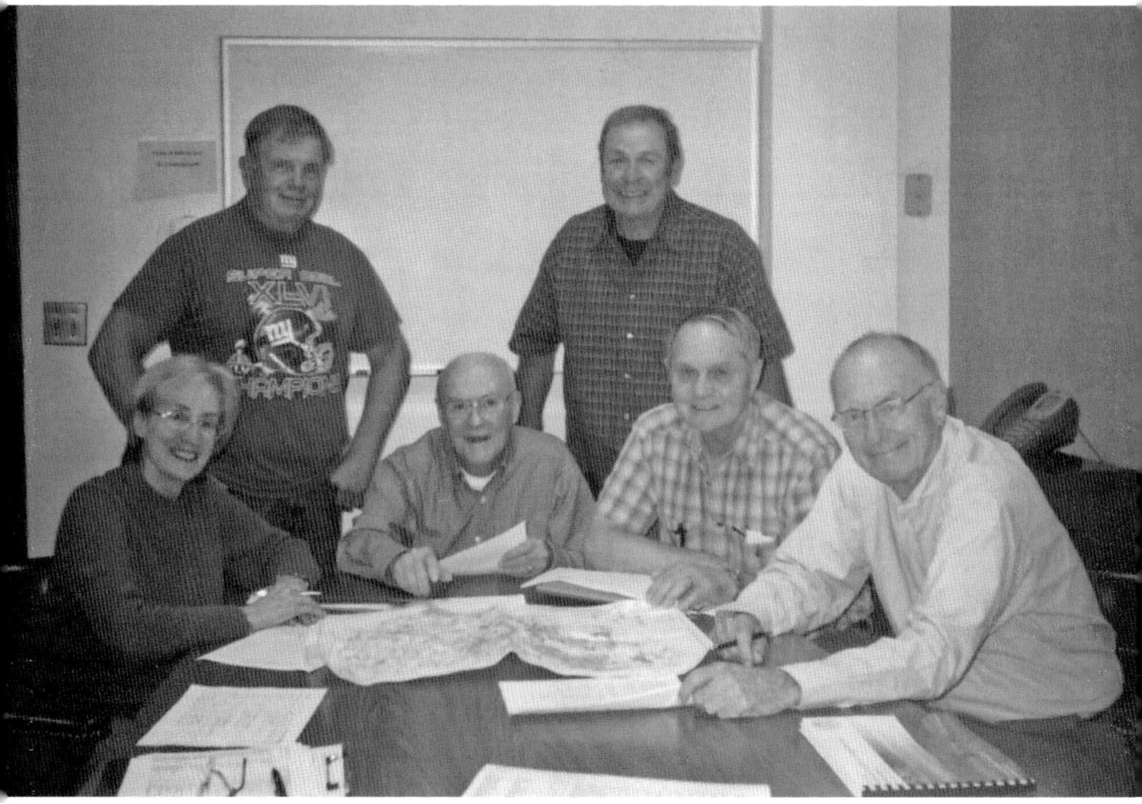

Rural Preservation Advisory Commission
The Rural Preservation Advisory Commission (RPAC) has developed an inventory of large or undeveloped parcels of land and evaluated them. The commission advises boards regarding open space issues and the town's rural character. From left to right are (seated) Lucinda Hunt-Stowell, Paul A. Palmer, Edward Wildman Jr., and chairman Edward W. Gore; (standing) vice chairman Gary Gollenberg and Edward A. Platt. Not pictured are Glenn Ackerman, Gary Giroux, Selectman Chad Landmon, and Jeffrey Manville. (Courtesy of Catherine Palmer.)

CHAPTER SEVEN

Popular Vote

Always vote for principle, though you may vote alone, and you may cherish the sweetest reflection that your vote is never lost.

—John Quincy Adams

In Southbury, it has rarely been difficult to enlist citizens willing to serve in political office, both in an elected capacity and in appointed positions. Boards, commissions, and committees are comprised of diverse groups of residents who share common interests and possess the expertise and willingness to use them for the greater good of the town.

Since Shadrack Osborne and the early colonists planned and implemented the form of government necessary to provide and enact rules and laws for the new community, it has been a necessity to enforce them for the safety of citizens.

As each generation took the place of its ancestors, many family descendants carried on the tradition of serving in local government. A review of the names of those serving the town over the past centuries shows members of the Stiles, Curtis, Hinman, Wheeler, Mitchell, Platt, Williams, Bennett, Green, Davis, Wildman, Cooper, and Hine families.

Since the adoption of the town meeting form of government, Southbury has been represented by both the Republican and Democrat parties. The majority representation on the town's boards has been determined by the choice of the voters for their representatives on the Board of Selectmen and other elected boards and commissions. Appointed members are representative of both parties and are appointed by their respective party. Although philosophies may differ in each party, bipartisan cooperation is necessary for the smooth operation of the town government's business.

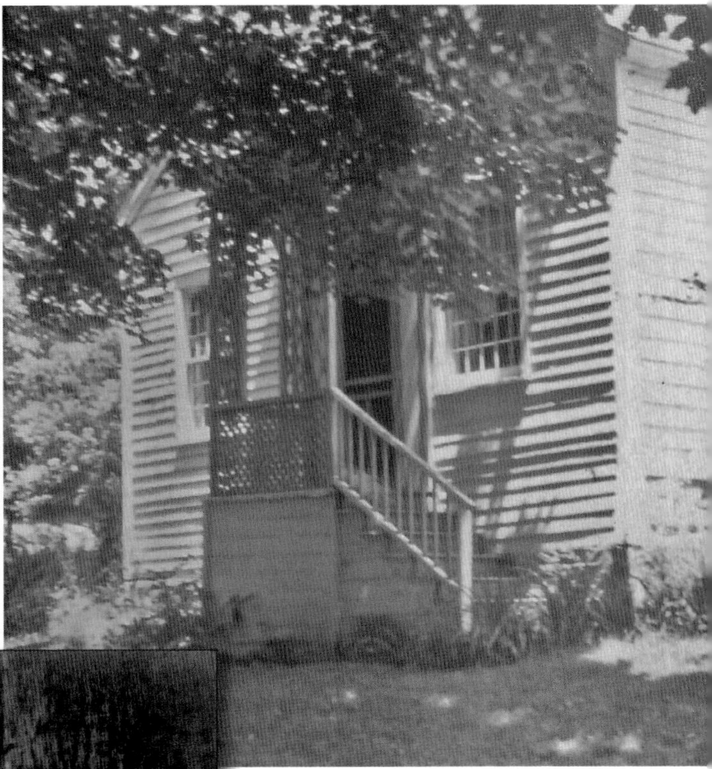

Shadrack Osborne
Shadrack was the first selectman of the town. He served from 1787 to 1788. He operated a store on a site near the Church of the Epiphany. In 1811, he paid the highest property tax in town. (Author's collection.)

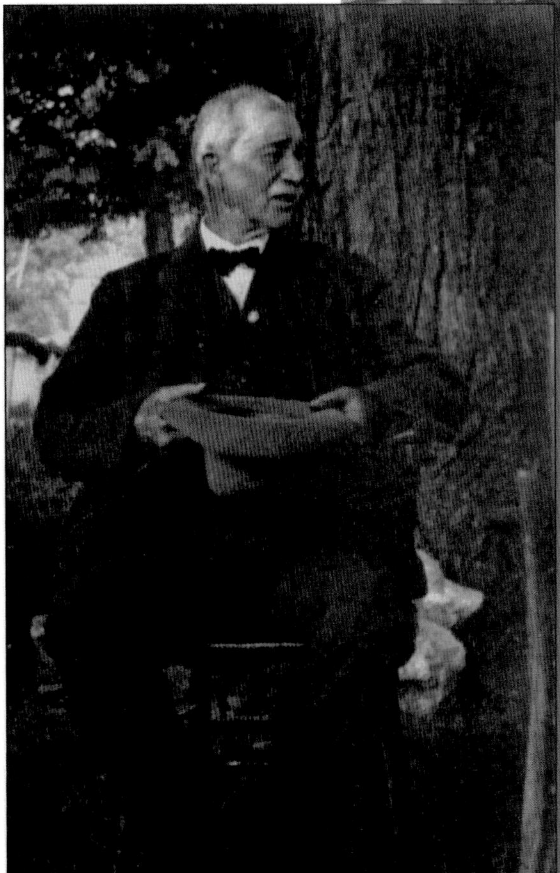

T.F. Wheeler
T.F. was a prominent Democrat and represented the town in the House of Representatives. On alternate years, he served as first selectman for 16 terms from 1885 to 1905 and as a member of the Board of Selectmen for 17 terms from 1887 to 1921. As deputy sheriff, he arrested a horse thief and confidence stealer and suggested that he be tarred and feathered. (Courtesy John Dwyer.)

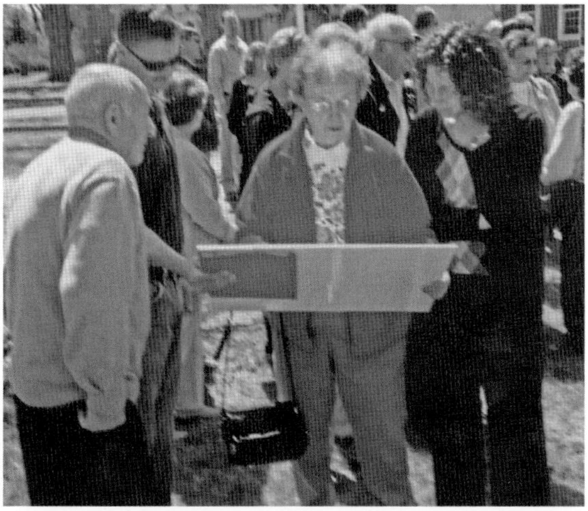

Alfie Candido Memorial Dedication
A memorial tree and plaque were dedicated in memory of First Selectman Alfio Candido at Bullet Hill School. Alfie was a veteran of the US Army and served in Korea. He and his brother ran a family business. Family and friends gathered for the Arbor Day ceremony in his honor. From left to right are Daniel Candido, Alfie's brother; Dan Messenger; Althea McGahie, Alfie's Bullet Hill School classmate; and Maura Kenney Stanko, Alfie's friend and a member of the Bullet Hill School Days board. (Courtesy of Catherine Palmer.)

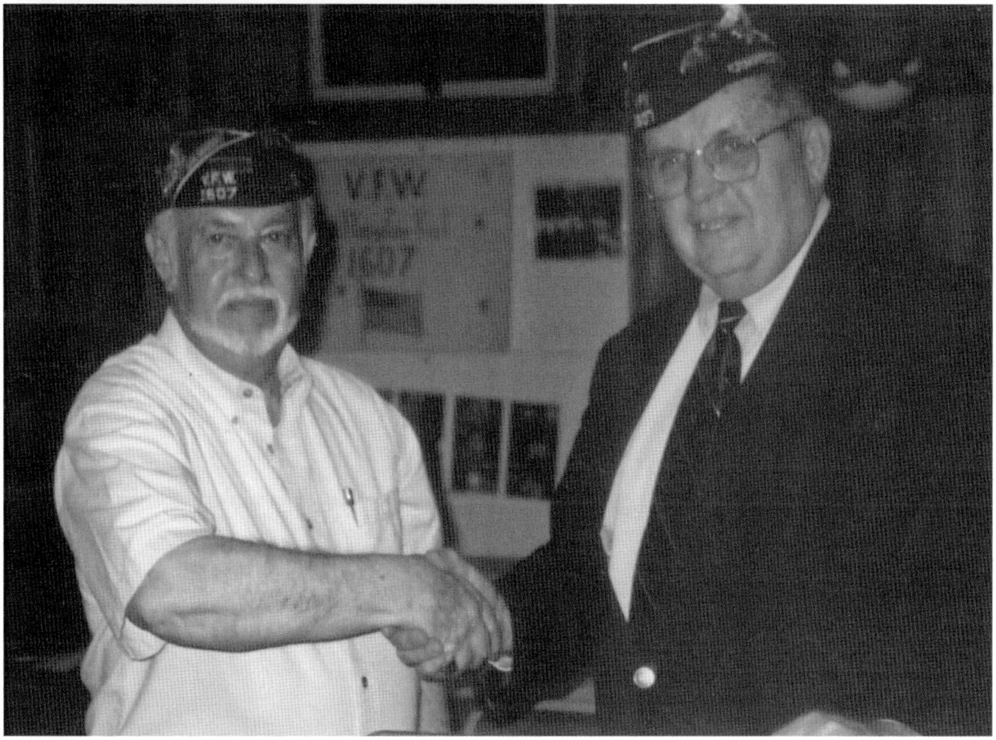

Former Selectmen and VFW Members
Pictured are former first selectmen and VFW members Samuel Green III (left) and Harmon Andrews. Samuel was selectman in 1968 and 1969. Harmon was selectman in 1983 and 1984. Southbury Veterans of Foreign Wars George Newton Post 1607 is comprised of veterans who encourage community service and a development of public interest in American history and traditions. Post members work closely with local schools to encourage both of these goals for students. Programs are presented on Memorial Day, students march in the Memorial Day parade, and veterans are honored during Flag Day ceremonies. The VFW also has annual fundraisers for the "Thank a Soldier" program that benefits veterans. Members include those who have served in Vietnam, World War II, the Gulf War, and Korea in all branches of the service. (Courtesy VFW Post 1607.)

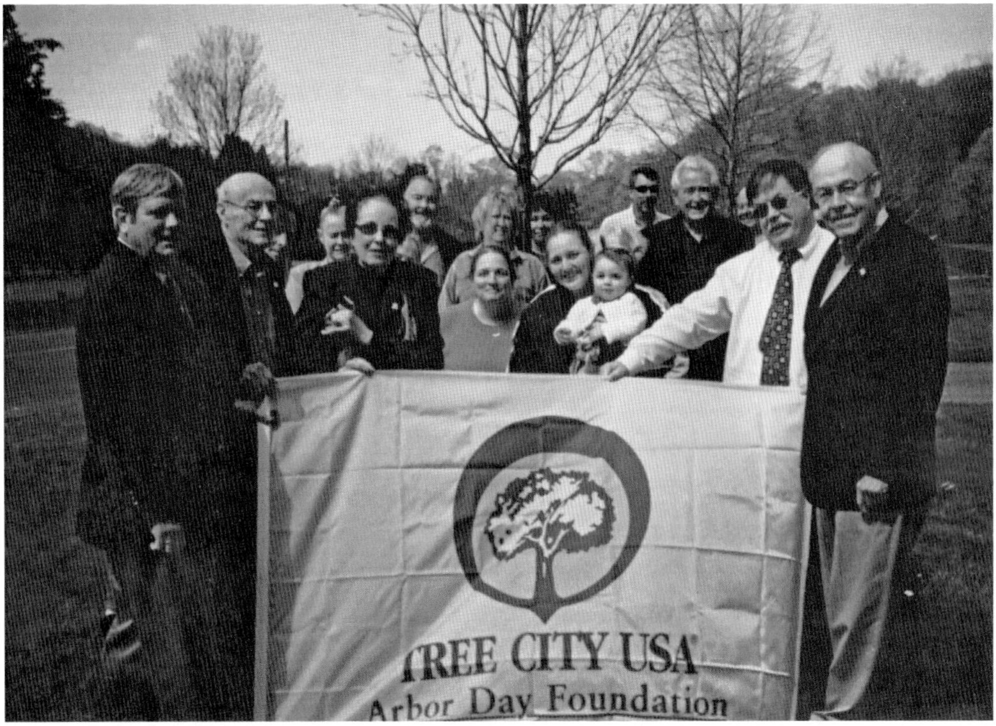

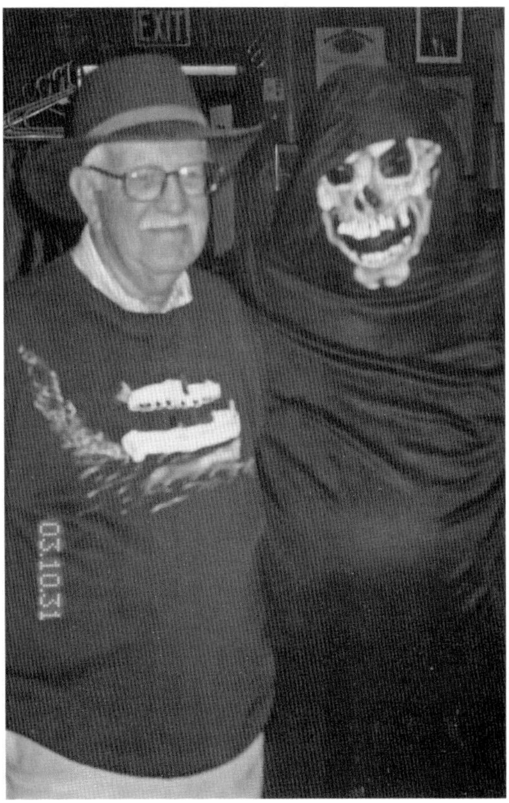

Three Selectmen Receive Tree City USA Award

Three selectmen who participated in an Arbor Day memorial are pictured here with members of the Cronin and Cody families and other families honored: First Selectman William Davis (far left), tree committee vice chair and past selectman Paul Palmer (second from left), tree committee chair Catherine Palmer (third from left), public works director Tom Crowe (second from right), and Selectman John Turk (far right). To qualify as a Tree City USA community, a town or city must meet four standards established by the Arbor Day Foundation and the National Association of State Foresters: a tree board, a tree care ordinance, a community forestry program with an annual budget of at least $2 per capita, and an Arbor Day observance and proclamation. (Courtesy Catherine Palmer.)

Joe Jameson

Joe Jameson served on the Southbury Board of Selectmen in 1972 and 1973. He has been an active 50-year VFW member. (Courtesy VFW Post 1607.)

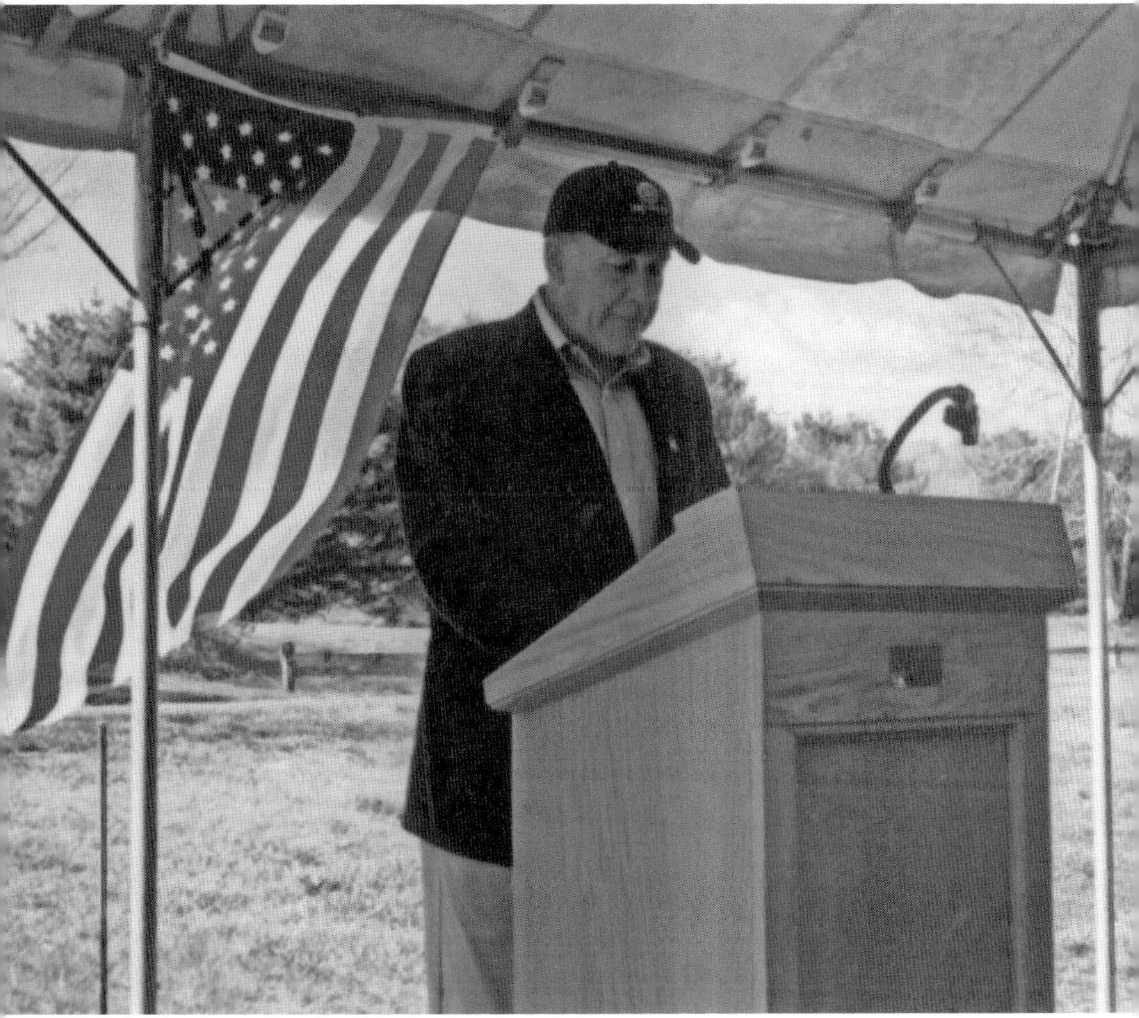

First Selectman Ed Edelson
Ed and his wife, Christine, have owned the Old Field Cornucopia Bed and Breakfast since 2004. Their home was built between 1818 and 1822. The interior was pictured in several Wallace Nutting photographs. The couple met more than 40 years ago when they taught in a private school in Connecticut. Prior to moving to Southbury, they lived in Bermuda. Ed has served on several boards and commissions and has been Southbury's first selectman since November 2011. (Courtesy Catherine Palmer.)

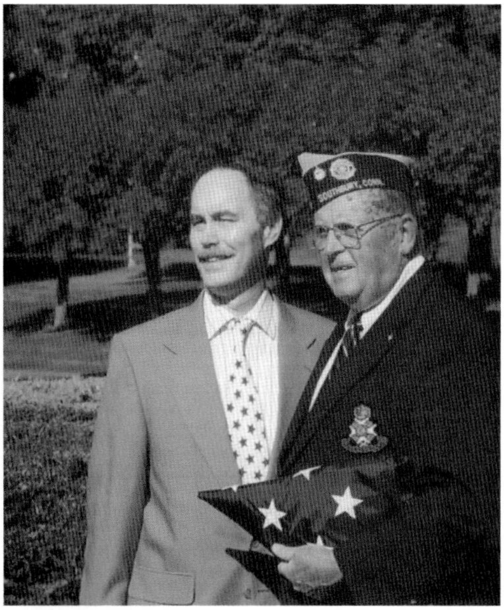

First Selectman and Connecticut State Representative

Arthur O'Neill (left), Connecticut state representative for House District 69, and former First Selectman Harmon Andrews celebrate Memorial Day. Representative O'Neill has a long record of service to the 69th district. He was first elected to the state House of Representatives in 1988. He was honored by the hospice community with the Excellence in Achievement for Public Service Award. He is a House ranking member on the General Assembly's Judiciary Committee and an assistant house Republican leader. Andrews was a commissioner of the Veterans of Foreign Wars. (Courtesy VFW Post 1607.)

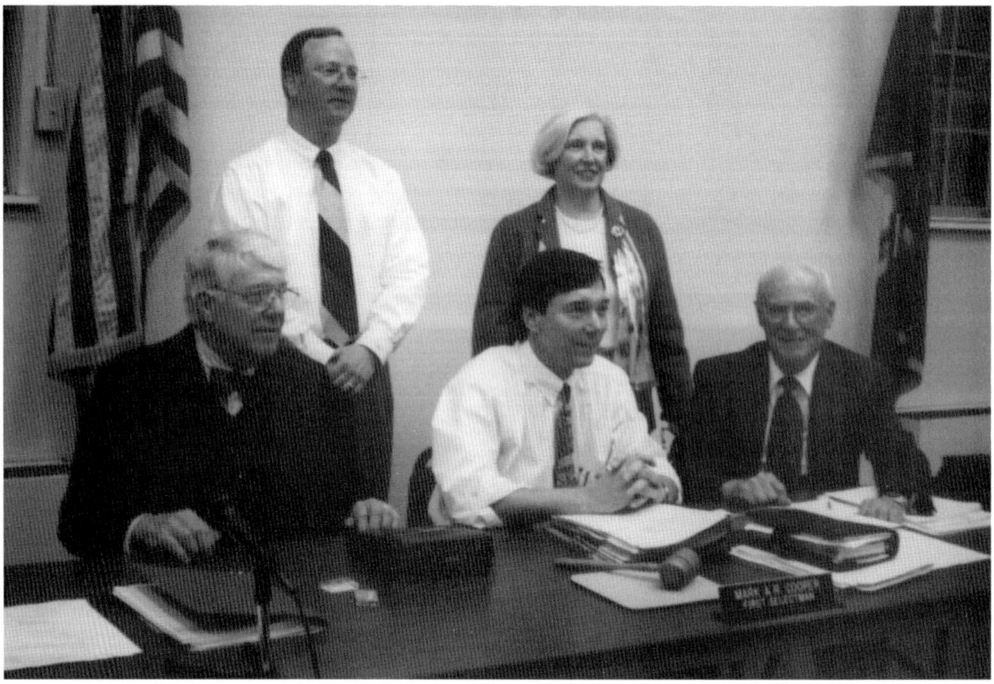

The 2003 Selectmen

The 2003 Board of Selectmen are, from left to right (sitting) Donald Briggs, First Selectman Marc Cooper, and Paul Palmer; (standing) Jeffrey Hughes and Carol Hubert. Not pictured is David Mathieu. Southbury operates under the traditional New England town-meeting form of government and under the guidelines of the town charter. Mark Cooper served as first selectman from 2001 to 2008. Paul Palmer was on the Inland Wetlands Commission for 20 years and was chairman for the last 10 years. Carol Hubert was chairman of the board of education for many years. Don Briggs was a longtime Board of Selectmen member. (Courtesy Catherine Palmer.)

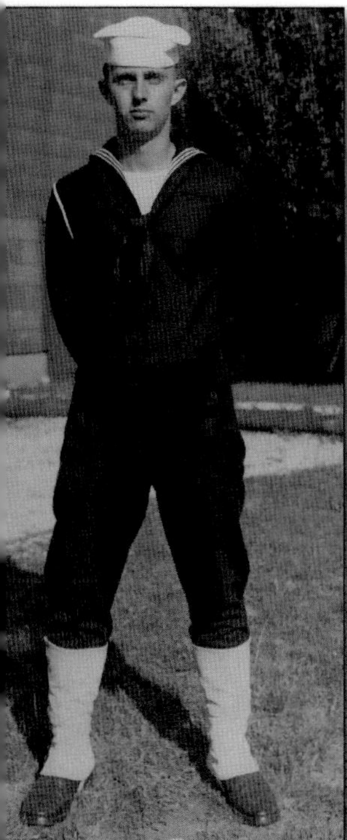

Sam Green III

Sam Green served as first selectman from 1968 to 1969. He has served the town in many roles and has been a longtime member and officer of VFW Post 1607 and American Legion Post 147. Sam joined the Navy at 18 and served on both an aircraft carrier and a destroyer antisubmarine ship that patrolled the east coast. Sam went to the University of Connecticut on the GI Bill. (Courtesy VFW 1607.)

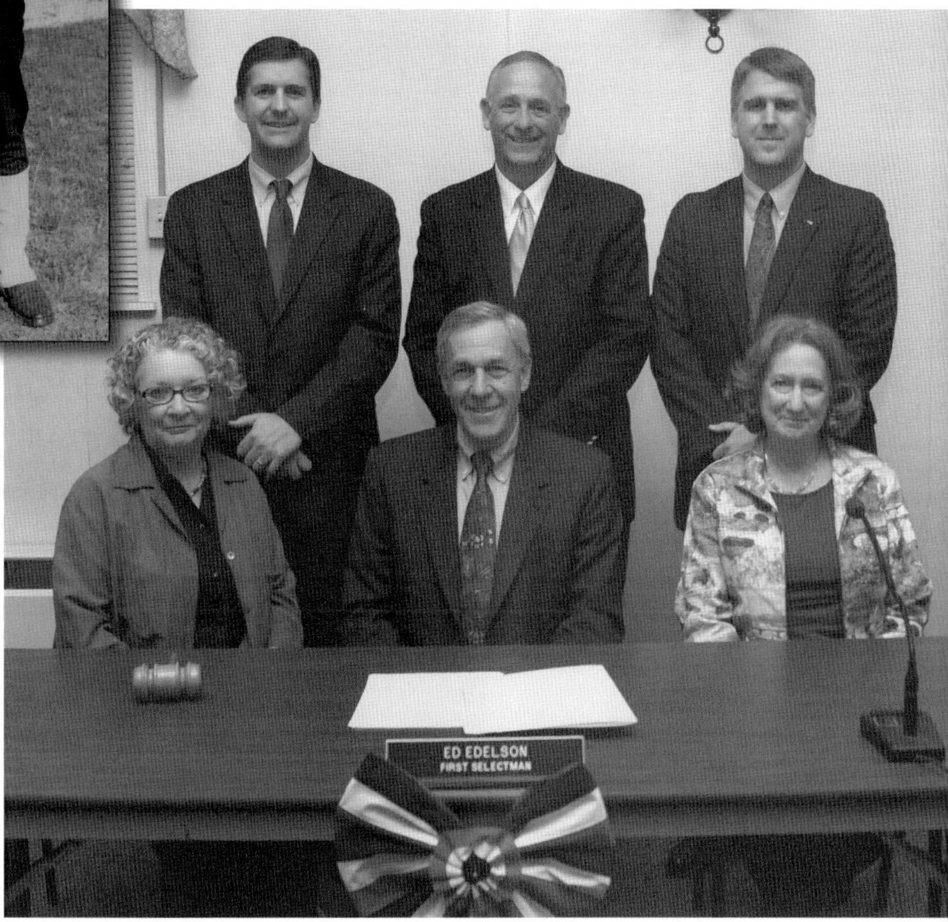

The 2012 Board of Selectmen

Pictured from left to right are (seated) Donna Pereira, First Selectman Ed Edelson, and Marcia Gore; (standing) Chad A. Landmon, Ronald J. Pugliese, and Edward H. Gittines III. The powers of the selectmen are conferred upon them by the constitution and general statutes of the state of Connecticut. Ronald J. Pugliese is an officer for the town of Waterbury. Chad Landmon is an attorney who served on the charter revision commission. (Courtesy Gosia Leidlich.)

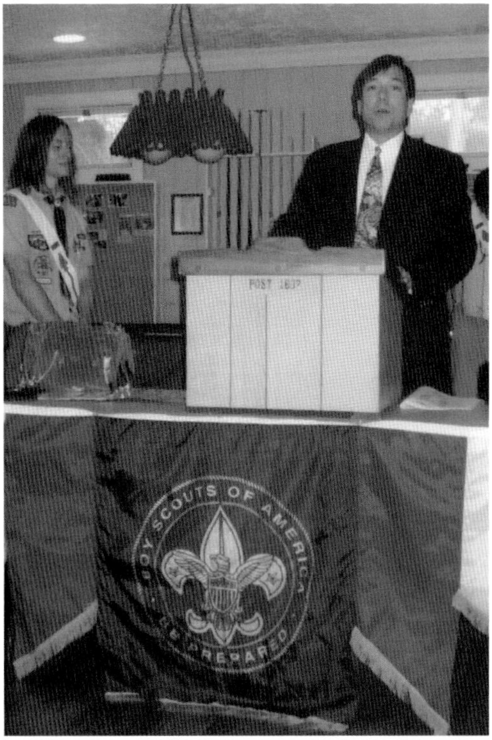

First Selectman Marc Cooper
Marc Cooper is a third-generation Southbury native. He served as chairman of the Water Pollution Control Authority, Inland Wetlands Commission, and Naugatuck Valley Council of Governments. He was a Board of Selectmen member prior to four terms as first selectman. He served on the board of directors of the Connecticut Resources Recovery Authority and Southbury Training School Board of Trustees. (Courtesy VFW Post 1607.)

First Selectman Edward R. Hveem
Mrs. Perry and Mrs. Cunningham, auxiliary members of VFW Post 1607, present a flag to former First Selectman Edward R. Hveem. He served as selectman in 1967. He also worked as the farm manager for the Southbury Training School. (Courtesy VFW Post 1607.)

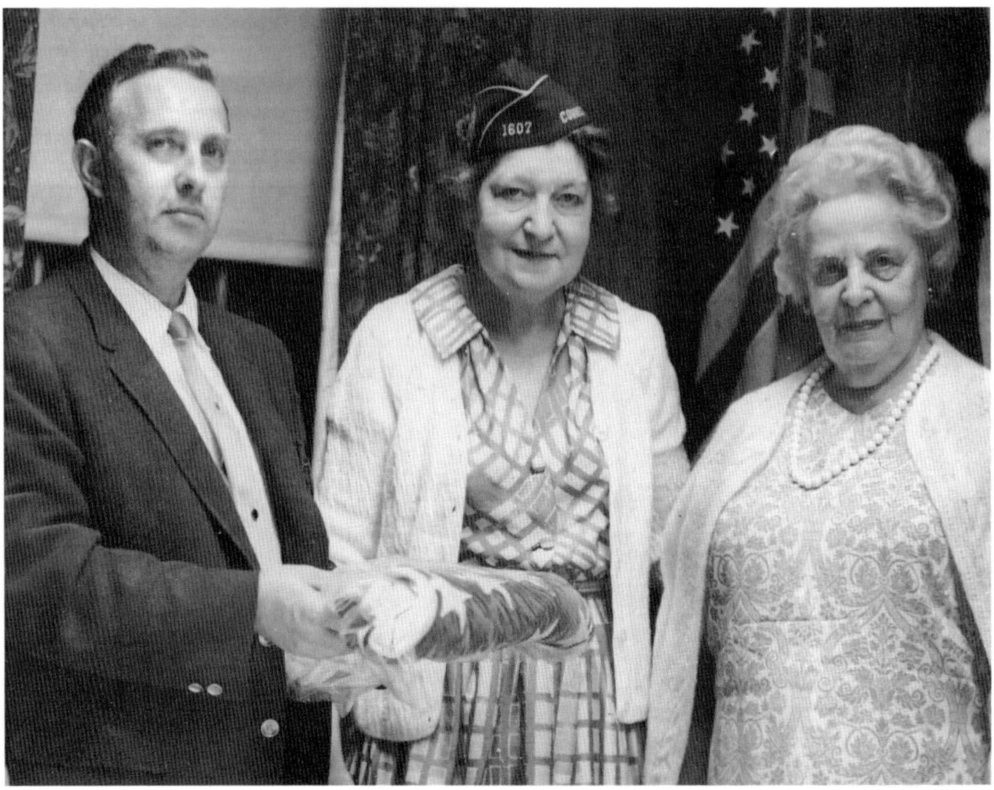

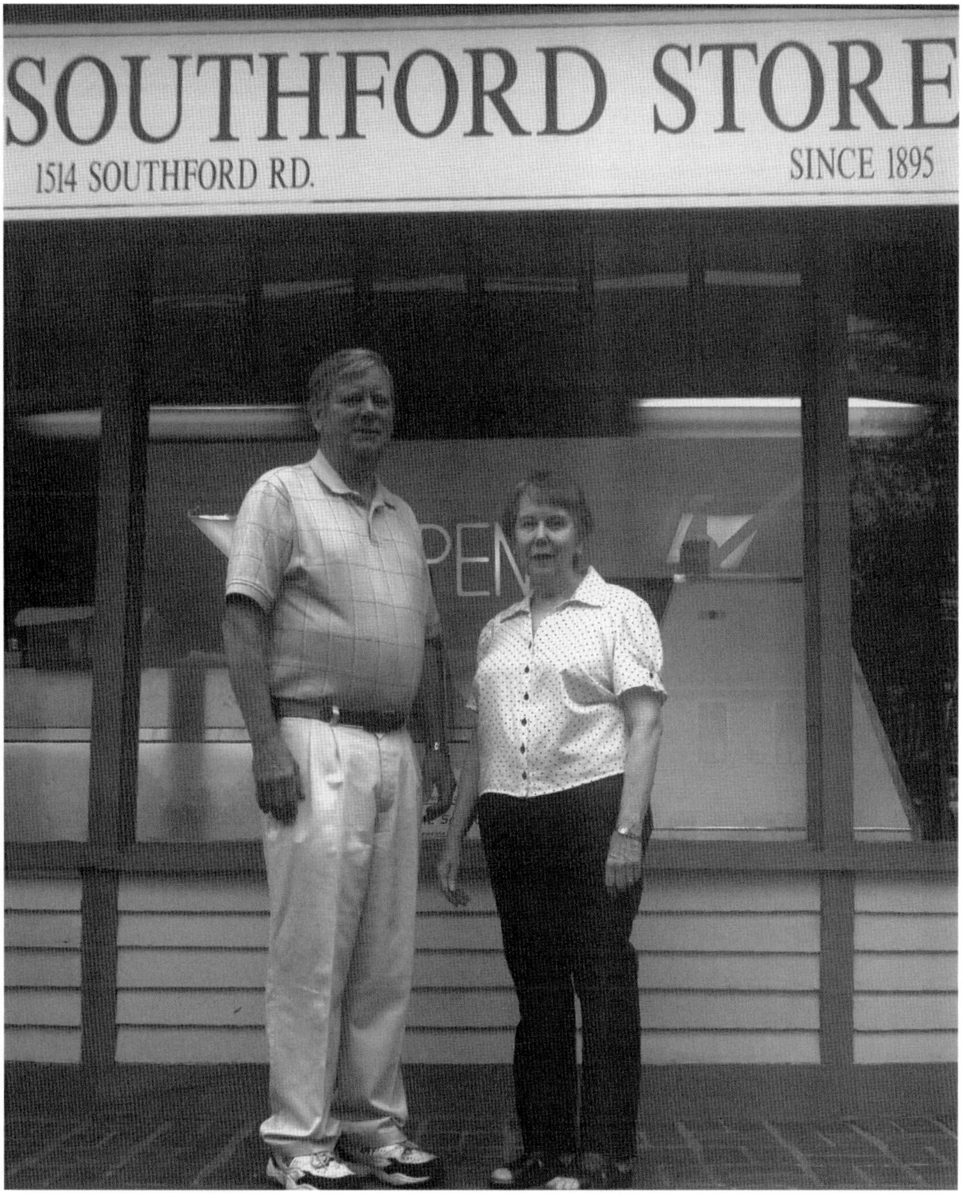

A Salesman Since Childhood
The Davis General Store in Southford has been in the family since 1895. Davis's mother was quoted as saying that Bill was a salesman from an early age when he filled a suitcase with old newspapers and got on his tricycle and sold them to neighbors. He took advantage of the town's new zoning code when Heritage Village was built and established a package store next to the family general store. An exciting happening at the store occurred when a young boy found a lottery ticket worth $10,000. His mother had to cash it since he was not 18 years old at the time. Bill served on both the Board of Selectmen and as first selectman. His great-grandfather John B. King was a foreman at the Diamond Match company. At the turn of the century, it was one of the largest industries in western Connecticut. Former First Selectman H. William Davis and his wife of over 45 years, Kayanne, are pictured in front of the Davis General Store. (Courtesy Andrew Skok.)

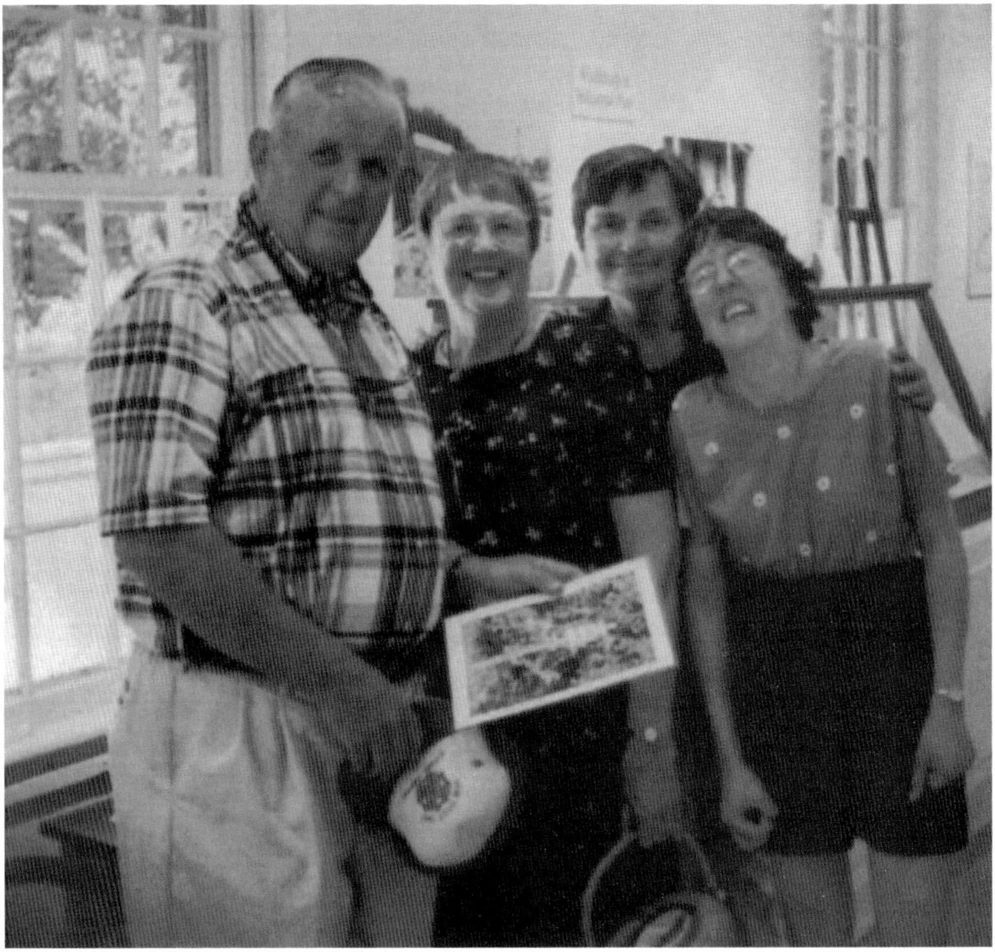

Former First Selectman Harmon Andrews
Harmon Andrews has served on innumerable town boards, commissions, and organizations. He served in World War II in the Merchant Marines, Infantry, Honor Guard, and National Guard. He has served as an officer of VFW Post 1607 and American Legion Post 147. Pictured from left to right are Harmon and Doris Andrews; Arleen Mitchell, Southbury Historical Society treasurer; and Amy Andrews. (Courtesy Catherine Palmer.)

CHAPTER EIGHT

Ring the School Bell

True terror is to wake up one morning and discover that your high school class is running the country.

—Kurt Vonnegut Jr.

The first accounts of Southbury schools were recorded in the Ecclesiastical Society records of March 30, 1741, which stated that schools could be established in different sections of town. According to Ancient Woodbury records, Bullet Hill School was established in 1762, and schoolmaster David Hicock's diary account records that he taught school at Bullet Hill in 1769. His 1770 class roster includes children's names from that section of town. Eleven school districts were eventually established throughout Southbury's 40.9 square miles: Bullet Hill, White Oak, Purchase, Pootatuck, Wapping Joint, Hull's Hill, Pierce Hollow, Kettletown, Southford, and South Britain, including Transylvania, which was often used both by Southbury and Woodbury, depending on the bordering population.

Learning to read, write, spell, and understand arithmetic were essential educational components. Slates, slate pencils, quill pens, and hornbooks accompanied the few textbooks of the day since paper was scarce. Students were expected to behave by both teachers and parents. If students veered from behaving, they were punished at school and at home.

Former student Jim Hine, also a historic buildings commissioner, was asked how to reconnect the school bell in the belfry with the school rope in the classroom when it would not ring for a visiting class. When he was a student at Bullet Hill School, he and classmates would often play a prank on their teacher and try to delay the morning bell by stealing up the stairs, climbing into the belfry, and unhooking the rope.

Early schools did not have today's heating and plumbing conveniences. Heating was furnished with fireplaces and, later, wood-burning stoves. Families were required to contribute wood for the fires, and if they failed to do so, their children were often seated at the farthest corner of the room away from the fire. Edmund Schade, a former district schoolteacher and member of the Southbury Historic Buildings Commission, told of arriving at school to teach and finding the ink frozen in the inkwells. Once he kindled the fire and the room warmed, the frozen ink melted on the desktops. He soon learned to keep the ink wells at a low level. The children who lived near the school brought a pail of water from their well and a communal dipper was used in the days before good sanitation. Convenience houses, also know as privies, were usually behind the school and were not too comfortable in cold weather. Although early students did not have today's conveniences, they were able to gain a solid education and become contributing citizens in their communities.

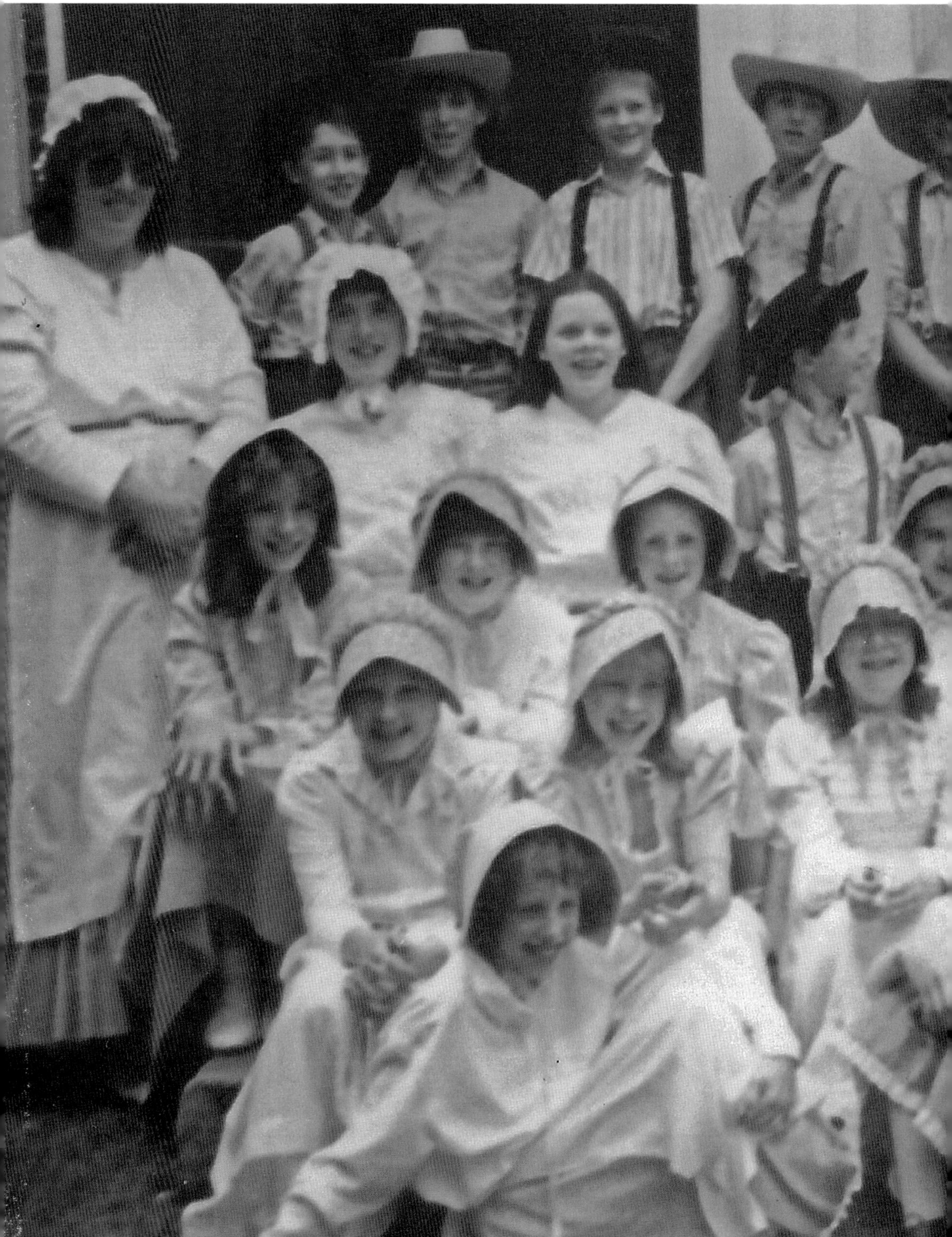

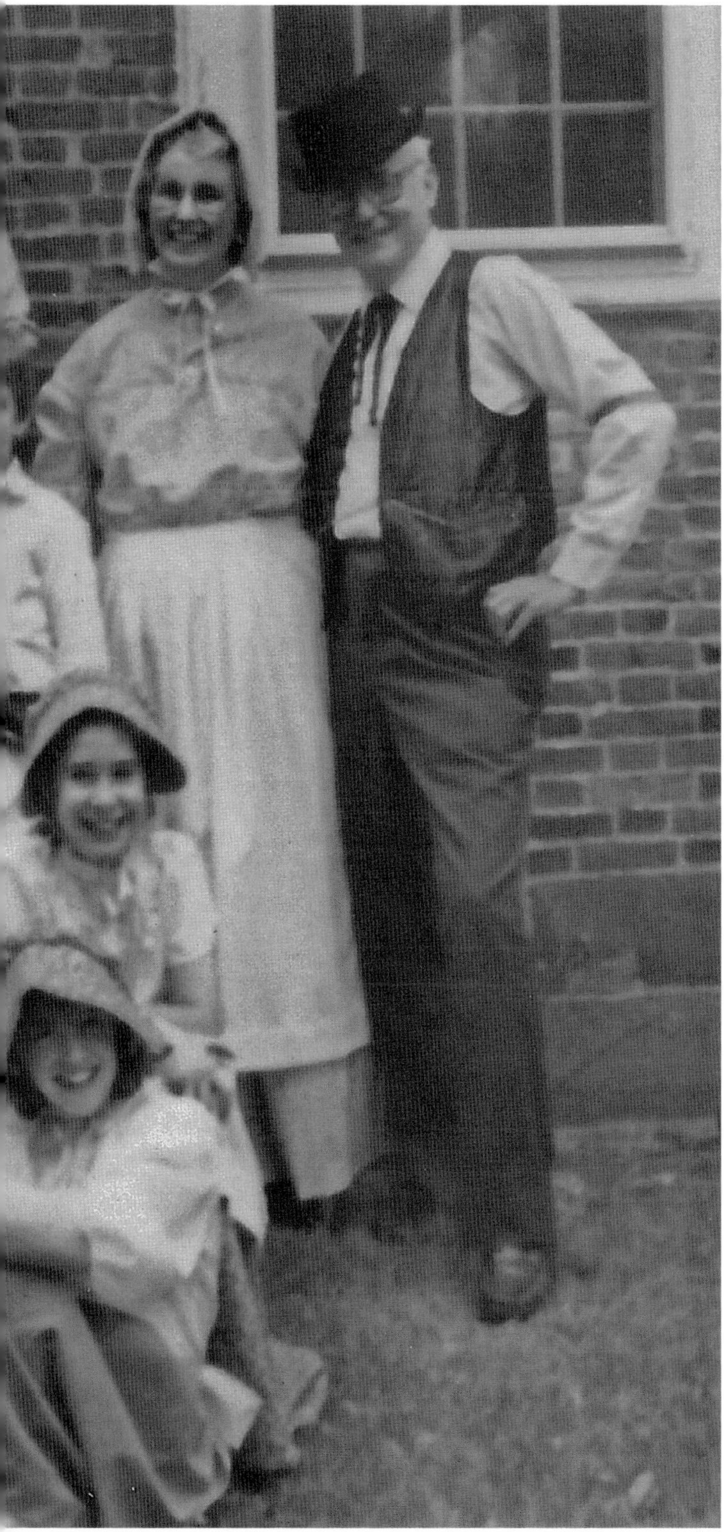

Catherine Palmer and the Living Museum Program
There are some people who were born to teach others, and Catherine is one of them. Named after her grandmother Catherine Chappell Gilmore, a one-room schoolhouse teacher, Catherine began teaching in 1966. In addition, she has spread her love of education and history by starting the Bullet Hill School Days Living Museum program in 1987. Here, Gainfield Elementary School students reenact a typical 1800s school day at Bullet Hill School. From left to right are (first row) Allison Brinley and Lauren Garille; (second row) Sarah Solsbury, Meg Hamill, Amy Belval, and Kristin Tolles; (third row) Danielle Riley, Megan Larsen, Mia LaFrance, and Amy Williams; (fourth row) docent Sue Matula, Noreen Nilan, Becky Matula, John Noonan, Kevin Kastelein, teacher and program founder Catherine Palmer, and selectman and docent Paul Palmer; (fifth row) Matthew Divine, John Thibodeau, Matthew Voity, Sean Doherty, and Todd Ritchie. (Author's collection.)

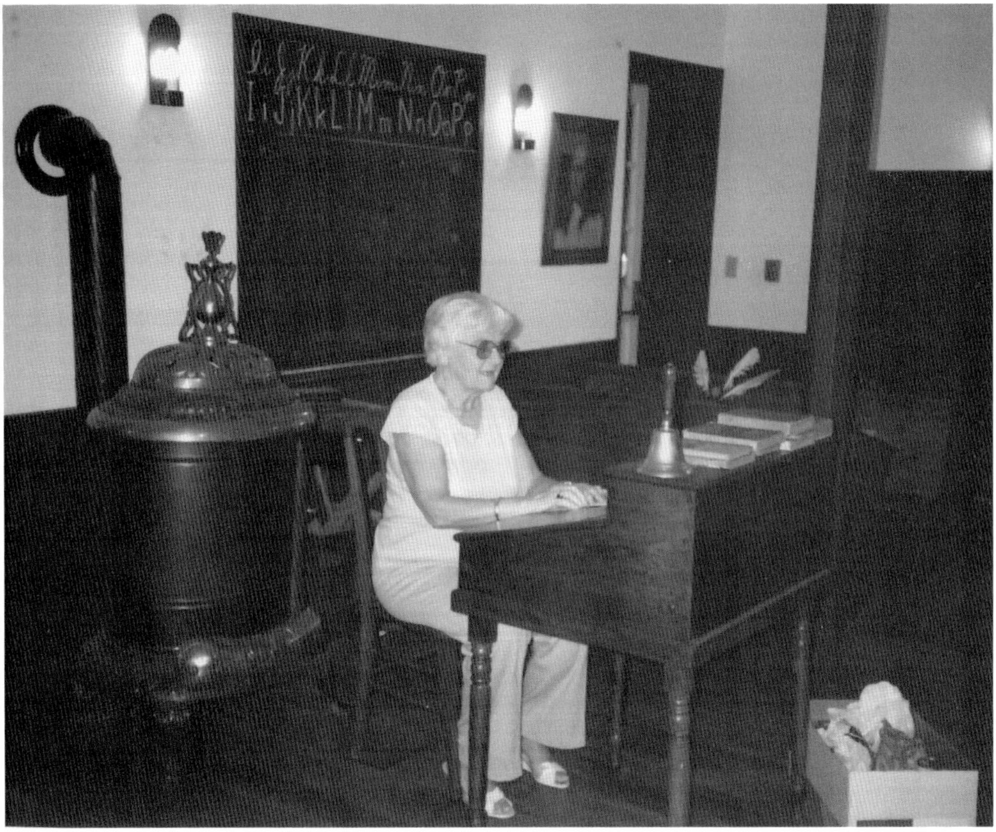

Frances Hunihan Davis
Fran was a one-room schoolhouse teacher at both Purchase Brook and Kettletown Schools. As a student, she was the White Oak School champion speaker. She grew up on Dublin Road, where many Irish people made their home. It was their custom to name places after their hometowns, and Irish railroad workers settled that area of town. Fran is pictured visiting Bullet Hill School. (Courtesy Catherine Palmer.)

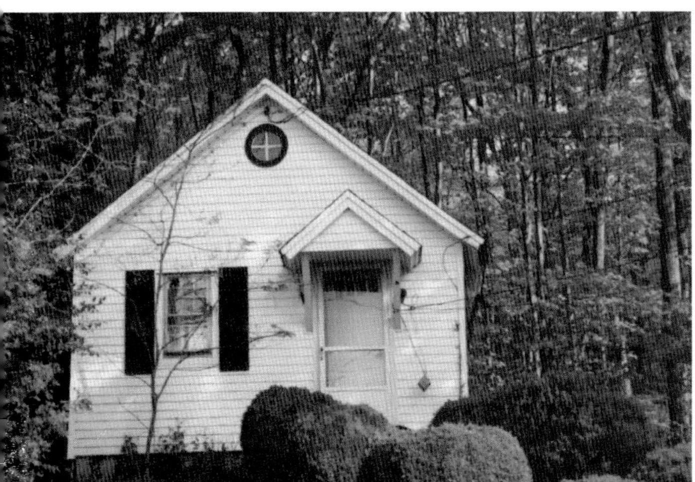

Kettletown School
Frances Davis also taught at Kettletown School, which later became a residence. It was built in 1860 and was the smallest of all the district schools. Frances made $894 per year teaching. Her mother came from Ireland at age 16. She later met her husband in Woodbury. Frances's father, John Denis Hunihan, was born here and was a farmer to the day he died. (Courtesy H. William Davis III.)

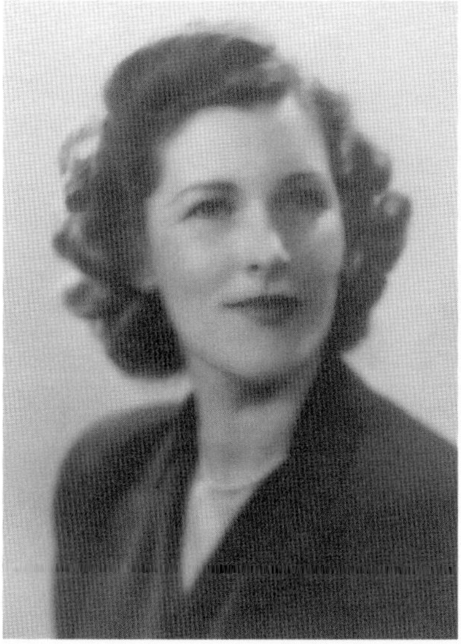

Mildred Davis, Teacher
Mildred Davis grew up in Southford in the house that is now the Southford Medical Center. As a student, "Mimi" was known as the champion speller. Born in 1912, she taught in one-room schoolhouses in South Britain and the Purchase. She never married, and she taught her whole life. At one time, women were not allowed to teach after they married. (Courtesy H. William Davis III.)

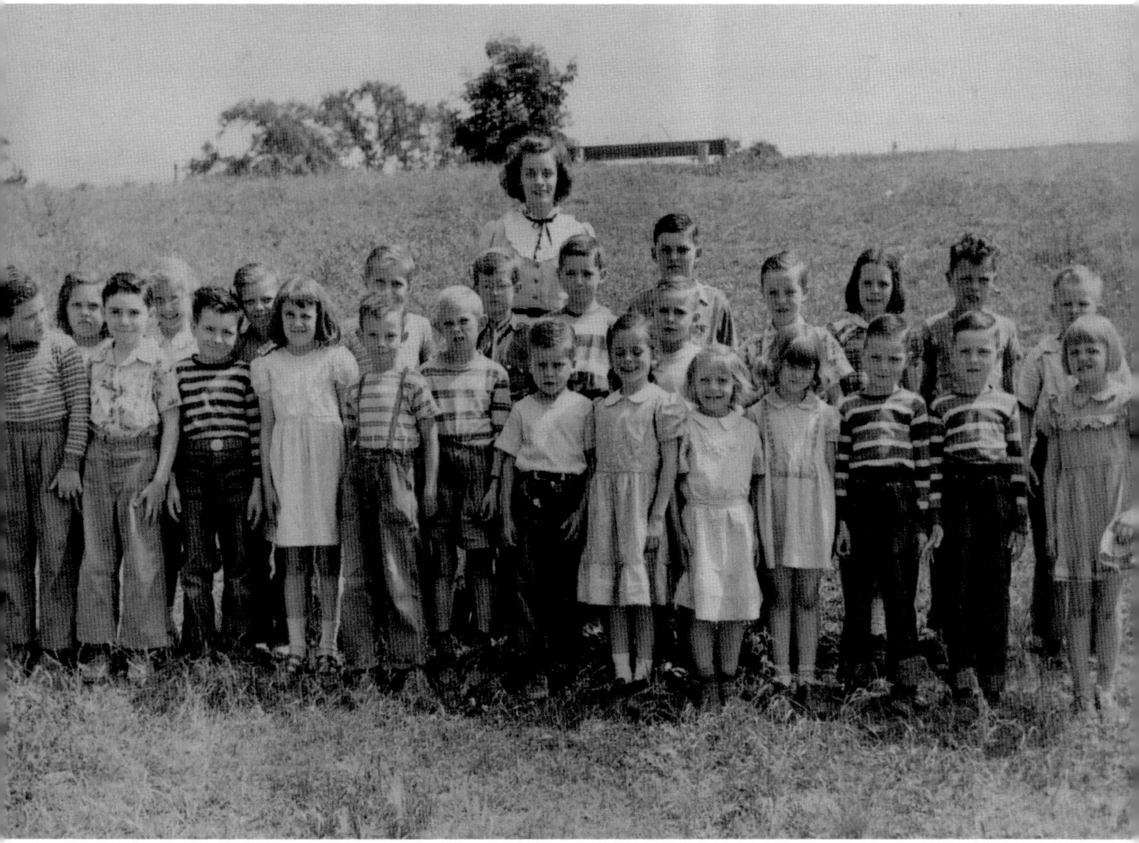

Dorothy Drum
Teacher Dorothy Drum is standing in the back of her students on the hillside bordering the Southbury Consolidated School in the late 1940s. She was a longtime teacher for the town of Southbury. (Courtesy Ed Wildman Jr.)

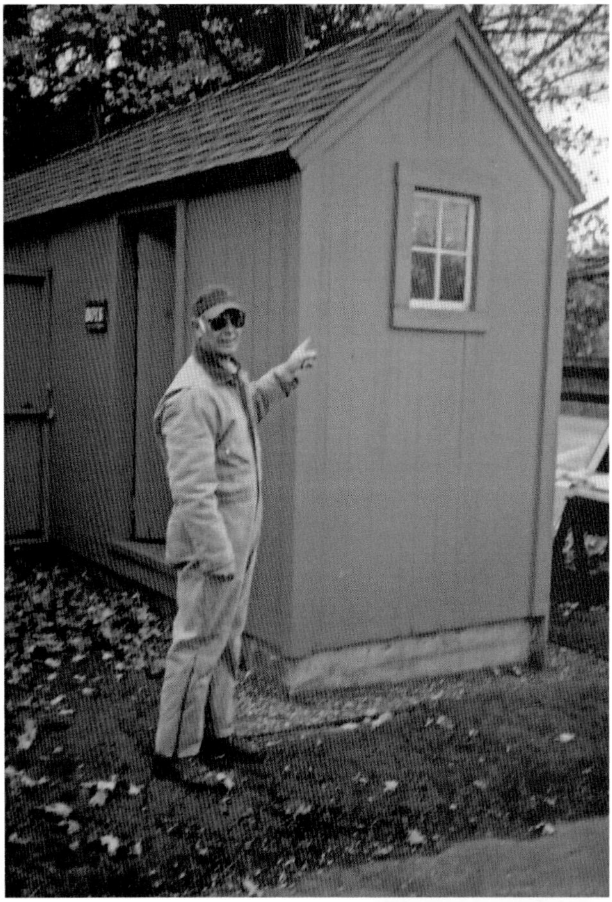

Robert Williams
Bob Williams, a local carpenter and restorer, is pictured at the completion of the Bullet Hill School convenience house restoration in 2003. Bob served many years on the Historic Buildings Commission and now volunteers as a consultant and as a restorer for the town's three historic buildings: Bullet Hill School, the Old Town Hall Museum, and the South Britain Library. (Courtesy Catherine Palmer.)

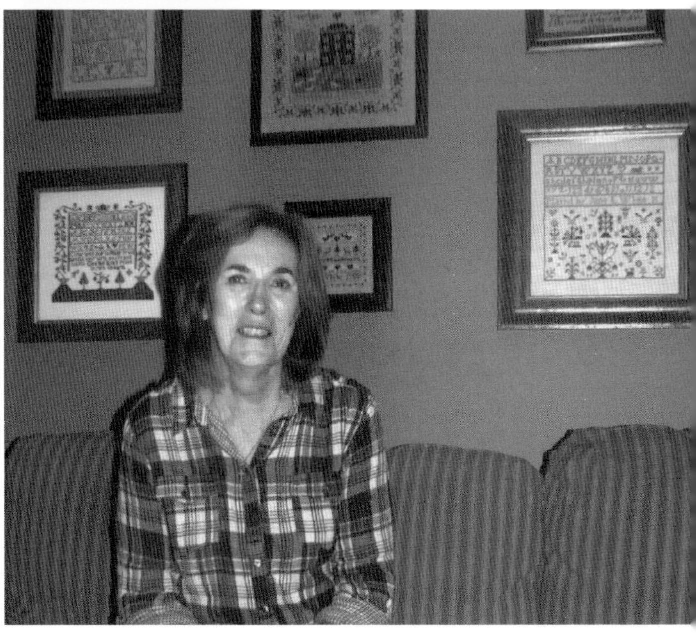

Third Generation Teacher Jane Ewald White
Jane, who teaches at Long Meadow Elementary School, is pictured with the replica samplers that she needlepointed. Her grandmother Gertrude Hand Hine taught at Bullet Hill School. Her mother, Ruth Hine Ewald, and her Aunt Ollie also taught in both Southbury and Woodbury Schools. Jane's classes have participated in the Bullet Hill School Days Living Museum program for many years. (Courtesy Andrew Skok.)

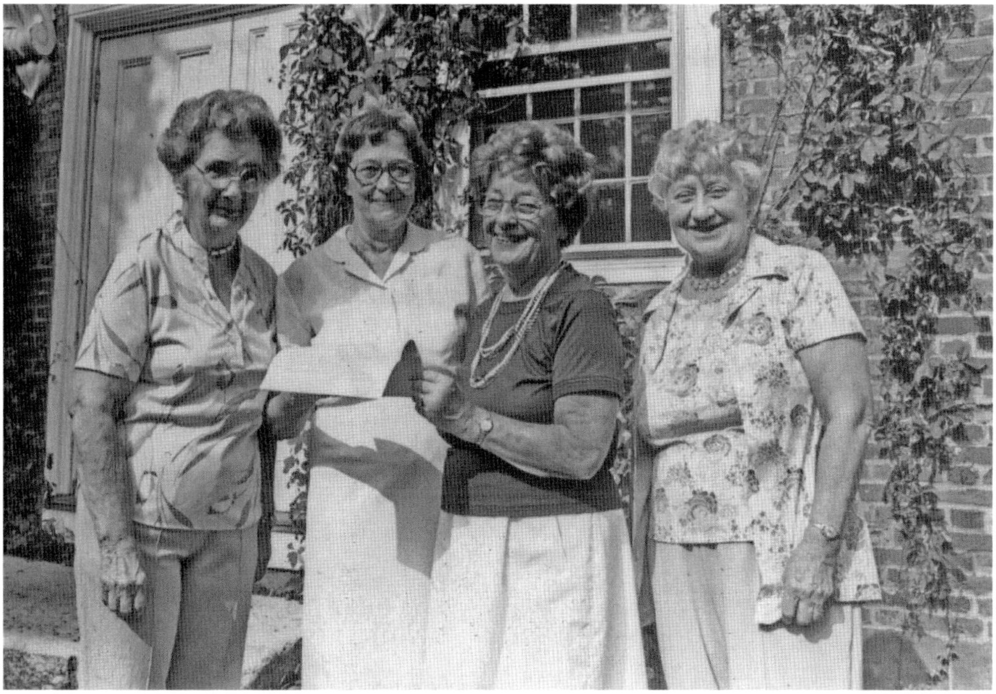

Vivian Tarbox with Three Cousins
Four Southbury natives, cousins, and Bullet Hill School District schoolteachers gathered together to share their many teaching days and family memories, making a positive mark on the young people of the community. Vivian was well loved in the community. In addition to teaching from the school curriculum, she taught her students about opera and *Bulfinch's Mythology*. From left to right are Evelyn Williams Hicock, Vivian Platt Tarbox, Julia Mitchell Schielke, and Doris Hotchkiss Solosy. (Courtesy Althea McGahie.)

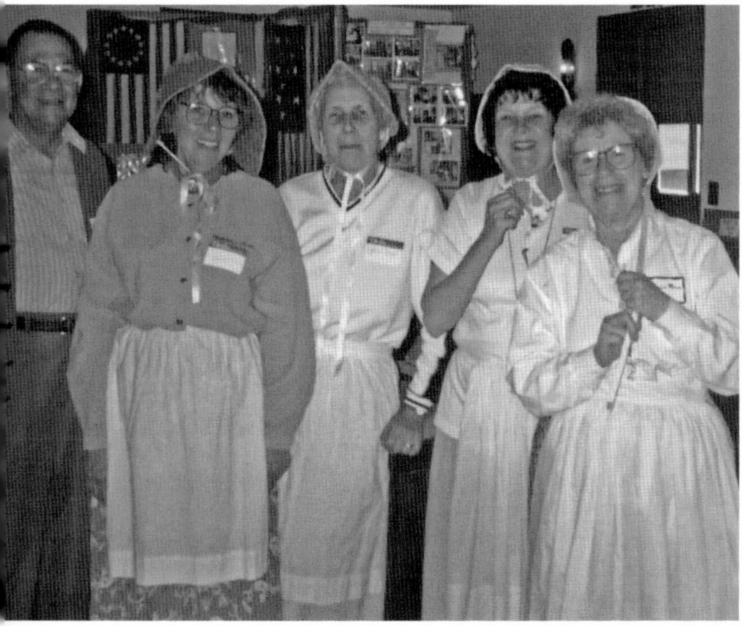

Celia Schwartz and Bullet Hill School Docents
The Heritage Village community has served many local programs. This is one example of its community service. Celia Schwartz is a gifted writer and reporter for the *Heritage Villager* newspaper. Sylvia Forbes served as a director of docents for many years. Volunteer docents welcome each visiting class. Docents pictured, from left to right, are Bill Bauserman, Helen Hanlon, Sylvia Forbes, Celia Schwartz, and Louise Pesca. (Courtesy Catherine Palmer.)

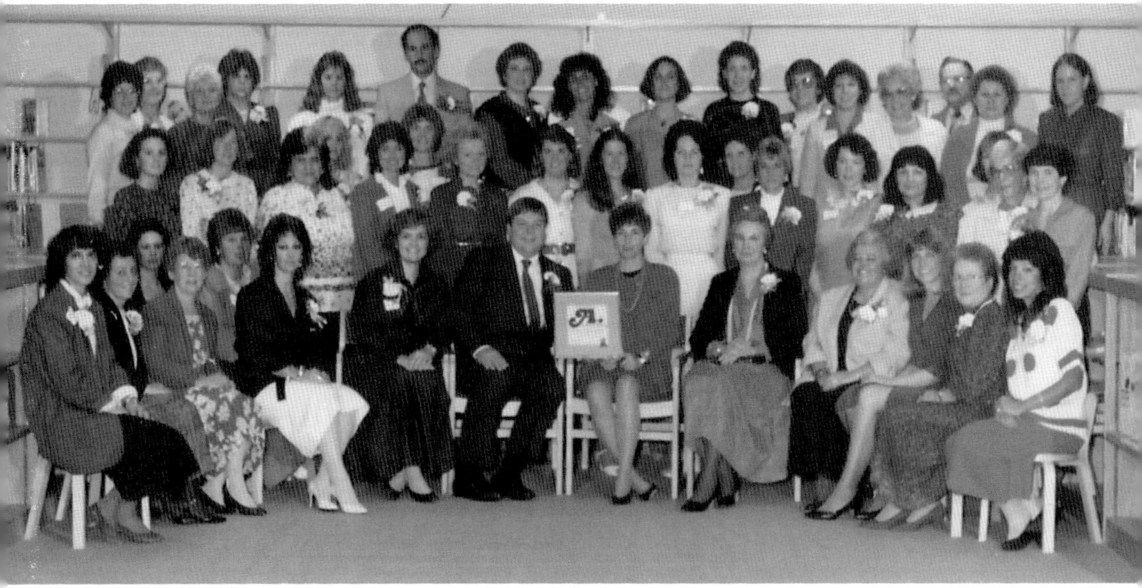

John J. Mudry and the Gainfield Elementary School Staff
Gainfield Elementary School Principal John J. Mudry and staff members were honored with the prestigious *Instructor* Magazine Award in 1987 from *Instructor* magazine editor Leanna Lansman. This excellence in education award was presented for Gainfield's outstanding curriculum and enrichment programs promoting optimum student achievement in all areas of learning. Gainfield Elementary School staff members pictured from left to right are (first row) Nancy Neal, Carmela Shanahan, (Sharon Pettit is behind Carmela), Evelyn Slason, Nancy Clement, Cindy Bethancourt, Christine Guiditta, Principal John J. Mudry, *Instructor* magazine editor Leanna Lansman, Cathy Palmer, Barbara Kane, Patricia Norman, Anne Pope, and Susan Fishman; (second row) Kathy Skinner, Gail McCleary, Erminia Sampieri, Eileen Ferrell, (Jeanne Gleason and Jackie Hunter are behind Eileen Ferrell), Francis Fillipelli, Maureen Campbell, Lynn Martin, Joyce Skowronski, Linda Carlson, Ruth Ann Ritter, Mary Johnson, Rosemary Mesaric, Elaine Kahn (Peggy Wildman is half hidden behind Elaine Kahn), and Evelyn Skowronski; (third row) Martha Millette, Gloria Gervais, Joyce Piskura, Cindy Spakowski, Michelle Oatley, Charles Iaiennaro, Stephanie Lynott, Sherri Cocchiola, Deborah Little, Judy York, Ginny Kowalski, Kathy Heran, Annette Rhoades, Bill Rhoades, Mary Pettit, and Ann Brittain. (Courtesy Gainfield Elementary School Archives.)

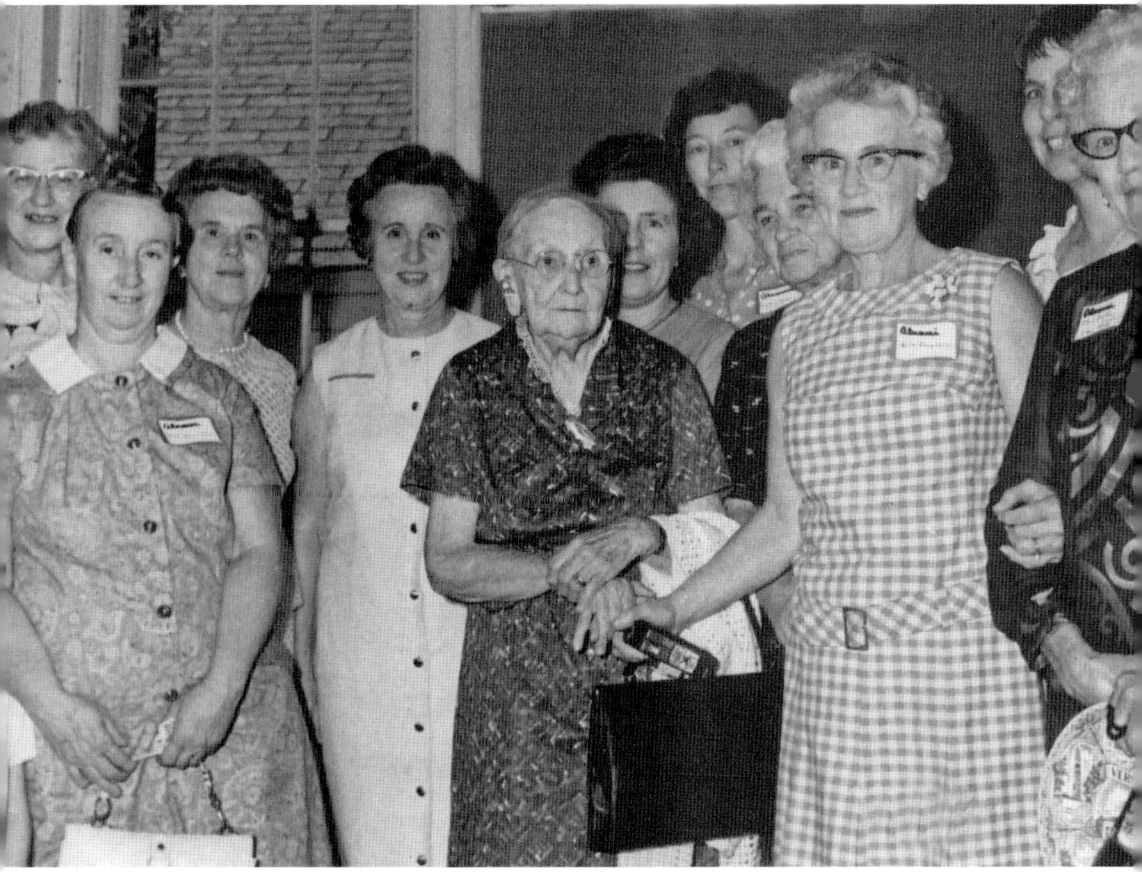

Teacher Flossie Hicock and Bullet Hill School Alumni, 1968

Shown are Flossie Hicock (center) and the alumni from the Bullet Hill School in 1968. From left to right are (first row) unidentified, Flossie Hicock (1902 teacher), Edith Dennis Warner, Ethel Bartow Loveland, and Harriett Stone Warner; (second row) Doris Hotchkiss Solosy, Katherine Stone Leavenworth, Esther Stone Katt, Lucille Grisgraber Terrell, Ruth Perry Ruben, and Virginia Hicock Harris. (Courtesy Bullet Hill School Archives.)

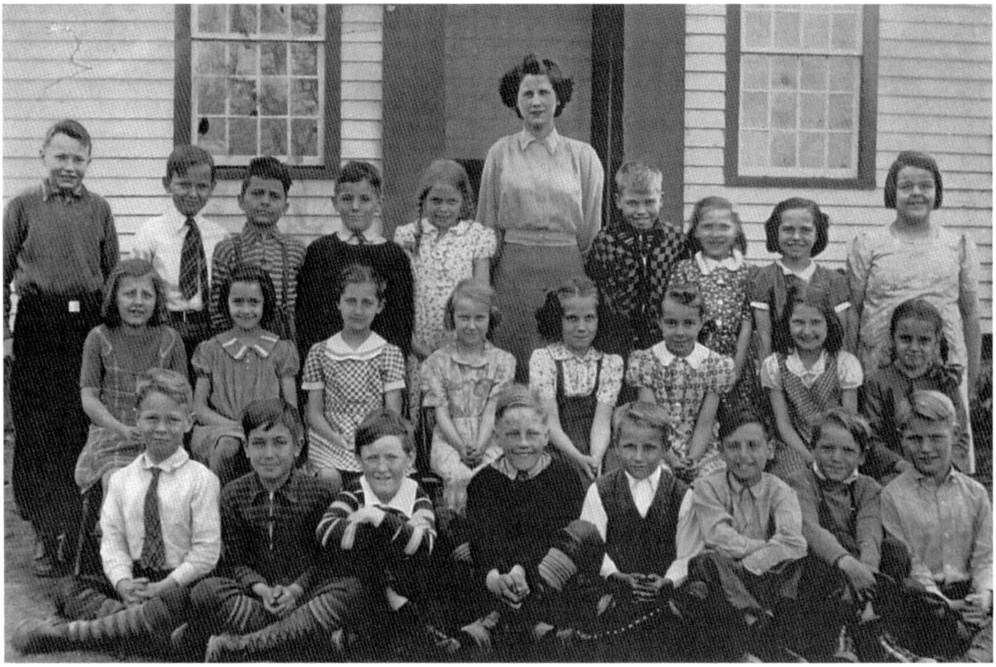

White Oak School Class c. 1930s
White Oak School was in the area of town where many of the first 15 families from Stratford settled. The Stiles family had several properties in the Ragland area, and descendants still reside there today. Children walked to school and the state law was that the distance should not exceed two miles. (Courtesy Arza Bennett Jr.)

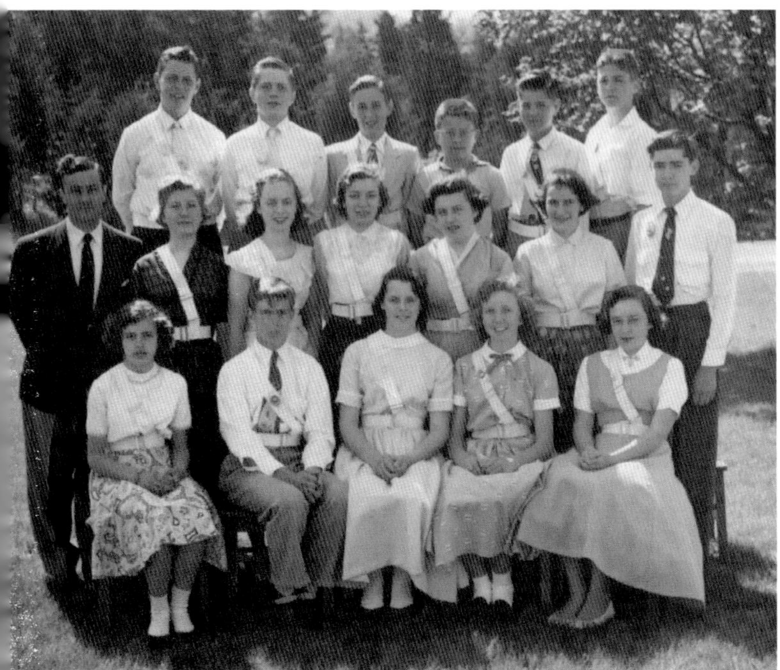

Thomas Pepe and Southbury Consolidated School
Southbury Consolidated School students are pictured with their teacher Thomas Pepe (second row left), who later became the Southbury superintendent of schools. When the remaining six of eleven original district schools closed in 1941, Southbury Consolidated School was built. Two hundred and four students in grades one through eight were transported by buses from town. This school is now Gainfield Elementary School. (Courtesy Ed Wildman.)

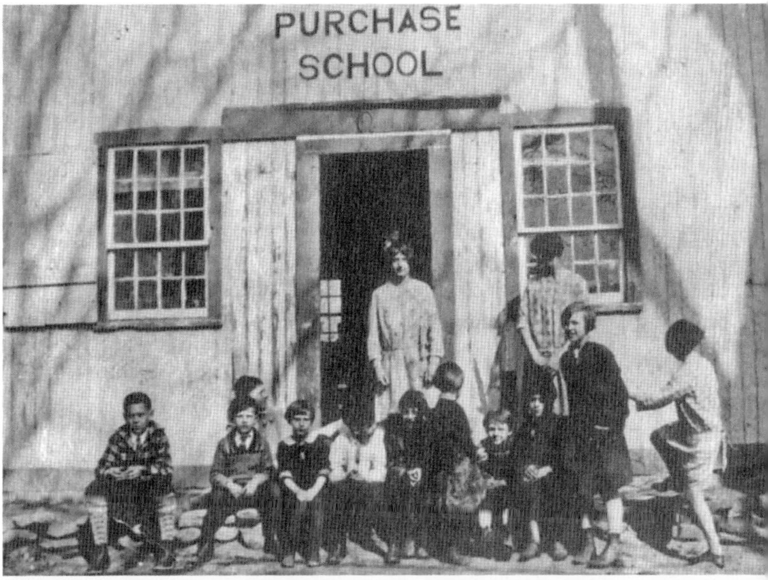

Purchase School Class, 1920s
Purchase School was in one of the more rural Southbury school districts. In 1941, during district school consolidation, most were sold. Purchase School was an exception. After years of vandalism, the deteriorating school became a public safety hazard. Southbury volunteer firemen burned it in a training exercise. The teacher's desk, bought when the school closed, was later contributed to the Bullet Hill School Museum. (Courtesy Ed Wildman Jr.)

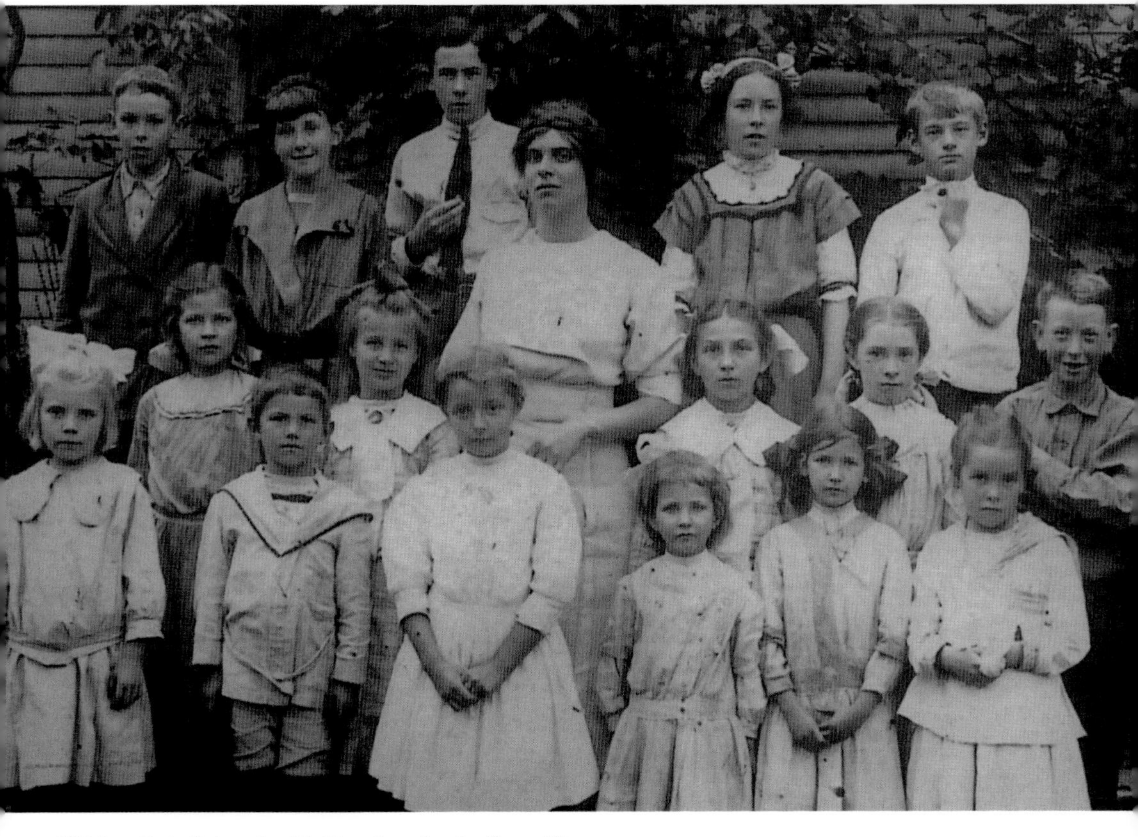

White Oak School with Teacher Janie Grey Pierce
Janie sold land for a park that was named after her with the request that the land be kept in its natural state. The park overlooks the Transylvania Pond setting and is located off Transylvania Road and includes 100 acres of woodland, trails, and picnic areas. (Author's collection.)

INDEX